The Rich and Other Atrocities

The Rich and Other Atrocities

BY

CHARLOTTE CURTIS

HARPER & ROW PUBLISHERS
New York, Hagerstown, San Francisco, London

Grateful acknowledgment is made for permission to reprint the following:

Articles from the *New York Times*. © 1963, 1964, 1965, 1966, 1967, 1968, 1969, 1970, 1971, 1972, 1973 by The New York Times Company. Reprinted by permission.

"Mafia Chic: The Last Delicious Days of Joey Gallo" is reprinted by permission of *Harper's Bazaar*. Copyright © 1972, The Hearst Corporation.

"Socially, Watergate Was a Bore" originally appeared in *Rolling Stone*, Issue #148, November 22, 1973. © 1973 by Rolling Stone Magazine. All rights reserved. Reprinted by permission.

FIRST EDITION

Designed by Patricia Dunbar

Library of Congress Cataloging in Publication Data
Curtis, Charlotte.

    The rich and other atrocities.
    Includes index.
    1. United States—Social life and customs—20th century. 2. Upper classes—United States.
I. Title.
E169.02.C85   1976   301.44'1   76–5121
ISBN 0–06–010931–9

---

76 77 78 79 80 81 10 9 8 7 6 5 4 3 2 1

For
Arthur O. Sulzberger,
Clifton Daniel
and
Harrison Salisbury

Contents

Preface

Society is just another name for that mélange of aristocrats, pacesetters and other rich overachievers who are forever exercising their money and power. Yet since even the rich drop out, die or retire on their laurels, the cast of society characters inevitably changes. There are always new people waiting in the wings.

In this book, which attempts to catch society in the act, the Vanderbilts, Whitneys and Astors share the pages with Hugh Hefner, Artie Shaw and the Maharanee of Baroda. The Duke and Duchess of Windsor add that much-sought-after cachet to the right parties. Truman Capote gives his celebrated masked ball for the then virtually unknown Katharine Graham, with a great to-do being made over who is and who isn't on the guest list. The Shah of Iran, in his own bid for international fame, sends out invitations to a party in the desert, rounding up a vast display of the world's titled and powerful. This is one kind of society.

Around the United States, waltzing is almost as big in Boston as the Cabots and the Lowells, whereas Houston offers up heart surgeon Denton Cooley (Michael DeBakey was in the operating room) in the name of charity. In the Bluegrass country, the makings of a mint julep (silver cups are better than glass) are as important as the thoroughbred race horses. New Orleans crowns yet another Mardi Gras queen and Charleston, South Carolina, festoons its ballroom with Southern smilax for the annual St. Cecilia Society Cotillion, whose ranks are closed to all but those who inherit membership. No amount of power or money can buy in. In Arkansas, the society event of consequence was the late Winthrop Rockefeller's annual livestock sale and house party. Grosse Pointe is an anthology of Fords, and Honolulu expects its old families to know and understand the hula.

New York, of course, is something else. In good times or bad, life in the upper regions consists of everything that's not nailed down, with Jacqueline Kennedy Onassis at El Morocco, royalty at an artist's pad in SoHo, Leonard Bernstein entertaining the Black Panthers, the Orbachs making spaghetti for mobster Joey Gallo, and the celebrated April in Paris Ball. Washington is politics, formal dinners at the White House and the chic of Georgetown, which watches the politicians come and go. All this is society.

If that isn't enough, there's always Las Vegas, where Caesars Palace dished up titled but blasé Europeans to give the gambling a little class; movie mogul Jules Stein's six-day Los Angeles party junket for six hundred of his closest friends; and the day David Frost rented a jumbo jetliner to take scores of his pals to Bermuda for lunch. This too counts as society.

Although an exact definition is elusive, society people are generally rich, fashionable, visible and sometimes well-bred, and regularly giving and going to elaborate parties. They are influential far beyond their numbers, their role inflated by their money and the ways they spend it.

By giving millions to found and support art galleries, museums, operas, symphonies, hospitals, medical research, parks, educational institutions and a wide variety of charities, they popularize one cause over another, affecting local and national cultural, health and educational priorities in ways no ordinary person or few groups can.

By wearing the newest fashions, decorating and redecorating their several houses, demanding exquisite foods from their personal chefs, and indulging in a frankly symbiotic relationship with the press, they create taste in this country, giving us Thorstein Veblen's conspicuous consumer as a role model.

What endures is the belief in America as Utopia, where all things are possible when, in fact, the reality has never jibed with the fantasy. The big rich, regardless of century, can and do live out the dream, thereby setting the pace and perpetuating the myth, while the poor, whether envious, resentful or even hating their economic betters, do not reject the dream. They aspire to it. Among the inalienable rights is "upward mobility," the leveling-up process. Until somebody pushes too hard. Then upward mobility becomes "social climbing" or "status seeking." But in the process, the overachiever sets the goals for nearly everybody else.

While professing a dedication to the principle of equality, Americans have consistently worked at being unequal. They close ranks, change rules and move onward whenever threatened by whatever leveling-up marauder appears to be gaining on them, which seems to have been constantly.

This will to move and change, whether aboard the *Mayflower*, the covered wagon, the automobile or the jet plane, coupled with an inventiveness of a restless people who consciously fled the traditions of the Old World while eagerly seeking the frontiers of the new, has produced a frankly neophiliac quality to American life. New and different is good. Old and familiar is boring. The safe conclusion, therefore, is that whatever society is at the moment is not what it is about to become. Which says as much about the current fascination with the doings of Diane von Furstenberg, Truman Capote, CeeZee Guest and the Vanderbilts as it does about *la cuisine minceur*, Ultrasuede, clingy dresses, dark red lipstick, turbans recycled from the thirties, the Hustle and backgammon.

In the hands of rich society figures, the dream of the good life, so basic to the national way of life, has ballooned into the pursuit of elegance and that goes a long way toward affecting the state of the economy. Elegance costs money. "Thank God," a Colorado prospector announced joyously, upon striking gold. "Now my wife can be a lady." And that just might be what society is all about.

C. C.

Acknowledgments

If politics is the art of the possible, then journalism is the art of attempting the impossible. Yet it is done 365 days a year against a deadline. If, in the process, journalists manage to report the facts that actually add up to the truth and illuminate the reality behind the appearance, theirs is a minor victory. Today's newspaper is a highly perishable product: it is tomorrow's garbage wrapper.

It should come as no surprise, therefore, that some stories in this collection are more finished than others. Those that have lasting validity owe as much to the perspicacity of the *New York Times* editors who assigned them as the reporter who wrote them. I am deeply indebted to such editors and to the unsung heroes of the copy desk.

I am grateful to my colleague David Schneiderman, who waded through hundreds of articles, sternly casting the weak aside; to Steve Heller and Thomasina Alexander, who helped with the pictures; to Robert Medina, who consistently tracked down obscure facts and located stories only dimly remembered; to Howard Goldberg and Muriel Stokes, who shouted encouragement; to Amy Bonoff of Harper & Row and, of course, to Simon Michael Bessie, who initiated this project.

Special thanks are also due the *Times*'s society and women's news staffs, and countless reporters, subjects of interviews and sources here and abroad.

C. C.

I

Their Playgrounds

*The all-year tan is a symbol of that
ability to be where the sun is regardless of season, and the rich, as anybody
who has tried to keep track of them is well aware, have more than their
share of tanned skin. And since they own second—even third and fourth—
houses in some of the world's most expensive palm-fringed resorts, they are
never at a loss for a place in the sun. In the winter, the assorted nabobs,
tycoons, moguls, magnates, biggies and fashion plates generally identified
with American society pack up their old and new money and head for Palm
Beach, Palm Springs, Arizona, Southern California, Mexico or the Caribbean. In the summer, they're off to The Hamptons, the lakes and mountains,
or Newport.*

*Palm Beach is $1-million houses, tiaras and a marathon of black-tie
dinner parties seven nights a week. Since Ruth Tankoos's death, it is perhaps
the only American beach resort where nobody who's anybody goes to the
beach, and in her day, the beautiful and gifted Mrs. Tankoos was always
considered just a bit eccentric when she abandoned the cocktail circuit,
armed herself with a beach towel and a book, and headed for her late morning swim.*

"But you'll get sand all over you," her friends used to exclaim.

*If Palm Beach is New York's elegant spenders, then Palm Springs be-
longs to the Los Angeles rich, a man-made resort in a desert full of movie
stars and visiting politicians. Newporters, by contrast, are not at all sure
about celebrities, but they do like visiting royalty and presidents who dance
well.*

*The Hamptons used to settle for good manners, a dedication to good
works, a decent competence on the croquet court and the proper cultivation
of hydrangeas. But in the late sixties and early seventies they became the
summer home of artists, writers and radical chic—the place where the rich
were forever drinking champagne on behalf of the disinherited and the dis-
enfranchised. The local potato farmers do not share in the social scramble,
but at least it's socially acceptable to swim in the Atlantic Ocean.*

Be it ever so homelike there was nothing humble about the *Carola,* the late
Colonel Leon Mandel's 121-foot yacht. Mrs. Mandel wrote her menus and
letters while the maid wore sunglasses, and life was rarely dull. They kept
a villa in Palm Beach just in case.
Jack Manning, *The New York Times* (1965)

Palm Beach

Society, which is periodically accused of having the zing of a wet tennis ball, has bounced back to life on America's most elegant sandbar. There is nothing relaxed, old-clothesy or understated about Palm Beach.

The little island playground, whose social structure is as stable as a Calder mobile, is the winter headquarters for some 25,000 of the country's richest persons, only a handful of whom are Old Guard aristocrats. The others, except for a couple of dozen families that try to lead reasonably ordered lives, seem to be constantly getting in and out of $2,500 French ball gowns, Rolls-Royces or the New York gossip columns. Third-generation millionaires and their actress and show-girl wives mingle democratically with new influential tycoons, former officers of the Junior League, Socially Registered philanthropists, international sportsmen, members of the nobility, diplomats, refugees from such summer resorts as Southampton and Newport, representatives of the best-dressed list and a sprinkling of entertainers.

On a typical day, a sizable segment of the community emerges from its palatial Mediterranean mansions shortly before noon and begins a round of activities that may last until dawn. It is not unusual, for instance, to lunch beneath an umbrella on the outdoor terrace at one home, have cocktails in the eighteenth-century French interior of another, and then sit down to a

5

formal dinner in the beach-house modern dining room of a third. And when the weather is good (the sun does shine now and then), the party people swim in one another's pools. Few go near the ocean.

"It's like a stage setting," said T. Bedford Davie, an articulate sportsman who collects clocks and jade. "I sometimes wonder what the real people are doing." Mr. Davie, son of Mrs. Paulding Fosdick, is a legal resident of Florida. He and his slim wife are not typical Palm Beachers. They do not like to go to more than three dinner parties in one week. "That's enough," said Mrs. Davie, who believes in traveling off season. "I like the outdoor life, and I can't enjoy it if I have to stay up all night."

Some—including three who have engaged publicity agents—work at dazzling one another, and some don't. In the end, however, the effect is the same. Such women as Mrs. Owen Robertson Cheatham and Mrs. Frank M. McMahon go out of their way to avoid the limelight, but people are always after them to come to parties, serve on charity ball committees and have their pictures taken. Both like to shop at the supermarkets for their groceries.

"I never want to get too involved," said Mrs. Cheatham, a New Yorker who was once president of the Augusta, Georgia, Junior League. "Then I have houseguests, and I feel as if I'm running a hotel." Mrs. Cheatham, whose husband is board chairman of the Georgia Pacific Corporation (wood products), is likely to cause a flurry of excitement, even on fashionable Worth Avenue, because she often appears in a Rodriguez of Spain scarlet ottoman suit with a large gold and diamond cotton boll in her lapel. Salvador Dali designed the brooch for her and the bracelet of gold fingers that is her wristwatch. She is one of the few women who do not wear slacks on the street.

"I do try to work for a few charities," Mrs. Cheatham said. "I think it's one's obligation." She has served on committees for two of the season's big charity events. She is also a member of the Church of Bethesda-by-the-Sea (Protestant Episcopal). "We had a dinner dance in honor of our diamond jubilee," she said of the sixty-five-year-old church. "There are some who think a dance is strange for a church, but they aren't Episcopalians."

Mrs. McMahon, a brunette, usually creates a stir, too. She is the wife of a Canadian oil and gas executive, mother, author of six books for teen-agers (under her maiden name, Betty Betz) and the mistress of Concha Marina—a Gold Coast showplace that belonged to the late Mrs. Isabel Dodge Sloane.

"I hate the word chic but I can't think of any other way of describing the informal luncheons people have on weekends," she said. "You don't call anyone until the night before. It's the kind of thing where the men have fun, too."

When the McMahons have such a party, there are Italian plates, wildly printed tablecloths, a buffet table heaped with food, lots of round tables and plenty of Bloody Marys. Thomas Cronin, the butler who once worked for Princess Margaret, sees that all goes as planned. The hostess is as casually dressed as her guests. She wears brightly colored tapered silk pants, a contrasting silk overblouse, pearls, tiny clusters of jewels at her ears and a hair ribbon.

"So many of these old houses are Spanish on the outside and French on the inside," Mrs. McMahon said as she strolled through a succession of drawing rooms. "Ours is an Addison Mizner. We've tried to make it comfortable."

Palm Beach was built by Henry Morrison Flagler, the Standard Oil multimillionaire. He arrived in 1893. A year later, he opened the Royal Poinciana, the first hotel here, and the real-estate boom was on. He also developed West Palm Beach on the mainland, calling it "The city I am building for my help." Mr. Flagler was followed by Mr. Mizner, who was responsible for the prevailing Saracen-Spanish architecture.

"Mizner was famous for forgetting to put things in houses," said Mrs. McMahon. "In our case, I think it was the stairs. They don't seem quite right."

Among other sizable estates are those of Mr. and Mrs. Loel Guinness, the Charles B. Wrightsmans, Mr. and Mrs. Michael G. Phipps, the Joseph P. Kennedys, the Stephen (Laddie) Sanfords and Mr. and Mrs. Herbert A. May. The Phipps establishment has separate telephone numbers for the main house, boat house, laundry, the Palace Cottage and the mushroom house. The Sanfords own Los Incas, a palatial seaside villa, which has several drawing rooms, a reception hall that's almost as big as the Waldorf-Astoria's main lobby and a trophy room. It is here, between tables made of elephants' feet, that the East Coast's indefatigable fund-raiser and her husband serve such drinks as the Sanford Sling—Dubonnet and lime juice over crushed ice —and talk up her various charity galas.

Mrs. May's Mar-a-Lago is even more incredible. It has 129 rooms and its own golf course. Until this season, it was the setting for regular square-dancing parties. "I'm not opening the house this year," said Mrs. May, who is the former Marjorie Merriweather Post Close Hutton Davies. "I'm going to be here only ten days."

Mrs. May, an honorary chairman of the Red Cross Ball, and Mrs. Jacques Balsan, the former Consuelo Vanderbilt, are among the resort's most cherished grande dames. Mrs. Effingham Townsend Irvin of New York and Mrs. John S. Pillsbury of Minneapolis are grande dames but are less well known. They have viewed Palm Beach from the top of the social order for years. "They call me a dowager," Mrs. Irvin said, "but I'm not, you know. I'm just a sweet little patroness of things." Mrs. Irvin, a friend of the legendary Mrs. Edward T. Stotesbury, is seventy-five. She sips an occasional Manhattan at the Colony Hotel, visits with other members of the exclusive Everglades Club and insists that "it's all very nouveau down here these days."

If this is the case, Mrs. Pillsbury has not noticed. She is a champion of civil rights, an art-collector and a tennis enthusiast, and has little to do with anyone except her friends. "I don't think I've been in a restaurant more than one or two times in all the years my husband and I have been coming here," she said. "We go to people's homes. We rarely even go to the club."

Some of Palm Beach's regulars prefer penthouses and yachts to mansions and hotels. J. Patrick Lannan, the Chicago investment banker, industrialist and art collector, lives in medieval splendor overlooking Worth Avenue, and Wally Findlay, the art dealer, lives above his gallery on the avenue. Mr. Findlay has two Rolls-Royces, a Bentley and a Buick, all of which are painted Cadillac white. "The Rolls white looks too much like a refrigerator," he said.

SAILING, SAILING OVER THE BOUNTIFUL MAIN

March 1965

No one in Palm Beach has more fun than the yachtsmen, those elegant adventurers who go down to the sea in ships stocked with Lowestoft china, crystal chandeliers and wall-to-wall carpeting.

When these wanderers have had enough of their pals on shore, they order more caviar, take their floating mansions out to sea and ignore the ship-to-shore radio. Once they are headed for the Bahamas, the Florida Keys or Miami, normal life resumes. Stewards serve them breakfast in bed. Personal maids, wearing uniforms and sunglasses, see that clothes are pressed. Chefs, whose domains rival those in the better New York apartments, whip up lobster mousse and cherries jubilee to go with the finest wines.

Finger bowls and casual clothes seem only mildly incongruous when the lady at the head of the table has pants on her legs and diamonds on most of her fingers. And if the ship is cruising close to shore, there is culture— black and white or colored television, sometimes both.

"My husband and I like being on the water," said Mrs. C. Hascall Bliss, the perennially tanned owner of the 104-foot *Maid Marian II.* "You either do or you don't. We're so crazy about it I sometimes wonder why we keep the house. We're never there."

The *Maid Marian,* the Blisses' home for nearly ten months a year, is one of the East Coast's most spectacular yachts—a French provincial town house on a hull. It has a pink and beige French drawing room, with one end walled in mirrors edged with delicate pink flowers and greenery; a library with paintings among the bookshelves; a turquoise dining saloon centered by a banquet table ornamented with opalescent glass fish from Paris, and what is believed to be the only baby blue, turquoise and white afterdeck.

"I love these colors," Mrs. Bliss admitted, looking directly at her husband, a retired business executive, for approval. "I always have."

She was sitting on a turquoise sofa. After she had spoken, the former Ruth Nash, daughter of the late Charles Nash, founder of the Detroit automobile company, patted a fat turquoise pillow. It was painted with a white inscription that read: DON'T CRITICIZE YOUR WIFE'S JUDGMENT. LOOK WHO SHE MARRIED.

The yacht's master bedroom, like a stateroom on the old *Queen Mary*, is turquoise, and so is the smokestack. But in one of the five bathrooms, the only turquoise is on a series of hand-painted seahorses. They line one of the basins.

"We seldom have more than sixteen for dinner," Mrs. Bliss said. "Everybody we know likes to sit down."

Deck-chair aristocrats try to avoid the complications of ocean storms, which tend to deflate the cheese soufflés, blow the men's custom-made yachting caps off into the sea and discourage some guests from consuming their share of the champagne.

"Everything's built in," Mrs. Bliss said. "But I do see that the flowers are all right."

Besides giant pots of healthy-looking pink geraniums and begonias, the *Maid Marian* usually carries such cut flowers as pink carnations and white chrysanthemums.

Colonel and Mrs. Leon Mandel have potted plants aboard the *Carola*, the 121-foot yacht Mrs. Mandel calls "our houseboat." But this vessel is better known for its arsenal. "We go shooting," said Mrs. Mandel, the former Carola Panekai-Bertini of Havana, one of the United States most honored target shots. "We spend the fall in Chicago, the spring and summer in Europe, and the winter in Palm Beach. We get quail forty minutes from here."

The *Carola* is Colonel Mandel's fourth yacht. His first, bought in 1930, was named for the *Buccaneer*—the ship William Randolph Hearst used to run news dispatches from Cuba to Florida during the Spanish-American War. When peace was restored, Mr. Hearst sold the *Buccaneer* to Colonel Mandel's grandfather. In World War II, Colonel Mandel, a retired retail merchant from Chicago, served in the Air Force. His yacht, the first of two named *Carola*, went to the Pacific as part of the Navy. He did not acquire the present *Carola* until 1951.

"I was a couple of years there without a ship," he said.

No such catastrophe is likely to befall Mr. and Mrs. James H. Kimberly. The Kimberly-Clark paper products heir ("I'm just a stockholder") and his wife have nine boats, all of which they keep in their backyard docks. "Now let's see," said Mrs. Kimberly, trying to remember which boat was which. "There's the *Gray Fox*; it's ninety feet long. And the *Blue Fox*; it's a fifty-one-foot sport fisherman. And the *Little Fox II*, which is an inboard speedboat, made of Fiberglass. And the sixteen-foot Boston whaler; that's the *Silver Fox*—the one we use for water skiing. And the thirteen-foot Boston whaler—*Foxy*—the only one that's just for me. What have I forgotten?"

The former Sharon Curran of San Francisco, a slender blonde who commutes to Europe to act in movies, paused momentarily to catch her breath.

"Oh, yes," she said. "The sailboats. There's the *White Fox*. And the *Sunfish*. Is that eight? No? Well, then there's one missing."

Mrs. Kimberly had forgotten the *Bimini Fox*. Her husband said it was a bonefish barge, and that he uses the *Blue Fox* for tournament fishing (blue marlin, sailfish and tuna). Their house, a pink stucco mansion that does not get much use, is called the Foxes' Lair. "I run all these boats myself," said Mr. Kimberly, a public-relations executive who wears a gold ring in his right ear. "When I can't, I'll take up croquet."

The Kimberlys, who have houses in Chicago and Neenah, Wisconsin, employ an oceangoing chef. But they are not strangers in their own galleys. They often cook and eat what they catch, or whip up hamburgers just for the fun of it.

Life is rarely as informal aboard the *Curlew III*, D. C. Elwood's 100-foot sailing ketch. "Everybody thinks 'cause you're in oil how easy it all is," said Mr. Elwood, shaking his head. "Well, it isn't. You don't hit every time."

Mr. Elwood, an introspective tycoon from Houston, shudders at the very thought that money in any form might be mentioned in his presence. He owns neither horses, ranches nor what he calls "cows," and if he has a ten-gallon hat, he keeps it out of sight.

"This feeling I have for the sea," he said, groping for words. "I don't know how you'd describe it. There's none of your fuss. It smells good. You don't get lonely 'cause there's too many things going on."

The *Curlew*, named for the wild bird found in Texas and the Northwest, is a million-dollar property with a crew of six. It has crossed the Gulf of Mexico ("That's like crossing the ocean") and sailed the length of the Mississippi River ("The most overrated piece of water in the world"). Its mainmast is as high as the *Maid Marian* is long, and all its place plates are vermeil or silver.

"I don't go ashore much," Mr. Elwood said, flicking an ash into a crested silver tray. "I don't have to. Most anybody wants to see me comes here."

PORTRAIT PAINTING: THE HEAVY INDUSTRY

March 1971

Hollywood's gone and New York is an urban crisis. But Palm Beach, that gilded land of the very rich, can still be depended upon to supply more than its share of the nation's glamour.

Besides being an impeccably kept tropical island with an opulence that fulfills some people's idea of the American dream, Palm Beach is a refuge for several thousands of the nation's multimillionaires. They have more diamonds, more Rolls-Royces, more mansions with more drawing rooms, more artwork, more servants, more ball gowns, more champagne and more money than the other 95 percent of the population. They also have more leisure time.

Yet sitting around isn't fashionable, and if they're not out playing golf and tennis, the rich are running boutiques stocked with $1,000 trinkets (Au Bon Goût now charges a $50 membership just to shop—a ploy that keeps the tourists from interfering with the big spenders); raising vast sums for charity ($700,000 from a ball isn't unusual even in these economically troubled times), and building and decorating palatial villas—which they then sell so they can build and decorate even more palatial villas.

Such households, with their sixty-foot rooms and twenty-foot ceilings, require vast amounts of art. Which may explain why painting, particularly portrait painting, is the resort's heavy industry, and why everybody who is anybody—from aristocrats and board chairmen to heiresses and tycoons—is either painting, having his portrait painted or buying art.

"We always have twenty portrait painters in town," said George Vigouroux, Jr., director of the Palm Beach Galleries. "I guess they make money."

Mr. Vigouroux started his gallery thirteen years ago. In earlier days, $400 for a painting was a fair amount of money. Today, he gets $1,200 as easily as a grocer gets $10. "The thing to do is to entertain the painters," he said. "We have a new show with cocktails and a new artist once a week for eighteen weeks. Every painter gets another three or four parties."

Totted up, that comes to something like seventy-two parties—just for Mr. Vigouroux's stable of painters. Yet his gallery, which represents sixty artists, including six portrait painters, is only one of twenty-three galleries in the resort. The largest is the Wally Findlay Gallery, which for years has made many millions off French Impressionists as well as Bernard Buffet, Nicola Simbari and Henri Maikes.

"Lord, how they buy," Mr. Vigouroux said of his friends. "They buy and buy till they don't have wall space for any more. Then they give their old paintings to the hospital so they can buy some more."

Mr. Vigouroux's sister-in-law, Mrs. Reed Albee, widow of the chain-theater owner, is one of the resort's newest and most enthusiastic painters. After perhaps four weeks in an oils class that includes Mrs. George Headley, Jr. (Barbara Whitney), she has produced two still lifes—two half lemons with two pomegranates in one and two Golden Delicious apples with a persimmon in the other. "I'd better paint something other than fruit or people will think I have a complex," she said.

Mrs. Albee, an early riser who sometimes holds coffee hours at 8:30 A.M., rents what she calls "just a tiny, tiny house"—a mansion with a living room that measures twenty-five by forty feet, a pavilioned terrace, a heated swimming pool and masses of pink geraniums and potted orchids.

"I'm here all alone with my maid, the butler and the cook," she said.

Her son, Edward Albee, the playwright, is expected for a spring visit. When the season ends, she will return to her Westchester home, accompanied by the portrait of herself that now hangs in her Palm Beach living room.

Guilford Dudley, Jr., paints, too, and it's probably a good thing. When President Nixon appointed him Ambassador to Denmark, he took some of his Palm Beach paintings to Copenhagen. That left him with wall space to spare.

"That's my Gainsborough portrait of Jane and Trevania," he said, indicating a painting he did of his wife and daughter. "It's soft and pretty."

The Dudleys, who have another house in Nashville, Tennessee, where he was president of Life and Casualty Insurance Company, redecorated the Copenhagen Embassy and added a swimming pool.

"Nothing like Walter Annenberg did in London," Mr. Dudley explained. But, according to Mrs. Dudley, "Everything except the tables and chairs are ours."

The Dudleys' chief contribution, however, had to do with the bomb shelter the Germans built into the Copenhagen residence which they occupied in World War II. The Dudleys knocked out the walls of the shelter, put in a dance floor and a stereophonic system, decorated the place to look vaguely like a stable, christened it a discothèque and promptly had a party in honor of Mr. and Mrs. Henry Ford 2nd.

"I wasn't sure it was dignified for an embassy," Mr. Dudley said, "but the Danes love it."

Mrs. Joseph H. King is too busy with golf and tennis to paint. Yet, like virtually everybody she knows, she's a collector. Her newest painting ("I didn't have a Van Dongen so Joe gave me one for Christmas") sits on a silk-covered chair in her black and white marble apartment—waiting for wall space. The Kings also have works by Jansem, Chambourg, Beauchant, Lorjou and Utrillo.

"I'd rather have paintings than jewels," she said. Mr. King has little time for Palm Beach. While his wife dashes around town in "my little car" (an $8,000 red Mercedes convertible), he is in New York, where he is chairman of Eastman Dillon, Union Securities and Company, Inc., the investment banking concern.

"When we're together, we're like two teen-agers," Mrs. King said. "We have a fun life even if we're separated from each other. We really like to talk to each other."

Mrs. Livingston L. Biddle 2nd's first love is French and Colonial antiques, but she's had her portrait painted, follows the art openings ("I'm mad about Keith Ingermann's paintings") and works for the Colonial Dames of America. "We raise money for scholarships and the Y.W.C.A. in West Palm Beach," she said.

The Colonial Dames is a women's club that has nothing to do with achievements—contemporary or otherwise. The only way to become a member is to have had an ancestor living on these shores not just before the American Revolution but before the Battle of Lexington. Even then, membership is difficult to achieve.

"Membership in the Daughters of the American Revolution won't necessarily work," she said. "Descendance from a *Mayflower* passenger or a lord of the manor would."

The Biddles are from Philadelphia ("There are so many of us you might as well call it Biddleville"). Their ancestor Nicholas Biddle was president of the Second Bank of the United States. And members of the family are forever being mistaken for one another. "When I was married, I had to have a blueprint," said Mrs. Biddle, the former Suzanne Hutchison Burke. The Livingston Biddles, and there seem to be dozens of them, belong to one of two Biddle family lines. Livingston, Jr., is not her husband's father but his cousin. Livingston 3rd is their own son and Livingston 4th is her husband's cousin's son.

Her husband's brother is the late Anthony Drexel Biddle. His sister is Mrs. T. Markoe Robertson, the former Cordelia Drexel Biddle Duke.

"It's enough to drive anyone crazy," Mrs. Biddle said. "I don't blame people if they can't make head or tail of us."

Life in the Stephen M. Sanford household is equally confusing. What with two Doberman pinschers, the Belgian shepherd, the King Charles spaniel puppy, and heaven knows how many little Jones terriers, the place is rapidly going to the dogs.

"I'm a dog person," Mrs. Sanford said, cuddling Duke, the puppy. "I like having them around."

King Charles spaniels, for people who aren't up on such matters, are royal dogs held in particularly high esteem in Britain, where royalty still matters. Some of the best ones have what is known as a Blenheim spot on their foreheads. It gives them special cachet. "That Blenheim spot business is silly," Mrs. Sanford said. "When I saw the litter, I took the baby without the Blenheim spot. I knew he'd have more personality, and he does."

Occasionally, the dogs bound around Mrs. Sanford's garden room, which shouldn't be confused with the white drawing room, the pink shell room overlooking the Atlantic Ocean or the arched ballroom that passes for an entrance hall.

The garden room is lined with perhaps thirty fishtail palms, dozens of potted chrysanthemums and all manner of wild game trophies.

"I like all sorts of animals," Mrs. Sanford said. "Some of them are far more pleasant than people." She likes diamonds and other jewels, too, and she has and wears plenty of them.

"Everybody else is terrified of robbery," she said. "I'm not really. The Dobermans and the police dog are vicious. Why, the police come in here with drawn guns. Everybody's afraid of them."

13

With burglaries and robberies of one sort or another (bandits with guns recently took the Bank of Palm Beach for $500,000 in cash), many of the women aren't wearing the jewels they used to.

"Not me," Mrs. Sanford said bravely. "There's nothing worse than having jewels you love and not being able to wear them. The only trouble now is that I'm afraid people will mistake mine for the Kenny Lane fake stuff."

IF YOU'RE NAUGHTY ON JUPITER ISLAND,
YOU'RE EXILED TO PALM BEACH

March 1967

Hobe Sound

There's no law against whooping it up on Jupiter Island, the remote and sufficiently elegant little winter resort just east of here. But hardly anyone does.

Peace, quiet and privacy are what the four hundred aristocratic inhabitants say they're after, even at the height of the season, and peace, quiet and privacy are what they get—in large doses. It's all right to get a little excited over a bridge game now and then, read a murder mystery, watch a late television movie, or foxtrot after dinner on Thursday until the midnight curfew. But aside from a purposely vigorous athletic program and the single $50-a-ticket charity ball the islanders allow themselves, that's pretty much it.

So much so, in fact, that the more adventuresome of the affluent residents, including the Island Club's president, John R. Drexel 3rd, and Mrs. Charles Shipman Payson, are likely to pop into their limousines, head for the bridge that spans the waters of Hobe Sound, and then hurry on down Route 1 to Palm Beach. Once they get there (at most, it's a forty-five-minute drive), Mr. Drexel, a descendant of the Philadelphia banking family, and Mrs. Payson, who loves her race horses almost as much as she loves her New York Mets baseball team, never do anything more daring than attend a few parties and see a few friends. But they, and such other temporary runaways as Spencer T. Olin, a director of Olin Mathieson Chemical Corporation, and Gordon Gray, chairman of the National Trust for Historic Preservations and a member of President Johnson's Foreign Intelligence Advisory Board— both of whom like to see what's going on in the Palm Beach art galleries—are suspected of actually liking Palm Beach a little. And by Jupiter Island standards, such thinking is akin to heresy.

The more conservative denizens tolerate such escapades, of course. But they're not very enthusiastic about them. Palm Beach, with its diamond-spangled marathon of luncheons, fashion shows, cocktail parties, charity balls, is not their cup of tea. And they like to think that being smaller and quieter,

Jupiter Island is the more exclusive, the more *recherché* and, therefore, the better of the two resorts. Mrs. Joseph Verner Reed, Sr., Jupiter Island's efficient mother superior, does not seem to subscribe to this thinking. She never says Jupiter Island is better—just that it's different.

"If we wanted all *that,*" she said, referring to Palm Beach, "we wouldn't live here."

Mrs. Reed, a tall, blue-eyed grandmother whose blond eyebrows and eyelashes show no signs of ever having been artificially darkened, is the daughter of the late Samuel Frazier Pryor and the sister of the present Samuel F. Pryor, who is never known as Junior. Her father, a member of a prominent Connecticut Republican family, was president of the Remington Arms Company of Bridgeport. Her brother, who divides his winters between Hawaii and Jupiter Island, is a retired vice-president of Pan American Airways. And she is president of the Hobe Sound Company. It controls the island through the land (nobody can buy without her approval), one of the few privately owned water systems and the Island Club.

In 1932, her husband, who is now executive producer of the American Shakespeare Festival, author and self-styled "angel for the difficult theatrical production," and a friend bought the island and a lot of property on the mainland. And then Mr. Reed bought his partner out.

"I'm too busy to have much to do with it anymore," Mr. Reed said. "Mrs. Reed runs it. I'm just the queen's husband."

As president of the company, a job she's had since World War II, Mrs. Reed is the only permanent member of the Island Club's board of governors. She has her own office in the clubhouse, a sprawling and comfortably furnished building. And on weekday mornings during the season—November 1 through April 15—she is there, smoking her little Dutch cigars, attending to business and chatting with the resident members. She alone decides who shall occupy which guest rooms in the clubhouse and where everyone shall sit in the dining room, and she has been known to arrange and rearrange her room and seating charts scores of times in an effort to head off what to her is some impossible juxtaposition.

She also polices "the Brig," a dormitory for prep-school and college students invited to Jupiter Island for spring vacations. These young people may stay as long as they're in bed with the lights off by midnight, up early in the morning for the sports, and generally behave themselves. If they don't behave—and this goes for adults as well as young people—they're in for a shameful drumming out. They're told they're leaving, a car is sent around to pick them up, and they're banished to Palm Beach.

"We have been saved here," Mrs. Reed says passionately, "by a lack of commercialism. We have a pro shop, a package shop, Western Union, the nurses' office, our theater and a library. Everything else is on the mainland."

Residents are either "sound people" or "ocean people," depending upon where their houses are. Ocean people tend to have grand houses with long driveways and vast gardens. They do not mind the wind, the roar and the dampness associated with life on the beach. Sound people live in less elaborate quarters and rave about the placid waters in their front yards and their views of the sunsets. The Reeds live on the sound. They share their comfortable white drawing room and its pale green, cream and orange furnishings with a pair of Pekingese dogs, a pot of purple orchids and Mrs. Reed's needlepoint stand. Mr. Reed arranges the flowers. "I like chrysanthemums," he said recently, sticking yellow and lavender ones into a tall vase. "They're beautiful."

Like twenty-eight of the 366 resident members of the club, the Reeds consider Greenwich, Connecticut, home. But Jupiter Island is almost as Middle Western as it is Eastern. Retired military figures, including General James A. Van Fleet (U.S.A., retired), commander of the United Nations troops in the Korean War, share the tropical hideaway with Frederick E. Jones, the Columbus insurance magnate; Frederick K. Weyerhaeuser, a St. Paul member of the timber family; and former Governor and Mrs. William Scranton of Dalton, Pennsylvania.

C. Douglas Dillon, former Secretary of the Treasury, is among those who have houses here, and the list includes James Paul Mills, the Middleburg, Virginia, horse owner and broker who's married to the former Alice F. du Pont; Gerald C. Holbrook, who flies his plane to Georgia for the shooting; James H. McGraw, Jr., former head of the McGraw-Hill publishing empire; and Edwin D. Etherington, who gave up the presidency of the American Stock Exchange to become Wesleyan University's twelfth president.

Residents are permitted to own dogs, Mrs. Reed said, and no particular style of architecture is required for the houses. "I think it would be deadly, absolutely deadly," she said, "if all the architecture were the same." This laxity has not, as might be expected, produced either an abundance of dogs or a wide variety of architectural designs. Most of the houses are either French or Italian in feeling, built around open courtyards, and behemoth in size. One of the more elaborate of these is the John B. Ford house, which is reputed to have cost $500,000.

Mr. Ford, a Grosse Pointe Ford who's invariably mistaken for a member of the automotive family even though he drives a big gray Bentley, is board chairman of the Wyandotte Chemical Corporation. He and his wife, a slim blonde who hardly looks old enough to be anybody's grandmother, built their house seven years ago. Their front hall, with its twenty-foot ceiling, white walls and marble floor, opens on to a terrace planted with huge trees, and the swimming pool is just this side of the ocean. Mrs. Ford grows her own calla lilies, manages the couple's social life without the help of a secretary, and admits that if she wants to buy what she calls good clothes she has to go to Palm Beach.

"Oh, but we seldom go there," she exclaimed. "I certainly wouldn't want to live there."

The Fords, whose evenings are devoted to going to or giving dinner parties that end around 11:30 P.M., are evidence that Jupiter Island doesn't have to be dull. Both are avid readers, are mad about the lecture series at the theater, and do a lot of walking. "You walk for exercise—not to get any place," said Mr. Ford, a distinguished-looking man who likes blazers with his pastel-colored slacks. "Everybody plays tennis, golfs or goes fishing."

From a fashion point of view, Jupiter Island is one of the few places where it is still safe for women to wear skirts that cover their knees, tailored dresses with waistlines and hairnets. Pants with flowered silk shirts are *de rigueur*, too, and it's perfectly all right not to wear any diamonds until dinner time. "We have no miniskirts, no paper dresses, and no vinyl dresses," Mrs. Ford said, obviously pleased. "We're a conservative group."

Jupiter Island's politics tend to be just about as conservative as its fashions. More residents share Archibald B. Roosevelt's interest in the Republican party than W. Averell Harriman's loyalty to the Democrats. Mr. Roosevelt, one of President Theodore Roosevelt's sons, has a white French house with a pink living room. He is in residence more regularly than Mr. Harriman. As President Johnson's Ambassador-at-Large, Mr. Harriman travels around the world and he is in and out of New York and Washington often. When he appeared here for what he said might be a seventeen-day vacation, nobody really believed him.

"He'll never be able to stay that long," said Peter Duchin, his godchild. "If he does, it'll be a miracle."

Mr. Duchin, the society orchestra leader whose wife is the former Cheray Zauderer of New York, recently was visiting the Harrimans between engagements. He played a charity ball in Palm Beach and was then going down to Miami to play at the Doral. In the meantime he and Mrs. Duchin were relaxing and taking tennis lessons. "It's not like anywhere else," Mrs. Duchin said, describing the island. "We don't do anything. We never go out. We go to bed early. It's so quiet. Ten days is just about enough."

The regulars stay a lot longer than that. Some arrive in November while others wait for Christmas, and there always are a lot of people around throughout April. March, however, is one of the biggest months.

"This is when our children and grandchildren come down," Mrs. Reed said happily. "We have a program of activities for them. We keep them busy."

The charity ball, which benefits Martin Memorial Hospital in nearby Stuart, was held recently. It raised about $15,000—peanuts by Palm Beach's $100,000 standards.

"But we don't go in for all that fund-raising," Mrs. Reed said. "We want a quieter life."

Warren Avis wanted a house "where you'd never see the servants," and he got it. His celebrated multilevel house overlooking Acapulco is so big you can't hear or see the houseguests, either. Which doesn't mean Mr. Avis is lonely. He has 150 people in at the drop of a hat.
William Sauro, *The New York Times* (1968)

Acapulco

The rich nomads who have given Acapulco what glamour it has achieved in recent years are neither hermits nor homebodies. Yet aside from an occasional shopping spree, they aren't out on the town giving the masses of tourists something to talk about.

What gaiety they do allow themselves is conducted almost entirely within the elegant confines of the marble *palacios* in the green hills above Acapulco Bay, and it often consists of nothing more spectacular than sitting around in bathing suits watching the evening sun sink into the Pacific. Such days, which usually start midmorning with sunbathing and swimming before a round of drinks, a salad and then a siesta during which several of the world's most beautifully preserved people actually take naps, are the good days.

And they are why Acapulco, like such beauty resorts as Main Chance and The Greenhouse, survives. It is a balmy, palm-fringed pause that refreshes as well as a place to vacation from other more socially strenuous vacations.

Mrs. Emi Fors, Mr. and Mrs. John Wendell Anderson 3rd and Warren Avis are among those who have cachet in Acapulco. Mrs. Fors, a Californian whose father gave her the money to settle in Acapulco fifteen years

19

ago, gives the biggest and most important private party of the season: a costume dinner-dance for 300 to 350.

"Next year, my party's going to be for Padre Angel Boys Town," she said. "It's an orphanage."

If Mrs. Fors carries out her plan, Acapulco will then have two charity balls a season. The only one so far is a multicharity gala usually held in the Hilton Hotel's gardens.

"It is time for this," Mrs. Fors said. "There are needs here."

Mrs. Fors, a handsome woman who likes six-mile walks along the beach, lives among giant cut-leaf philodendron, bougainvillaea, bright paper flowers and white wicker furniture in an airy, multilevel house with parquet white Carrera marble floors and a panoramic view of the harbor. Her sunken mosaic bathtub is gold and white, while Mrs. Anderson's is cream outlined with pink.

"I'm mad about it," Mrs. Anderson said. "Just look at the view."

Mrs. Anderson's bathroom is cantilevered out toward the bay, and the view, as she indicated, is extraordinary. So is her library—built of stone and outfitted with records rather than books—and the waterfall that rushes through the house.

"The waterfall gets very noisy," she explained. "We have to turn it off in the afternoon. It begins to get on our nerves."

Mrs. Anderson, the former Lisa Ferraday, is not, as she put it, "just knocking myself out as a people collector." She and her husband, a Grosse Pointe tubing manufacturer, consider themselves day people ("Sometimes we get up at eight o'clock"). And if there's anything they can't stand, it's too many late nights. "That's not what we're here for," said Mrs. Anderson, who regularly outfits herself in little shifts and gold hoop earrings. "We like the tiny little frogs, the lizards, the sun."

"The part I accept with the greatest joy is the siesta," said Mr. Anderson, who takes one whenever he can.

"Yes," said his wife. "That's when I sit quietly with the help and do the menus or go and have my fittings."

Life at Warren Avis's cliff house apparently is more hectic, with guests coming and going to sun, sip something cool and swim. On a typical day, the host, an industrialist who has sold his rental car business, is likely to be padding around in bright orange shorts.

"I can handle 150 people at the drop of a hat," Mr. Avis said, adding that he himself designed his stove and a pantry that's open to anyone who wants to fix himself a drink or a snack. "I wanted a house where you'd never see the servants, and you don't."

The Avis establishment is so big and so intricately designed that guests in the same general area aren't necessarily visible to one another. The nearest thing to a front door is a gate with a bell at the top of a long and involved stairway that begins up the hill—somewhere above Mr. Avis's roof. But what you do see are terraces leading to other terraces, all of which overlook the bay, a telescope for Mr. Avis to identify pals on the yachts that come to call, several comfortably furnished marble living rooms and a bullhorn.

Mr. Avis needs the horn to call anyone who has wandered off somewhere—say to the beach 150 feet below. But it apparently is never used to call the gang in to dinner.

"We aren't that formal," he said.

JUST A LITTLE HOTEL-SIZE STONE AND MARBLE HIDEAWAY FOR THREE

March 1968

Casa de Lisa is a gigantic, multilevel sprawl of stone and marble that's regularly mistaken for a fortress. But it isn't a fortress at all. It's merely the extravagant hotel-size hideaway Mr. and Mrs. Carl Renstrom built themselves for the two months a year they spend in sunny, tropical Acapulco. The Renstroms could have been like some other American multimillionaires, who rent hotel suites for $100 a day or houses for $200 or $300 a day. But that's not their style. They like to stay in their own houses, which is what they are accustomed to doing in such places as Miami, the fishing country of northern Minnesota, at their fly-in camp in Ontario ninety miles northeast of International Falls, Minnesota, and in their native Omaha. So the house was inevitable.

Once they decided they liked Acapulco, they just had to build. The project involved four years, 162 tons of marble, countless pillars, arches and stair steps from old churches and monasteries, and heaven knows how many hundreds of thousands of dollars. But it apparently was worth it.

"We love it," said Mrs. Renstrom, a freckled blonde with big blue eyes. "It's the only Mexican colonial house in Acapulco."

It also is the only house named for Lisa Renstrom, the couple's eight-year-old daughter. She has polished black marble floors in her bedroom and her own big, round, sunken bathtub—just like her mother's and father's.

"We bought the lot from Lana Turner," Mrs. Renstrom said.

"It was exactly what we wanted," Mr. Renstrom added. "It's got everything."

Mr. Renstrom, a gray-haired athletic man who can do scores of pushups when he's in the mood, is the son of a Swedish immigrant. He was born in Omaha, where he was a Fuller brush salesman. Before long, he was developing and selling liquid solder. After that came the empire.

"I was in haircurlers in 1935," he said. "It pays to get into millions of women's hair."

It certainly did. He is still known as "the haircurler king," although he sold out to Rayette-Fabergé. His financial ventures include major real-estate investments in Mexico and great chunks of Omaha, where his company recently won the garbage disposal contract.

"I read in the paper where Japan has this machine that turns the garbage into stone," he said happily. "I'm investigating."

In the meantime, he's fishing, exercising and sunning himself at Casa de Lisa. When he resorts to his own sauna bath, which is big, roomy and windowed so it has a spectacular view of Acapulco Bay, he always comes away smelling faintly of cedar. The cedar walls were imported.

"I can't spend as much time here as I'd like," Mr. Renstrom said. "But we try to get away for a weekend now and then."

The couple travel in their own Lear jet, with Mr. Renstrom in the pilot's seat. Sometimes they bring in American beef—Acapulco not being at all famous for any of its meats. They don't have to bring in their water. "We have our own purifying plant," Mr. Renstrom said.

The Renstroms also have separate apartments for guests (fourteen could live in the house without running into each other except on the terrace around the swimming pool), a thatched-roof coffee house explicitly for watching the evening sun go down, four full-time gardeners (each with his own thatched-roof house), a cook, a houseboy who doubles as chauffeur and two maids.

"We keep the staff all year around," Mrs. Renstrom said.

And what happens during the ten months when the Renstroms aren't in residence? Not much. Richard M. Nixon was permitted to borrow the house. But, unlike most of the other big houses here, Casa de Lisa is not for rent.

When they're here, the Renstroms are what are known locally as quiet people. This means that they're not much interested in parties, night life or visiting other people's houses. When they want to see people, they invite them in. They have a lot of houseguests.

"We live in our bathing suits," said Mrs. Renstrom, the former Elizabeth Anderson. "This is not a place where you have to wear clothes."

The house, with its high Spanish arches, its carved wooden doors, its miles of plain marble floors, its pots of brightly colored bougainvillaea and its unexpected views of the bay, is purposely undecorated and very easy to keep up.

"You can clean the whole thing with a hose," Mrs. Renstrom said. "The water isn't going to hurt the marble."

And so it is with people who live in a marble fortress on a mountain top.

If he wasn't in Switzerland or the Sahara, Truman Capote spent his winters in his Palm Springs house, writing *Answered Prayers* on a portable typewriter. He and Maggie, his bulldog with the unusual appetite, have since moved closer to Hollywood.
Gary Settle, *The New York Times* (1970)

Palm Springs

The movie stars who frequent this remote and elegant sand pile try to be polite to everyone who comes to visit. They'll play golf with a man even if he is President of the United States. In recent years, almost anyone who wanted to be welcomed has been—politicians who win elections, Broadway luminaries, sports champions, labor leaders, millionaire industrialists, Socially Registered Easterners and royalty.

President Kennedy was here as the guest of Bing Crosby, and former President Dwight D. Eisenhower and his wife are expected again this winter. But it's the film people who set the pace. They were the first true resort lovers here, and it is they who made the desert chic. The stars organized most of the country clubs, directed the construction of golf courses over what had been nothing but sand, and built the first piano-shaped swimming pools. Such old-timers as William Powell fell into the pool of Raymond Loewy, the industrial designer, long before New Frontiersmen took up the sport.

The stars also created their own uniform. Charles Farrell, Janet Gaynor's leading man in *Seventh Heaven* (1927) and amiable founder of the Racquet Club, does not look down on anyone who wears a coat and tie at midday. He's too democratic. But his own attire—brick-pink shorts, a yellow sport shirt and black alligator shoes—is far more acceptable. "When the New Yorkers started coming out, they wanted to dress," Mr. Farrell said. "So we made

25

Saturday night black tie at the club. It's requested, but not required. We've never really had 100 percent black tie, not even on New Year's Eve." The leading ladies have contributed standards of taste, too. Besides Capri pants or short shorts with high-heeled gold shoes, they made it almost mandatory to wear enormous diamonds in the morning. Then, with typical logic, they decided jewelry was a crashing bore and stored all but their wedding rings in safes.

"It gets so hot here one has to adapt," said Zeppo Marx, youngest of the Marx brothers. "My wife plays golf in her swim suit so she can jump into the pools beside every hole." Mrs. Marx, a lithe blonde who once was a model, could not indulge herself in this fashion if it weren't for the way in which Palm Springs residents arrange their homes. First comes the country club, then the golf course. And finally at the edges of the fairways, barely out of range of the flying golf balls, come the houses and backyard pools. There are about three thousand pools here, one for every six people.

Phil Harris and his wife, Alice Faye, the former actress, have such a house and pool, but it's protected from intruders by a wall. The Harrises are among the thirty-five stockholders who developed Thunderbird Country Club. It is as fashionable as Eldorado, La Quinta and Tamarisk Country Clubs or Smoke Tree Ranch, also in Palm Springs. The Harrises, like at least half the celebrities here, live reasonably quiet lives. They're usually asleep by 9:30 P.M.

"You either like the desert or you don't," Mrs. Harris said. "I love it. I never go into town unless I have to."

"Town" for the Harrises and such home owners as Alan Ladd, Bing Crosby, Bob Hope, Red Skelton and Dinah Shore means Los Angeles. But to Frederick Loewe, the composer, or to Floyd Odlum, president of the Atlas Corporation, and his wife Jacqueline Cochran "town" could be New York or a foreign capital. To Dan Thornton, a former Governor of Colorado, it always means Denver. The Thorntons have a house in a cove some seven hundred feet above the Coachella Valley floor. They like it in the mountains with the desert spread out before them.

"Dan here's put out if he can't have steak three times a day," said Mr. Harris, his good friend.

Aside from patients in out-and-out health resorts, people in Palm Springs probably pay more attention to how they look and feel than any other group in America. They are universally tan and athletically versatile. Theoretically, the social season runs from October to June, but there's rarely a night, except in midsummer, when someone isn't having a cocktail or dinner party. Each club has its opening party, and there are more parties held in connection with the continual parade of sports tournaments. And then, when it seems as if peace may prevail, Frank Sinatra's helicopter drops out of the sky with a new load of party people.

Either that or someone organizes a charity gala, one of which was named for New York's April in Paris Ball. The diamonds come out of the safe (the police chief once estimated that $20-million worth of jewelry is displayed during a mildly celebrational dance at the El Mirador Hotel), and unless it's platinum, all that glitters is gold.

"This is absolutely the only place to be and the time of year to be here," said Mr. Farrell, whose home is not far from the Racquet Club. The club, which shares Palm Springs' tennis players with the Tennis Club, has just had its opening cocktail party. This annual gathering no longer has what used to be Mr. Farrell's special touch. In the old days, before he became Palm Springs' mayor and his wife made him stop, he inaugurated each season by dressing in white tie, top hat and tails, and somersaulting into the swimming pool.

PALM SPRINGS: TRANQUILLITY, DESPITE GO-GO REPUTATION

March 1970

For some years now, Palm Springs has been having what it calls a "golden era," and although nobody seems to know exactly what that means, it has been interpreted as signifying that at long last "the Springs," as the regulars call it, has arrived.

Rich Easterners, who were never quite sure how to approach the movie stars who built and run the resort, own houses here these days, and the desert is littered with Texas tycoons, aristocratic San Franciscans, Middle Western industrialists, European nobles and people who play golf with presidents.

The late Dwight D. Eisenhower was by no means the first President to pass through the Coachella Valley, but it became his winter home, and after him came John F. Kennedy (who never stayed very long), Lyndon B. Johnson, Richard M. Nixon and—to the great joy of at least some of the residents—Vice President Spiro T. Agnew.

The Vice President was here not long ago, playing golf, sitting in the guest of honor's chair at dinner parties and commiserating about the state of youth in America, and as Mrs. Pollard Simons said after he left, "He really brings out the politics in you." Mrs. Simons, who may or may not be political, is a dazzling creature who looks as if she presides over a coral and marble palace with gilded bathroom fixtures and a sunken swimming pool, and of course she does—with a cook and a houseman to help.

"Each year I have a project," she said. "This year, it's avoiding one."

As a result of this thinking, she and her husband, who's in real estate, insurance, construction, oil and all the other enterprises suitable to a proper

Texan, are living the typical quiet desert life. He plays golf. She swims, makes her own mayonnaise, pleads with the florist for the long branches of yellow forsythia that must be flown in from Los Angeles, and is grateful their days are not cluttered with luncheons, dinners, cocktail parties and benefits. "We can get all that back in Dallas," Mrs. Simons said.

Or in Jamaica, where Mr. Simons owns the Tryall Club and they are building a house. Or almost anywhere except Palm Springs which, despite its go-go reputation, is perhaps the only important American resort where dinner jackets and evening dresses are rarely seen and almost everybody who is anybody is asleep in his or her king-size bed before midnight.

"You'd be surprised how many people get up early," said Mrs. Paul Zuckerman, widow of a New York stockbroker. "Why, I can get most of my telephoning done before nine o'clock."

Mrs. Zuckerman gets up early to paint miniature pictures, sew on her needlepoint and work in what her friends consider one of the prettiest gardens in Palm Springs. At the moment, the lawns beneath the palms and mimosa around her pool are an array of daisies and petunias, but some of the petunias are pink. "I'm going to change that," Mrs. Zuckerman said. "All the flowers should be white. They light up better at night." Two gardeners come in three times a week to look after Mrs. Zuckerman's yard. Yet nobody's figured out how to get it through the dry summer heat. "You just learn to live with it," she said. "You know the grass and the flowers are going to die every fall. Everything has to be put in all over again every year."

Mrs. Zuckerman's house is white with white floors. She has two living rooms: one with pink, coral and green prints, the other with a zebra rug and a Coromandel screen. She uses them both for big parties. "We all use the same party helpers," she said. "What you do is get on Myrtle's list. It's almost like being in the *Social Register*."

Myrtle is the statuesque Myrtle Bennett, the former Cotton Club dancer who left Harlem thirty years ago. During the day, she presides over Truman Capote's house. At night, she caters the dinner parties that matter. Bennett Cerf, the book publisher, is high on her list, and so are Kirk Douglas and Henry Ittleson, Jr., the banker.

Besides Mr. Capote, Miss Bennett's charges include his bulldogs, eight-month-old Maggie and ten-year-old Charlie. Maggie is the talk of Palm Springs. After eating Princess Lee Radziwill's sable coat last season ("I could have heard Lee's screams a mile away," Mr. Capote said), she started off this season with several of Mr. Capote's shoes and went on to an entire bale of pralines a friend had sent from New Orleans, Mrs. Johnny Carson's pink slippers and a trio of potted poinsettias. The bulldogs are here for the winter because several years ago Mr. Capote decided he liked deserts.

"I tried the Sahara," he explained, "but you couldn't get anything to eat or read. The last place I thought I'd end up was Palm Springs."

But now (when he isn't working on his new book or enchanting the inevitably casually dressed habitués by turning up for dinner in his rainbow-striped wool cardigan with the fluffy orange scarf) Mr. Capote raves about the blue sky, the lavender mountains, the dry air, the warm days and the cold nights. "It's the perfect place," he said from among the pillows and furs tossed over the leather sofa in his highly personal living room. "It makes you feel good."

Aside from the climate, the golf (twenty-six courses with plans for a twenty-seventh), the tennis (at either the Racquet Club or the Tennis Club) and the early hours, what makes the denizens feel so good is those periodic trips to the Spa. The ritual there involves forty-five minutes of eucalyptus steam, seven to ten minutes of pure hot steam, a mineral bath with water swirling around, a cold shower and then a massage.

"Afterwards you feel as if you've really accomplished something terrific," said Mrs. Doris Vidor, daughter of the late Harry Warner of the movies. "You feel just great."

Mrs. Donald S. Stralem, wife of a New York banker, says she feels great, too, but that "four weeks of nothing is all I can take. After that I can hardly wait to get back to New York." Mr. and Mrs. Stralem have been coming to the desert since 1935, a year before the Racquet Club, the resort's most socially important institution, was organized. Louis A. Benoist, the San Francisco vintner, is an old-timer, too, and there are days when he misses the coyotes that came out of the hills at night to howl at the moon.

"We still hear the quail," Mr. Benoist said, "and six raccoons come for dinner every night and wash themselves in the pool."

The Benoists live in a series of little pink brick houses in the foothills, forty-nine stone steps above the road and perhaps a thousand feet above the desert floor. They arrive in March and stay until June. "We live a quiet life," Mrs. Benoist said. "We are here for Christmas, then to Puerto Vallarta for maybe two months, then back here, and then to Virginia for the summer."

Mr. and Mrs. Joseph H. Hirshhorn live quietly, too, in a house filled with works from his multimillion-dollar art collection. There are Calder sculptures on the end tables, a Matisse figure on the coffee table and at least six de Koonings, including the painting in the kitchen.

"We play house here," said Mr. Hirshhorn, the mining and oil in-dustrialist. "I'm up at six or six-thirty making the coffee and carrying out the garbage and Olga goes to classes and makes meatloaf."

Last season, Mrs. Hirshhorn had French classes at the College of the Desert at 9 A.M. This year, she's taking design and composition at 8 A.M. And while other resorters drive about in Cadillacs and Jaguars, she drives a rented Mustang. Her husband rides a tricycle.

"It's a way to exercise," he said.

The Hirshhorns have homes in Cap d'Antibes in the South of France, Greenwich, Connecticut, and New York. But their chief concern is the house they are building in Washington. They want to live there, Mr. Hirshhorn said, "so we can be near the collection." He has given his art works, which he persists in calling "my nine or ten thousand items," to the Smithsonian Institution, which is building a branch to accommodate them.

By contrast with the Benoists and the Hirshhorns, Mr. and Mrs. Michael Nidorf are pure Southern Californians. He is a retired television executive. She is Louis B. Mayer's widow. They are on the party circuits either here or in Beverly Hills. "At night we go to dinners and movies," Mrs. Nidorf said. "That's about all there is to do." The residents show movies in their own projection rooms or rent theaters for films they ship in from Hollywood.

"I do not go to the movies," said the elegant Maggie, Baroness van Zuylan. "I play cards."

The baroness, who speaks four or five languages fluently, is new to Palm Springs this year and one of the few women who regularly wears dresses and diamonds. She says she finds the desert as exhilarating as Paris, where she has a town house, or the Netherlands, where her castle feels empty unless there are twenty-five or thirty guests. The trouble here, she says, is that no house is as large as her castle.

"I need more rooms," she moaned. "How can I entertain properly?"

The baroness, who has space for four houseguests without anyone's having to double up, is an Egyptian with a Belgian passport. Her husband was a Dutch diplomat. She has been everywhere and seen everything. But when she first arrived, she was in something of a dither. The mansion she rented was handsome enough (white with lots of mirrors, several living rooms and a pool), but no push buttons to summon the chef and maid she brought from Paris. Mr. Capote finally told her that, in Palm Springs, one either yelled at the top of his lungs or used the intercom telephone. The baroness is using the telephone.

Las Vegas gets them all, of course, not the least of them being Baron Arndt Friedrich Alfried Krupp von Bohlen und Halbach, the munitions heir (right), who partied with Olene Alvarez (left) and Clifford S. Perlman (center), whose company owns Caesars Palace.
D. Gorton, *The New York Times* (1971)

Las Vegas

After seventy-two hours of festivities, the score at Caesars Palace today was two $100,000 galas and a surprise wedding down and a plane trip to the Grand Canyon to go, but as William S. Weinberger said, "I can't see why anyone would get excited. It's like this every day."

Mr. Weinberger is president of Caesars Palace, by no means the least of the big, brassy gambling establishments for which this neon-gaudy town is famous, and he's used to every day being New Year's Eve. But "the royals," as some twenty elegant and titled Europeans imported for the hotel's fifth anniversary celebration came to be known, were more than a little undone.

"What can happen next?" asked Prince Maxim Cröy, a young banker from an old French family. "We do not have things like this in Munich." What they don't have in Munich is invitational four-day parties with the host—in this case Caesars Palace—picking up the tab not just for air fare to and from Europe, but also meals, rooms and social excursions. Predictably, a lot of the royals were quick to accept.

The group, mostly young German and French nobles, was new to the frankly-good-for-business junket, and they kept asking, "Why me? Why was I invited?" Nobody gave them a straight answer, of course, but Caesars Palace hoped they would add glamour and class to their party, and they did. They were not expected to gamble. By late Thursday, after a yachting trip to Hoover Dam and a banquet that ended with waitresses in brief togas massaging their aristocratic necks and backs, the royals were being joined by a thousand American guests. This list included tycoons who had flown in on their own planes, movie stars, big gamblers who ignored everything except the gaming tables, Joe Louis, Pancho Gonzales, the sheriff of Los Angeles County, and a man who insisted he was Aristotle Onassis's nephew.

The main event (crap-shooters happily clutching wads of $100-bills probably would not agree) was "Winter Wonderland," the anniversary extravaganza. The first of these twin dinner-dances was held in a vast ballroom the hotel calls "The Coliseum."

Harry Finley, the Los Angeles decorator, aimed for "an ice palace in the desert when it's 110 degrees," and he got it. Everything—from the walls, ceilings, carpeting and dance floor to the tables, chairs, two thousand chrysanthemums and scores of live doves cooing away in cages—was white. Six hundred freshly cut Oregon evergreen trees were covered with shredded Styrofoam snow. Mirrored domes spattered reflected "snowflakes" against the wall. And bubble machines blew snowflakes into everybody's face.

"Fantastic," exclaimed Princess Veronique de Rachevsky, widow of a Cinerama executive. "Fantastic, I tell you." The French princess found Hoover Dam "fantastic," too. She hadn't yet seen the Grand Canyon. "For a European to come to Las Vegas is such a change," the princess added, glancing at the skimpy hot pants, brocaded dinner jackets and flashy plaid shirts some of the Americans wore. "I came here straight from Monte Carlo. It's so different. It's like going to the moon."

Countess Hugues de Montalembert was in culture shock, too. So was the Marchesa Idanna Pucci di Barsento, niece of the Florentine couturier Emilio Pucci. "In France," she said wide-eyed, "a title is a terrible strike against you. Nobody takes you seriously. My husband and I hide ours when we do movies. Here, it is unbelievable. You'd think I was a queen. Everyone calls me 'Princess' or 'Princess, sweetie.'"

"Yes, and they slap you on the back," said Countess Marthe de la Rochefoucauld, who belongs to an old, rich and highly respected French family.

Crowds of tourists, some still holding paper cups filled with coins for the slot machines, lined up outside the ballroom to watch the formally clad guests arrive. "Which one is Princess Grace?" one woman yelled. "Who's that?" a man demanded when the curvaceous blonde Princess Hannelore von Auersperg drifted in wearing turquoise satin and feathers. Her husband, Prince Alfred von Auersperg, is a member of Austria's deposed royalty. She was regularly mistaken for a Hollywood actress.

Between Les Brown's band and Leadfeather's rock group, neither the royals nor the Americans managed much conversation at dinner. And few of the royals danced.

"It's entirely too strenuous," said Baron Arndt Friedrich Alfried Krupp von Bohlen und Halbach, the Krupp munitions heir, who may very well have been the richest visitor. The baron, whose wife wore pink satin, a diamond tiara and nearly $1-million in other jewels, has $125-million stashed and an annual allowance of $500,000.

"We're just ordinary people," he said, smoothing the ruffles that went with his purple velvet dinner suit. "We are honored to be here, but it's so embarrassing. They won't let us pay for anything."

Baron von Bohlen und Halbach watched the dancers. He was surprised when Clifford S. Perlman, chairman of Lum's, the conglomerate that owns Caesars Palace, ditched his dinner jacket and tie and then swung Princess de Rachevsky around the dance floor. Prince Albrecht of Liechtenstein, nephew of the ruling Prince Franz Josef of Liechtenstein, danced, too. But mostly he and his long-time sweetheart, Miss Mylene Tullio, a model and former Miss France, kissed and held hands.

By last night, Prince Albrecht and Miss Tullio were married. They unexpectedly slipped away between parties (she in flower-printed black chiffon hot pants and he in slacks and a T-shirt), headed for the downtown marriage license bureau, said their vows to a justice of the peace, and were back again in time for cocktails. Mr. Perlman gave a reception for them complete with champagne, a three-tiered cake and a bridal bouquet on only two-and-a-half-hours' notice. The couple spent the rest of the evening at the second of the "Winter Wonderland" galas.

"We thought it would be amusing to be married here," the newly wed princess explained. "It's just as interesting as France."

Betty Friedan wrote *The Feminine Mystique*, founded the National
Organization for Women and took the women's liberation movement to
The Hamptons. At one meeting, Ms. Friedan did the talking and Ethel
Scull did the "right on's." The Hamptons also have other activities.
Michael Evans, *The New York Times* (1970)

The Hamptons

CROQUET TIME ON SOUTHAMPTON'S
CLOVER AND GRASS COURTS

August 1964

A band of serious-minded sportsmen gathered on Mrs. Lloyd H. Smith's spacious lawn here one afternoon last week, selected mallets and wooden balls from a collection in a small field house, flipped a coin to determine the order of play, and then took to two immaculately tailored fields. It was croquet time again in Southampton.

The game, which attracts such regulars as the board chairman of Condé Nast Publications, Inc., the late Governor Al Smith's daughter and the Duke of Marlborough, is as entrenched here as privet hedges and blue hydrangeas, and just as English. The Jacques of London croquet set ($169.50 at Abercrombie and Fitch) is considered standard equipment. And the English game, described in a yellow folder entitled "Rules and Layout for the Game of Croquet as Played in Southampton," is more complicated than its American counterpart.

"What we're doing here is a kind of turf chess," John Lavalle said between shots. "It requires strategy. A game lasts fifty minutes or longer." Mr. Lavalle, the big, gray-haired portrait painter, was teamed with Louis Gourd, a wiry and deeply tanned stockbroker. They were playing against Charles Winn, retired Army officer and brother of Lord St. Oswald of England, and

37

the duke. The latter is here for his annual visit with his mother, Mrs. Jacques Balsan.

"Bert here is pretty good," Mr. Lavalle said, referring to the sixty-six-year-old duke. "He was champion in 1962. You have to watch out for him."

As Mr. Lavalle spoke, John Albert Edward William Spencer-Churchill bent himself into a right angle and then swung his mallet in a wide arc. His croquet ball went rolling through the third wicket and down the field. It was a five-foot shot that put him within perhaps two strokes of the fourth wicket.

"Good shot, Bert," Mr. Lavalle said admiringly.

All the players, including another foursome on the second croquet field, were informally dressed. Mr. Winn wore dark orange slacks, an outsized yellow T-shirt and a floppy straw hat with the brim rolled back. The duke, who chomped on a long cigar, was in green—acid-green silk slacks and a forest-green shirt. Mrs. Carman Messmore was the lone woman player.

"We don't have a court, but we play all the time," said Mrs. M. Dorland Doyle. "It's terribly chic to have two courts. The winners from one court can play the winners of the other." Mrs. Doyle, a small blonde in a red suit, was sitting in a white chair on the sidelines with two other spectators —Milton W. (Doc) Holden and her husband. Mr. Holden, New York's perennial man about town, was keeping score.

"People who think this game's easy just don't know," said Mr. Doyle. "I walked three miles in two and a half hours of play in a single game. I know because I wore a pedometer."

"That isn't just a piece of lawn, either," Mrs. Doyle said, eying a court. "It's like a putting green. Look how smooth it is."

"I've had an indirect telephone call from Westhampton," Mr. Lavalle told the onlookers. "I understand they want to play us."

"They do," said Mrs. Doyle, turning to her husband. "But we don't know anyone down there."

"Well, it's very unlikely we'll play them," Mr. Lavalle said, leaning on his mallet. "They may not even play the same game we do. Does anybody know?"

Nobody answered, so Mr. Lavalle returned to the game, which he and Mr. Gourd seemed to be winning. Mrs. Doyle went on to describe the Southampton croquet tournament.

"It's four years old," she said. "Mr. Holden has given the winners beautiful old croquet prints. My husband and I gave silver cups last year. Everyone has to draw for partners. The winners' names go on a plaque."

Mr. Doyle, the duke and his daughter, Mrs. Edwin F. Russell, are among the champions. Mr. Holden has won twice. Mrs. Smith is not only a champion but the croqueteers' den mother. She has iced tea delivered to the players every afternoon there is a game. "Sometimes that's seven days a week," Mrs. Smith said on the terrace of her house. "It all depends on the weather."

GARDINERS ISLAND:
REFUGE FOR THE LORD OF THE MANOR
September 1964

Robert David Lion Gardiner, this country's only lord of the manor who still owns his manor, leaped from the back of a battered blue pickup truck, picked his way through a thicket of young oak trees and emerged on a knoll where beach grass pushes up through the sand and raspberries grow wild. Then he stood, hands on hips, looking back first at Gardiners Island, which has been owned by his family since 1639, and then across the stretch of choppy, blue-gray water that separates his domain from Long Island.

"That's America over there," he said, pointing a bronzed finger toward the horizon. "I feel very removed here."

Mr. Gardiner, the first Gardiner in nearly fifty years to use the island as his personal playground, is usually involved in twentieth-century affairs. But when he is in residence, which is never more than two days and a night at a time, he seems removed from what is now called "the American mainstream."

In the fall, the Gardiners intend to have their first hunting parties. They will go after duck, pheasant, wild turkey and deer, which bound across the green meadows and into the largest stand of white oaks left in North America. The island also abounds with ospreys, which wheel ceremoniously above large twig nests, and with rare warblers and other wildlife. Talk of politics, business and fashion does creep up in the comfortably furnished pink-brick manor house, but the tall, muscular aristocrat and his friends come here to commune with nature and history, and Mr. Gardiner never forgets it. For some, a day here is like a visit to a museum.

"We get into the truck and drive all around, looking at everything," said Mrs. Gardiner, the former Eunice Bailey Oakes. "Mr. Gardiner talks about the history of the island and tries to make sure everyone sees a deer. The tour takes about two hours."

A day on the island begins with lunch at the Gardiners' palatial East Hampton house ("The summer people come and go. We Gardiners are here to stay") or at the nearby Devon Yacht Club. Then Mr. Gardiner and his friends climb aboard the *Laughing Lady,* his power cruiser. It takes them across Gardiners Bay, which separates the northern and southern claws of

Long Island. Only once in the year and a half since he stopped leasing his island has there been a full-scale party in the manor house. It was held a few weeks ago.

"There were thirty of us in three boats," Mrs. Gardiner said. "The Devon Yacht Club catered the lunch. We sat around afterwards and talked. Then we went on the tour, had some drinks and went home. We don't have any servants on the island, so we can't do anything very elaborate."

A caretaker looks after the property, patrolling the beaches and enforcing the *No Trespassing* signs. The 3,300 rolling acres of wilderness, beaches and well-kept fields have been part of the United States since shortly after the American Revolution. And although the property is surrounded by water, which Mr. Gardiner calls "our moat," the retreat is only three miles from Long Island and about a hundred miles from New York. The manor house, built in 1947, has such comforts as electricity, a ship-to-shore radio-telephone and running water.

Mr. Gardiner, who jokes about his family's no longer having the privilege of appointing the clergy or chopping off people's heads (a power they never had), is equally up to date. He likes the idea of being the six-teenth successive lord of the manor ("Sometimes I feel very feudal") and occasionally glories in his ancestors' accomplishments ("Sam Houston was in love with Julia Gardiner Tyler, which is why Texas is in the Union"). But he has never been one to live in the past.

"I like living in the twentieth century," he said. "There's a sense of adventure about it."

He is involved in at least two contemporary financial ventures. One is the World's Fair, of which he is an active director. The other is the Gardiner Manor Shopping Center. The latter was developed on land in Bay Shore that has belonged to his family for more than three hundred years.

"Such excitement," he said. "Such a wonderful way of using land in terms of 1964. My ancestors raised sheep; I build shopping centers. My ancestors had tenant farmers; I have tenant owners."

The fifty-three-year-old businessman also owns a small marina that is patronized by tenant boat owners, and an additional estate, Sagtikos Manor, in Bay Shore. He is a Democrat ("It's very un-Suffolk County of me") and a graduate of Columbia University ("I did brilliantly in modern languages. I just barely passed physics") and he is listed in the *Social Register*.

"Most old families don't amount to much today," he said philosophically. "They lean on their ancestors or worship them and don't do anything. Some-where along the line they had bad luck. Or they didn't adapt. A lot of times it was a matter of adapting."

The Gardiners protected their land in Revolutionary times by having representatives with both armies—the Americans and the British. They have been adapting ever since.

"We had slaves and when that ended, we could not count on agriculture to keep us going," he said. "We became interested in business and industry. My Aunt Sarah bought General Motors when it was a new thing—only 25 cents a share. I'm trying to do the same—to build something. I just bought Comsat."

Lion Gardiner, the first lord of the manor, could never have conceived of a communications satellite. But in his way, the dapper, seventeenth-century Englishman was progressive. He did not believe in witches and would not let townspeople in what is now East Hampton dunk a suspected witch in the town pond. Lion and his wife came to this country in 1635—fifteen years after the *Mayflower*. He was a military engineer who had been born on the Isle of Wight. He built Saybrook Fort at the mouth of the Connecticut River, commanded it and fought Indians for four years, and then looked around for a place to settle. Manchonake Island, which he renamed Isle of Wight and which later became Gardiners Island, cost him "one large dog, one gun, some powder and shot, some rum and several blankets, worth in all about five pounds sterling."

"He wasn't a Puritan," said Mr. Gardiner, himself an Episcopalian. "He wasn't discontented. He came here to do a job. He liked the country and stayed."

Charles I, the Stuart king, made Lion the lord of the manor, and before the first Gardiner died, he had amassed 78,000 acres of land. Mr. Gardiner owns in excess of five thousand of those original acres.

"Before Sears, Roebuck joined my shopping center, they wanted title research to make sure I owned the property," he said. "I had the original Indian deed and the royal grant. We never had occasion to get a modern deed."

The Gardiners live on Fifth Avenue in New York in the winter and in the gray stone mansion in East Hampton in the summer. He has just had a swimming pool built behind the house, although his wife cannot swim. He spends a lot of his free time working in the gardens and works out with barbells. His boat flag is a red skull and crossbones on a yellow ground.

"I wouldn't have anything else," he said of the flag. "Captain Kidd left his treasure with Lord John Gardiner, Lion's grandson. The Gardiners returned that treasure. I have a document showing that everything was there but six diamonds."

LA CAUSA: THE GRAPE PICKERS AT COCKTAILS

June 1969

The United Farm Workers, fighting for recognition of their union and contracts with California table grape growers, took what they call *la causa* to the frankly rich residents of this conservative summer resort. Andrew Imutan, the first vice-president of the union, and a team of bluejeaned organizers and longtime supporters, accepted an invitation to mingle with the elegant Southampton regulars at what amounted to a combination rally and elaborate buffet supper.

Mrs. Giancarlo Uzielli, the former Anne Ford, was chairman of the benefit. Mrs. Robert F. Kennedy emerged from more than a year of mourning to serve as honorary chairman. The committee was made up of liberals of one sort or another, only a few of whom summer in Southampton. And the party was given by Andrew Stein.

"I believe in the cause and I wanted to do something," he said simply.

Mr. Stein, a young Assemblyman from Manhattan's Upper East Side who usually spends his summer weekends playing touch football and tennis, is the son of Jerry Finkelstein, chairman of the Struthers Wells Corporation, a diversified concern involved in desalinization and other projects. His father also publishes *The New York Law Journal* and the *Civil Service Leader*. And the Finkelstein-Stein home, with its indoor trees and outdoor swimming pool, is not small. In fact, it was the biggest house Mrs. Imutan had ever seen.

"It has a place for servants to sleep," she said wonderingly, as women in silk pajamas and diamonds and men in bright pants and blazers streamed through the house and out onto the lawn where the bars were. "We couldn't even afford the curtains."

Mrs. Imutan, whose blue pants and pink cotton shirt were no more bizarre than Heidi Vanderbilt's shocking pink silk pants suit, stood at the edge of the crowd, obviously awed. She said she had never before seen uniformed waitresses pass hors d'oeuvre on silver trays.

"I didn't know if I was allowed to pick up anything or not," she said of the little watercress and crabmeat sandwiches. "I thought maybe it was only for the millionaire guests. It's the first time in my life I came to this kind of party."

The Imutans' three boys were less reluctant. The youngsters threaded in and out among the seven hundred guests, staring at them. And when Mrs. Kennedy arrived without much fanfare, they followed her around with an Instamatic camera.

"She's very pretty," said twelve-year-old William Imutan, after she shook his hand. "She wanted to know how old I was."

Mrs. Kennedy, in a short pink dress with gold and diamond bracelets, moved quietly through the crowds, shaking hands with friends mostly from campaign days. When guests said it was nice of her to come, as they almost invariably did, she smiled, and inevitably answered, "It's nice to be here."

Aside from that, some comments about how the ocean dampness was wrecking her hair and an occasional reminder that César Chavez, the union head, and his cause had been close to her late husband's heart, Mrs. Kennedy hugged Rafer Johnson, the track star turned movie actor, and Antonio Muñoz, the Spanish banker. After perhaps an hour of small talk and drinks (during which Mark Goodson, the television producer and *causa* sympathizer, remarked that he found the party "more than a little incongruous," and Joel Sirkin, a Harvard Law student who is serving as a union organizer, deplored the use of a mariachi band on such an occasion), Mr. Stein ran his hand over the mess the damp wind had made of his black hair, escorted Mrs. Kennedy and Mrs. Uzielli up onto a floodlighted stone terrace, adjusted the microphone and attempted to call the party to order.

He never really succeeded.

Mr. Imutan, a quiet, gentle man in tan pants and a blue and tan plaid sport shirt, asked everyone to shut his eyes and pretend for a few minutes that he was a farm worker's wife. He talked about breakfasts of tortillas and baloney sandwiches at 3 A.M., days picking grapes in the fields when that was possible, and the need for money to support both the strike against the growers and the boycott of grapes in stores. Only a few guests, including Mrs. Kennedy, paid much attention. Anita Colby, the model known as "The Face," was being hugged and kissed by an admirer as Mr. Imutan talked, and off across the lawn there were knots of conversation. Miss Vanderbilt had reason to whisper, however. She was circulating with pledge cards she was trying to get filled.

Senator Fred R. Harris of Oklahoma spoke briefly (and gave $100), and so did Frank Mankiewicz, the late Senator Kennedy's press secretary and now a political news analyst, and Peter Edelman, a one-time Kennedy aide. And then Mr. Stein announced some of the contributions. The Uziellis had started the fund with a $1,000 contribution. Huntington Hartford, the Great Atlantic & Pacific Tea Company heir who picketed one of his own stores because it was selling grapes, gave $1,000, although he couldn't attend the party. And W. Averell Harriman, President Johnson's representative at the Paris peace talks, sent a pledge for $500.

"I understand there's a man out there who'll give us $10,000 if four others will give $2,500 cash," Mr. Edelman announced.

He got lots of conversation, at least three cries of *"Viva la huelga"* ("Up with the strike"), and no takers. But Abe Schrader, the dress manufacturer, came up with another $1,000 and Newton D. Glekel, chairman of Beck Industries, Inc., the shoe company, agreed to give $1,500—the largest single gift. Mr. Glekel, like several other important contributors, had been carefully cultivated by several committee members. They had been expected to give a lot more. But, as one man said, "they'll never give if it's public and announced."

Another theory had it that making the gifts public—announcing them not just to the press but in the presence of Mrs. Kennedy—would up the ante considerably.

The final tally, made up mostly of $100 contributions, was $20,500, which is still all right for a cocktail party on a Saturday night in Southampton, but the committee was disappointed. It had hoped for $100,000, which was only reasonable considering that Mr. Stein had spent about $3,500 on his party.

And by the time most guests left, the pickets in front of the Stein residence were gone. They had carried signs with such slogans as "Boycott Communist goods, not grapes" and "Grapes Si, Chavez No." But there weren't any aristocratic old Southampton residents in that group, either.

SOUTHAMPTON IN SUMMER

June 1970

At this stage, Southampton is azaleas against the cool shock of emerald green lawns. The sun, hardly a pale rumor above the Atlantic beach, is bright enough to burn some of New York's more aristocratic noses. The palatial houses are open again. The summer season has begun.

Vietnam? It's not a topic of conversation in an enclave that dotes on golf scores and spends considerable time elucidating the white walls, hot colors and splashy print theory of interior design. Neither is the recession.

But life behind the privet hedges is not without its little chores. When the ladies are not grappling with such problems as whether or not to serve grated onion with the caviar (and what to wear while eating it), they are struggling to even up their tans, improve their tennis or keep up with all the parties. At the Walter G. Dunnington house, for instance, the hundred-year-old ponderosa lemon trees are giving the residents pause. Mrs. Dunnington never really feels properly decorated until the trees have been moved from their winter greenhouse to their places beside the terrace door.

"The whole balance is off," she moaned from the edge of what must be one of the handsomest rose gardens on Long Island. "It's been too cold to move them. The door just doesn't look right without them."

Off balance it may be, but the house, a vast white frame structure with formal and informal drawing rooms, is elaborately landscaped on the outside, very decorated on the inside and the repository of a somewhat special array of inanimate animals. Mr. Dunnington collects elephants, which accounts for the ceramic tables. Mrs. Dunnington collects lions, one of which is made entirely of white feathers. And Coriolanus, their Cavalier King Charles spaniel, snoozes under tables laden with zebras and flower arrangements.

Southampton houses tend to have names (Tanglebrae, Children at Play, Puffin Hall, Colonnades), and the Dunningtons' is no exception. The retired lawyer and his wife call it The Return.

"My father's family were among the first arrivals in 1640," Mrs. Dunnington said. "I'm the thirteenth in a direct line from Thomas Sayre. The Return means the return of the native."

Miss Julie Kammerer, a former president of the New York Junior League, hasn't a name for her newly acquired house. But as she looked about its gutted interior the other day, she thought The Wreck might be appropriate. "I have an endless number of contractors drifting in and out," she said. "I only hope I see some progress before the end of summer."

Miss Kammerer is a weekender and a sports activist. She may be found on the golf course in the morning, at the Beach Club for lunch and a swim, and then out on the tennis courts in the afternoon. She belongs to the Beach and the Meadow clubs, which take a decidedly more tolerant view of gentile single women than they do of male or female Jews.

"Southampton is a pretty big place," Miss Kammerer said. "You don't see the same people at every party."

She's right, of course. The aristocratic Murray-McDonnell clan, whose Irish Catholic progenitor was the utilities tycoon and inventor, have their own three-hundred-acre compound. The croquet gang, which uses the English pronunciation (CRO-key) as well as English rules, sticks by its velvet grass courts. But when Colonel Serge Obolensky gives his annual cocktail party ("I always expect about 960 of my best friends"), virtually everybody who's anybody shows up.

On a good day, and it was a cool sunny evening this year, that group includes an assortment of elegant New Yorkers interspersed with displaced Texans, Newport refugees, titled and untitled Europeans and Russians, diplomats, Dina Merrill (and her husband, Cliff Robertson, Southampton's resident film stars), Philadelphia Main Liners, Mark Goodson (the resort's only truly debonair television tycoon) and members of the international set.

The fashions at such parties are as ecumenical as the guests. Mrs. Donald Chipman, wife of the taxi man, appeared at the Irving Hotel's opening party in Adolfo's long ruffled flower-printed skirt and green checked gingham shirt, whereas Mrs. Donald Nelson, the ebullient widow of the World War II production chief, was in a short Pucci print.

And at Colonel Obolensky's, there was Mrs. Lloyd H. Smith, the Humble Oil heiress, in a very formal red chiffon evening gown, a chinchilla jacket and masses of diamonds, while Mrs. James Van Alen, the Newport sportsman's wife, was in pants, an Australian wool poncho, a red yarn hair ribbon and rings of diamonds and rubies.

"I've been fishing," Mrs. Van Alen explained, although she needn't have.

The host was in baby blue and yellow plaid cashmere trousers, a blue blazer and patent loafers. Mrs. Robertson wore what appeared to be American flag patchwork. And Mrs. Louise Dâle Pistell, former wife of the conglomerateur, was in such a rush she still had her bathing suit top under her Pucci shirt.

"Almost anything goes these days," Mrs. Iva S. V. Patcévitch said. "About the only thing you have to wear is shoes. We're very big on shoes." Mrs. Patcévitch, wife of the Condé Nast chairman, was referring to the signs shopkeepers on fashionable Jobs Lane have been putting in their windows.

They all demand shod feet on the assumption that only hippies go barefoot and that the elimination of bare feet automatically eliminates hippies from the shops. But the rule doesn't work—mostly because expensively shod social leaders have been known to remove their shoes in protest.

"We used to be fairly conservative about fashion," Mrs. Patcévitch said. "Five or six years ago if your shorts were a few inches above your knees, you were sent home. I don't think anything's too short today."

WOMEN'S LIBERATION IN THE LONG ISLAND SWIM

August 1970

Everything at the women's liberation party had gone pretty much according to plan. Then Representative Patsy Mink, Democrat of Hawaii, disappeared when she was supposed to speak, and a woman shed her blue jeans and dived into the swimming pool. After that, things were never quite the same.

The cocktail reception was a Women's Strike for Equality benefit. It was held in the sculpture-filled gardens around Mr. and Mrs. Robert Scull's starkly rectangular summer compound. By 6:30 P.M. perhaps a hundred gaily clad guests had arrived.

"All I see are the committed, their husbands and the press," Betty Friedan, author of *The Feminine Mystique*, said as she surveyed the crowd. "I hope at least some of them are paying guests."

Mrs. Friedan, founder of the National Organization for Women, was co-hostess along with Mrs. Wyatt Cooper, the former Gloria Vanderbilt, Mrs. Richard S. Coulson, the former Edith De Rham, Mrs. Scull and the writer Gloria Steinem. Mrs. Cooper failed to show, reportedly at the insistence of her husband.

"We had flak from some of the husbands," Mrs. Friedan said. "One man tore up his wife's invitation. I must say Bob Scull's been very nice." She is serious about such issues as abortion on demand, child care centers and equal pay for women. Yet it was her attire, a long red baby dress with teeny white polka dots, puffed sleeves and deep, deep décolletage, that caused the comment.

"You've liberated your dress," said Mrs. Coulson, author of *How Could She Do That*, a crime book. "You are really liberated."

Mrs. Coulson, like some of the other "sisters" sipping drinks and eating

46

little sandwiches there on the lawn, was fashionably liberated, too. She wore a flesh-colored body stocking, a long white see-through caftan and no bra.

"I chucked bras six months ago," she explained.

By this time, Mrs. Mink, whom Mrs. Friedan enthusiastically called "a real heroine of the movement," had arrived. The diminutive heroine won that accolade by taking on no less a personage that Dr. Edgar F. Berman, former Vice President Hubert H. Humphrey's physician and a member of the Democratic Committee on National Priorities. Dr. Berman had insisted that such factors as the menstrual cycle and menopause (or what he called "the raging hormonal imbalance") make women emotionally unfit for top executive jobs. Mrs. Mink, backed by scores of practicing physicians and psychiatrists, said he didn't know what he was talking about. The fight was on. The upshot was Dr. Berman's resignation from the committee and between five hundred and six hundred "overwhelmingly" supportive feminist letters on Mrs. Mink's desk. Yet Mrs. Mink, flown up from Washington especially for the party, denied she was a women's liberationist.

"I don't like to fit myself into any particular stereotype," she said.

Mrs. Mink also opposed bra burning as a way of calling attention to women's rights ("I don't see that anything can be accomplished by that"), wasn't sure why guests considered August 26 such an important date (NOW and other women's lib groups expect to spend the day—the fiftieth anniversary of women's suffrage—in nationwide demonstrations in support of their cause), and said that although there was some discrimination against women, each woman must work to eliminate it in her own way.

"Just because I'm interested in women doesn't mean I'm for women's liberation," she said as her little daughter, Wendy, looked on nonplused. "I support all groups when what they do coincides with what I believe in."

When Mrs. Mink appeared on the lawn with Mrs. Scull, both women were besieged with guests who wanted to meet the Congresswoman and congratulate her. At the edges of the crowd, other party-goers were getting a little restless.

"I paid $25 for liberation and $25 to see the Sculls' house," said Dr. Robert Gould, a psychiatrist, "and the house is locked up."

"This is my first feminist party," said Mrs. Lilian Rixey, a grandmotherly Bridgehampton summer resident. "I'm waiting for something to happen."

Tammy Grimes arrived while Mrs. Rixey was talking. The actress, who guessed she was liberated ("You're freer in the theater. There isn't as much discrimination against an actress"), was bra-less. But she wore a voluminous green caftan shirtwaist dress, so virtually nobody noticed. At about the same time, Mrs. Timothy Cooney, the former Joan Ganz, was admitting that it was her husband who'd interested her in the cause.

"He's the feminist in the family," said Mrs. Cooney, the president of the Children's Television Theater, which produces "Sesame Street."

47

"I was the Uncle Tom. I'm late in the movement. I see it differently now. This strike zeros in on good issues. It's important and serious. If I'd been an ugly woman with brains I wonder how far I'd have gotten?"

At this point, Mrs. Friedan went to the microphone beside the Sculls' swimming pool and called the party to order. She thanked the Sculls for the use of their yard and said it was "time to finish the unfinished revolution of American women.

"They must be liberated from menial housework," she cried, hitching up her plunging décolletage. "In the churches, we must get them out of giving church suppers and into preaching the sermons. In politics, they shouldn't be looking up zip codes but be the powers. No more of this obscenity of one woman in the Senate.

"Nor the obscenity of women in industry," she said. "Their average wage is little more than half what men get. They are the last hired and the first fired. We've got to break this up."

Mrs. Friedan went on this way for perhaps ten minutes, noting that "it's fine to be a mommy, but you have to be a person first," demanding "her-story not just history," calling for participation in the August 26 women's strike, and explaining that the party was "a great event—a political event and not just a fashionable event to get women into the paper."

William J. Goode, professor of sociology at Columbia University and president of the American Sociological Association, was next. He talked about what could be the new spread of power. "Men won't be quite the center of attention they were in the past," he said. "It might be a great gain for men if women had power and weren't so full of rage."

His remarks, delivered in a blue velvet suit with a multistriped shirt, were greeted with male and female bravos. Then it was Mrs. Mink's turn. Mrs. Friedan introduced her, the crowd applauded and she failed to materialize.

"She's gone," somebody shouted.

"You're not serious," Mrs. Friedan said, looking pained. But Mrs. Mink had gone, apparently without a word either to Mrs. Scull or to Mrs. Friedan. Miss Steinem was summoned to take her place.

She was discussing Dr. Berman's resignation when Jill Johnston, dance writer for the *Village Voice*, stripped to her denim shirt and black panties, and dived into the pool.

"It's hot," Miss Johnston said as she surfaced and removed her shirt.

"You're proving nothing," cried a voice in the crowd.

Miss Johnston, who was bra-less, went right on swimming. "It's really nice," she said, reaching the deep end. "I didn't even pay $25."

Mrs. Friedan muttered something about "One of the biggest enemies of this movement . . ." The rest was drowned out by the crowd. Miss Steinem tried to speak, too, but without success.

"It's a great pool," Miss Johnston yelled as she reached for a plastic surfboard, rolled over on her back and floated for a few seconds.

"We *are* going to be a big political issue," Mrs. Friedan shrieked into the microphone. "And now some of us will sing for you."

The sounds of "Liberation Now" came over the loudspeaker amid shouts of "Right on!" Miss Johnston, who'd finished four laps, climbed out of the pool, accepted a towel Mr. Scull held for her and tripped off into a zinnia bed. Everybody was talking all at once.

"I always say if you have a pool, you have a pool," Mrs. Scull said, shaking her head.

Yachting caps and diamonds are always *de rigueur* at the America's Cup races in Newport, and it's always better to follow the action from aboard your own floating mansion. The late Raymond W. Marshall and Mrs. Harold W. Brooks had a perfect view from Mr. Marshall's *Charay Mar II*. Carl T. Gossett, Jr., *The New York Times* (1964)

Newport

Money is still in style in America's social capital, especially if it's inherited. The best money goes back so many generations nobody is quite sure where it came from, but staid old Newport tries to be democratic toward outside millionaires. It accepts a new one every few years. Which is not to say that seating arrangements at the big dinner parties are what they used to be. When President Chester A. Arthur visited, he sat on a hostess's left. A financially more impeccable Vanderbilt was on her right. Today, the place of honor goes to position, not money. Kings, princes, a president or two, and a long list of ambassadors have had their turn at the Newport hostesses' right. But more often than not, the chair goes to a fourth-, fifth- or even sixth-generation Newporter, some of whose bank accounts are down to their last few millions.

A sure sign of social acceptance in this world that treasures family background, excellence of education, good manners and the Republican party is a second invitation to Wakehurst. The first summons, usually for tea and issued only after the prospect has been carefully considered, gives Mrs. Louis S. Bruguière, palatial Wakehurst's elderly mistress, a chance to examine the candidate at close range. A second invitation, to lunch, tea or dinner, signals approval. Mrs. Bruguière is a handsome woman who dresses more like the late Queen Mary than like somebody's eighty-year-old grandmother, and her ways

51

are decidedly grand. Tea in Wakehurst's immense candlelit hall is a formal, eighteenth-century ritual. Footmen, wearing her yellow and black livery, pass among the eight or ten guests bearing trays of sandwiches and little cakes. The butler helps, too, and sometimes there's a parlor maid.

On opening day of the eighty-three-year-old Newport Casino's invitational Lawn Tennis Tournament—a week-long event that marks the peak of the summer season here—Mrs. Bruguière viewed the proceedings from the comfort of her black Rolls-Royce. She had had her chauffeur park the car within a few yards of the grass courts on which the qualifying rounds were being played. Everyone else had to sit on folding chairs. Mrs. Bruguière's dress was lavender that day, not much lighter than the color she rinses into her elegantly coiffed hair. And she wore a black and white pearl ring, ropes of pearls, a diamond bracelet and a pince-nez. Among younger Newporters, she is affectionately known as "the purple people eater." She inherited part of her money from the Van Alens and part from the Vanderbilts.

The presiding genius of the Casino and therefore of Tennis Week is James H. Van Alen, Mrs. Bruguière's outgoing, informal and tireless son. During this frenetic week Mr. Van Alen stalks about the green shingle and frame verandas, towers and fences of the Casino making sure all is as it should be. Only rarely does he pause in the president's box to watch a match. "If the Casino were self-supporting, I wouldn't be so white-haired," he said recently. "If it isn't one thing, it's another."

The Casino, designed by the architectural firm of McKim, Mead and White and opened in 1880, was built because of an insult. James Gordon Bennett, publisher of the *New York Herald,* commissioned it because of an affront to Captain Candy, a polo-playing friend. The story told here has Captain Candy riding past the exclusive Reading Room when a member challenged him to ride his horse into the club. Candy took the challenge, and guided his steed up the steps and into the bar. Outraged, the Reading Room's governors withdrew the captain's membership. Bennett, equally outraged, resigned from the Reading Room and ordered his own club.

"The band on my hat has the Casino's colors," Mr. Van Alen said. "They're the same as our flag out front." His hat is straw, and the grosgrain ribbon is green, yellow and white. The rest of his daytime clothes are like all the other men's—sport shirts with open necks, sport coats that contrast with the slacks, bright socks and comfortable shoes. White is required on the tennis courts. And in the evening, as one Newporter put it, "we all turn back into gentlemen again"—complete with black tie.

"This town's friendly to new people," said Mrs. George Henry Warren, the gray-haired president of the Preservation Society of Newport County and one of the community's busiest women. "It doesn't look down on people. Some of the most popular people live simply, very simply."

Mrs. Warren, who has been coming here for forty-five years, is the wife of a third-generation Newporter. She usually wears pink dresses or slacks, Dior perfume and a flag-shaped diamond pin set with a sapphire circle and a ruby cross. "When you have sailboats and yachts and things, you have a little flag you fly," she said. "This pin is our flag, a St. Catherine's wheel. My name is Katherine with a K."

Mrs. Warren leads the fight to preserve eighteenth-century Newport as well as the big, nineteenth-century and twentieth-century houses people can no longer afford. She wants to revive the cultural spirit this resort had in the days of Henry James and Edith Wharton. She would like to see the Elms, a mansion her organization rescued from commercialization, play host to the New York Philharmonic.

"People think we're rich here. Well, we're not really," she said. "Taxes have taken care of that. We have substantial contributors but there is not enough money for our work."

Aside from one or two energetic souls, society does not do much here in the mornings. At noon, it emerges from the imported silk, marble and crystal-lined cocoons that are the chateaux, castles and mansions it calls "summer cottages," and heads for the Spouting Rock Beach Association. This ultra-exclusive territory is more familiarly known as Bailey's Beach. Society suns, swims and lunches among the cabanas or around the pool, then moves on to the Casino, the golf club or home for a nap. There are few cocktail parties.

"Washington and Southampton always have gangs of cocktail parties," said Mrs. Albert B. Dewey, the chatelaine of Easterly. "I'm so glad we don't do that here."

Occasionally someone asks someone else to drop by for a drink about 5 P.M., but even this is not a custom.

"I never go to cocktail parties," said Mrs. Van Alen, a striking brunette and gracious hostess. "It ruins the whole day."

Social Newport spends five or six nights a week at dinner parties for eighteen to eighty guests. Most gatherings start at 8:30 with cocktails. Dinner is usually served at nine, and it is often followed by dancing. At Beaulieu, which has been owned by an Astor and a Vanderbilt, it is customary for Mr. and Mrs. Wiley T. Buchanan, Jr., to invite fifty or sixty for dinner and another 150 in later for dancing. The exquisite French chateau has an entrance hallway from which one can see all the way across the house and lawns to the Atlantic Ocean. Along the way are Aubusson rugs, a collection of Fabergé pieces, some Renoir sketches and a desk that once belonged to King George V of Britain.

"We have this little orchestra that comes in and sits under the stairway," said Mr. Buchanan, Chief of Protocol during the Eisenhower Administration. "It works out wonderfully—everyone dances right here in the hall."

Tennis Week afternoons are still devoted to tennis, and the shaded stands around the Casino's courts contain members of the distinguished old families, some of whose names are not widely known. Countess Anthony

Szapary, daughter of Countess Lâszió Széchényi, was there one day with her husband. Countess Széchényi, the former Gladys Vanderbilt, leases the Breakers, the most elaborate of Newport's summer residences, to the Preservation Society for $1 a year.

There are court-side seats, too, for Harold Stirling Vanderbilt, the yachting strategist and racing helmsman who successfully defended the America's Cup three times; Mr. and Mrs. Harvey S. Firestone, Jr., of the tin and rubber clan, Mr. and Mrs. John R. Drexel 3rd, Mrs. John Barry Ryan and many more.

AMERICA'S CUP: MANEUVERS WITH NEWPORT'S FLEET

September 1964

Aside from the excursion boats and Navy destroyers, nothing on Narragansett Bay these days compares to the three-hundred-foot yachts of the 1920s and 1930s. But Newport need not hang its head in shame. When this rich old seaside resort wants to, it can muster and launch what may well be the world's most impressive fleet of privately owned yachts.

Such a fleet is here for the America's Cup Races between the British *Sovereign* and the American *Constellation*. The luxurious pleasure craft, some of which have palatial interiors, are owned by descendants of the East Coast's most celebrated yachtsmen as well as affluent newcomers from as far away as San Francisco and Seattle. And when scores of such vessels sail out and around the race course in the Atlantic, it is a sight fit for a Morgan or a Vanderbilt.

Former Postmaster General Arthur Summerfield's boat may be only eighty feet long, but its deck is covered with removable carpeting. Frank Freimann, chairman of the Magnavox Company, has wall-to-wall music aboard the seventy-foot *Magna-Mar*. And Laurance Rockefeller's yacht, which is usually at neighboring Fishers Island, is an elegantly reconstructed PT boat—one of the fastest vessels on the bay.

Then there is Mr. and Mrs. C. Hascall Bliss's *Maid Marian II*, a 104-foot oceangoing hotel, and there's nothing dowdy about Raymond W. Marshall's *Charay Mar II*, either. A ninety-eight-foot floating mansion that cost $1-million, she has three bedrooms (one is pale pink with hand-painted birds on the wall), indoor and outdoor living rooms, color television, showers with both salt-water and fresh-water spigots, an elaborate dining room, a stainless-steel galley and pantry and a crew of seven. Thirty guests could be aboard without bumping into one another. "I live here in the winter," Mr.

Marshall said of his yacht. "I put her in at the Palm Beach Yacht Club. I don't need to go to a hotel."

Mr. Marshall, a hospitable and vigorous sailor from Greenwich, is a transportation tycoon. He manufactured locomotives in his youth and later founded Alaska Airlines. Today he is chairman of the board of the Kansas City-Caw Valley Railroad and president of the Polychem Corporation, a concern that produces industrial detergents. Sixteen guests viewed the race with him on opening day.

"Everybody's just supposed to relax and do what he pleases," Mr. Marshall said as he welcomed his friends aboard. "We'll have lunch at two o'clock."

The *Charay Mar II,* like the other big yachts, left port at about 11:30 A.M. She sailed majestically out of the Narrows past Castle Hill, flanked by sailboats of every size and description, power cruisers and at least one motor-powered rowboat. By 12:30 P.M. she had reached the starting line, and five minutes later, when the race began, she joined the spectator fleet that was circling the triangular course. Most of Mr. Marshall's guests were on their second Scotch and water.

"It's marvelous how much there is to see," said Mrs. Harold W. Brooks, adjusting her binoculars. "That looks like Winthrop Aldrich over there." She was looking at guests aboard the *Topsail.* The *Charay Mar* had just overtaken the *Panda,* a huge auxiliary schooner that once belonged to Vietnam. Mrs. Brooks, a senior member of the Newport summer colony, was far more enthusiastic about the proceedings than the late Ring Lardner had been in his day. He thought the America's Cup was "about as exciting as watching the grass grow." To Mrs. Brooks, it was "thrilling, just thrilling." She was dressed so she would be neither cold nor windblown. She wore navy wool slacks with two matching sweaters and medium-heeled red shoes. She had settled a white turban of veiling over her brown hair and pinned the fabric together in front with a diamond brooch. Her arms and hands were protected by elbow-length white cotton gloves, and she had multiple strands of pearls and sapphires to keep her neck warm.

"Don't you just love it, all this fresh air?" she said to a man who was concentrating on the race. "I think it's too, too marvelous."

Luncheon, consisting of platters of cold turkey, ham, three kinds of salad, baked beans, macaroni and cheese, chocolate cake and coffee, was served exactly when Mr. Marshall said it would be. Everyone ate a little something, although some downed seasickness pills before they would go near the food. The buffet was prepared by Mr. Marshall's French chef. His previous employer was Harold S. Vanderbilt, recognized internationally as the greatest strategist and racing helmsman yachting has ever known.

"The Commodore was the first Vanderbilt to have a yacht and she was a giant," Mr. Vanderbilt said. "The Commodore was my great-grandfather.

My grandfather wasn't interested in yachts. My father was William Kissam Vanderbilt. He had two big yachts—the *Valiant* and the *Alva*, which was named for my mother. I am my family's first sailor."

Mr. Vanderbilt learned to sail when he was eleven or twelve. He puttered around Newport harbor in a fourteen-foot boat, "looking for mines the government put down during the Spanish-American War." Neither contract bridge, which he invented on an Atlantic Ocean crossing in the late 1920s, nor sailing kept him from performing his duties as an executive of the New York Central Railroad. The tall, ramrod-straight skipper successfully defended the America's Cup in 1930, 1934 and 1937. "Sailing is like everything else," the modest perfectionist said matter-of-factly. "Practice makes perfect. You've got to know your boat. No two of them are alike."

Mr. Vanderbilt has a tiny silver America's Cup on the mantel in his library. It is a copy of the twenty-seven-inch-high, bottomless silver trophy that has remained in American hands since 1851. If *Constellation* does as well as she is expected to, Mr. Vanderbilt will be among the winners. He is a member of the syndicate that owns the twelve-meter defender.

Walter S. Gubelmann, an Oyster Bay, Long Island, industrialist, is manager of the syndicate. During the races, he and his wife (her racing clothes are often red, white and blue) have been on the *Chaperone*, the large power launch that serves as *Constellation*'s tender. The British Ambassador, Lord Harlech, the former Sir David Ormsby Gore, and the Royal Navy share the *Decoy*, a British frigate, with such Newporters as Mrs. Hugh D. Auchincloss. George D. Widener was aboard an American destroyer.

"I might have considered staying home if this thing worked," Mr. Widener said last week, as he pointed to a telescope set up in his seaside drawing room. "But I don't have much choice. I can't see anything from here." He saw his first America's Cup race in 1908—in the days when his father, the first George Widener, steamed up and down the East Coast and across the ocean in the 270-foot *Josephine*. After his father's death (the elder Mr. Widener went down with the *Titanic*), the present Mr. Widener owned sailboats and a small schooner. He has always tried to be here for the America's Cup, but his real interest is his race horses.

The America's Cup flotilla has been escorted by nearly a dozen aircraft, including a blimp and two helicopters.

On Saturday, one of the twin-engine planes will contain Mrs. Louis S. Bruguière. The incredibly grand octogenarian will have her two pilots fly over the starting line, circle the watery course a few times, and then head back for the landing field. She expects to be home in time for tea.

"It's so much more comfortable that way," she told one of eleven Newporters she has invited to accompany her. "There aren't all those dreadful breezes."

The dinner Mr. and Mrs. James H. Van Alen gave here last night looked a lot like an Astor family reunion, and in a way it was. John Jacob (Jackims) Astor 3rd was there along with his daughter, his son and two of his former wives. He didn't run into a former fiancée until later at the Tennis Ball. "We'd hoped John could be with us," Mrs. Van Alen said shortly after eighty-six formally clad guests had trooped out of the foggy weather and into her baronial house. "He doesn't get here very often." By his own choice, the elusive Mr. Astor rarely gets anywhere very social these days. He lives in Miami, where he's never been much for big formal parties and lots of small talk. And when he walked through the front door, accompanied by his first wife, Mrs. Ellen Tuck Guest, more than one of the Van Alens' friends were visibly but silently startled.

The party was in honor of Mr. Astor's only daughter, pretty, blond Mary Jacqueline (Jackie) Astor, who made her debut on Long Island in June. And Miss Astor's mother, Mrs. Sonio Coletti-Perucca (the former Gertrude Gretsch—Mr. Astor's second wife), was in the receiving line.

Mr. Astor kissed his daughter and shook hands with Mrs. Coletti-Perucca. And then he stood there, a tall, heavy-set man with spectacles, quietly talking with Mrs. Van Alen.

His son, William Astor, an investment banker who commutes between Morristown, New Jersey, and Wall Street, was off in the drawing room with his own wife, the former Charlotte Fisk of Green Bay, Wisconsin. "I guess there are lots of us," he said later. "It's hard to keep track." Besides the Astors themselves, all of whom are descended from the John Astor who parlayed a $200 loan into a fur and real-estate empire, the festivities involved Stephen Spender and Mrs. Joseph Daugherty, who are Astor cousins.

By the time Mr. Astor arrived, Mr. Van Alen, whose grandmother was an Astor, had already played "My Shining Hour" on his guitar. He was busy welcoming guests and seeing to it that they got drinks.

"I like to get in there and help out with the music," he said happily. "If they'd play in the right key, I'd play the piano."

The bass man and the electric guitarist whom Mrs. Van Alen had hired to entertain during cocktails apparently didn't play in the right key because Mr. Van Alen went off to the drawing room to see what was going on. He had a white carnation in the lapel of his dinner jacket and dime-size amethyst studs down the front of his starched shirt. His wife, who was done up in Balenciaga's periwinkle blue crepe, a diamond pin, diamond earrings and a wreath of gold and diamonds in her black hair, bought the studs in Latin America.

"I'm in the middle of swimming-pool building," she said. "The one by the dining room is outdoors. Now I'm having another one put inside at the other end of the house. I need someplace warm to do my exercises."

If anyone set a new fashion note, it was Christopher L. Norrie, whose father, Lanfear B. Norrie, is the retired mining millionaire. Young Chris, a liberal-arts student at New York University, showed up in a fitted ten-button double-breasted black rajah coat with a stand-up collar.

"It's the newest thing from Pierre Cardin," he said. "The hardest thing was to find a white ascot. I have a Marine Corps T-shirt underneath."

Mrs. Walter S. Gubelmann, whose husband's syndicate successfully defended the America's Cup in the 1964 yachting races, didn't say what she had on under her completely beaded sheath dress. But every time she poked the largest of what must have been hollow plastic beads, she sounded like a cricket.

"It's fun," she said, pushing first one bead and then another. "But some of them don't work."

After dinner, which started about 9:40 P.M., everybody went on to the Tennis Ball at the Newport Casino. And it was here, beneath a giant ball of fresh flowers and little lights, that Mr. Astor encountered Mrs. John Jermain Slocum, the former Eileen Gillespie. She was engaged to him before he married Mrs. Guest, who was supposed to have been only a brides-maid. There also was a frenetic frug contest, during which Senator Claiborne Pell's daughter, Dallas, got so carried away she lost an earring. Victoria Leiter, daughter of Washington's Mrs. Oates Leiter, was a winner although she fell down once. And at one point, it looked as if Mrs. Slocum, whose husband is associated with the United States Information Agency, just might outshake the younger generation.

Wiley T. Buchanan, Jr., did not enter the frug contest. But he and Mrs. Buchanan, who'd broken two fingernails helping to install the big yellow and white plastic daisy decorations, stood on the sidelines—watching appreciatively.

"I'm exhausted," Mrs. Buchanan said. "I'm not sure I ever want to be on a decorations committee again."

Countess Anthony Szapary said she was tired, too. And yet she came to the dance early in order to see how the tables looked. Before the other guests arrived, she was inside the party tent picking leaves and fallen flowers off the plastic grass that had been put over the real grass on the Casino's main tennis court. Prince Philip and Prince Nicholas of Liechtenstein, the Pells' house guests, were among the younger party-goers. Nobody except the youngest and prettiest of the long-haired girls seemed to find them very special.

Saratoga Springs is the summer racing capital, but the circuit includes
Aqueduct and Belmont Park, each with its attendant social forays. The late
Elizabeth Arden was a fixture at the tracks. Here, she dances with Leslie
Combs 2nd at the once fabled Belmont Ball. She also had her horses
rubbed down with cold cream.
Bert and Richard Morgan Studio Photo (1954)

Saratoga Springs, New York

There are supermarkets and parking lots where the elegant old hotels used to be, but society has not deserted Saratoga. There probably is more blue blood here this month than at any other resort in the United States. It is centennial year, the hundredth anniversary of thoroughbred racing in Saratoga. This celebration, including a boxing match, a music festival and a bridge tournament, may stimulate tourism, but it is the thoroughbred horses and the twenty-four days of racing that bring the Whitneys, Vanderbilts, Phippses, du Ponts, Sanfords, Bostwicks, Bradys, Paysons, Von Stades, Haneses and Clarks home to Saratoga every August. Many of these families have been coming here for two and three generations. The high point of the season is reached when yearlings from all over the country are sold at auction.

These regulars like Saratoga, according to Mrs. Stephen Sanford, "because it's Saratoga," and their lives revolve around one of the most charming tracks in America. The Victorian clubhouse is a rambling, old, white, gabled structure festooned with red, white and purple petunias, red and white geraniums, and ivy. The paddocks, lawns and a park of ancient elms are in back. And the grassy infield is punctuated by gardens and a lagoon. Swans waddle about, sunning themselves, and a fountain spits streams of water into the air except when a race is in progress.

Not many representatives of the old families get to the 7 A.M. breakfast workouts. But by noon, when the mist has lifted, they have visited their stables, consulted with their trainers and jockeys, and are ready for lunch. They seem to prefer one another's company and it is traditional to have luncheon at the red-and-white-clothed tables at the track.

By 2 P.M., post time, the owners have taken over rows A and B—the $120-a-season clubhouse boxes. They sip Saratoga Geyser, one of the bottled waters for which this combination horse-and-health spa is famous, and they place a few $5 bets. It is a society in which the reading of the *Morning Telegraph,* a racing newspaper, is a daily ritual.

Until her death, Mrs. Isabel Dodge Sloane was known as the First Lady of the Turf. She owned Brookmeade Stable and the champion Sword Dancer. The title has since passed into modestly unwilling hands—those of Mrs. Charles Shipman Payson, a blue-eyed grandmother who does crossword puzzles between races.

"I don't think there is such a thing as First Lady of the Turf," she said, almost fiercely. "There are too many women who own horses now. I don't even want to think about it."

Mrs. Payson, who has little use for so-called society, is the daughter of Payne Whitney. He left his children an estimated $194 million. Her mother, founder of Greentree Stable, was credited with helping to keep the sport of kings a sport. Her gray-and-white frame house on Myrtle Street now serves as the Paysons' Saratoga headquarters. Mrs. Payson's grandfather was William Collins Whitney, a traction magnate, the first of the horse-owning Whitneys, and a onetime part-owner of the track. Besides Greentree, which she co-owns with her brother, John Hay Whitney, Mrs. Payson owns the New York Mets baseball team. Several of her horses, including Shut Out, who won the 1942 Kentucky Derby, have names inspired by baseball.

"Mother was crazy about baseball," Mrs. Payson said. "I guess it runs in the family."

Cornelius Vanderbilt Whitney is here, too, with his petite blond wife. He is Mrs. Payson's cousin. He bought his stable from his father, the late Harry Payne Whitney, sold it in 1937 and then reentered the sport two seasons later. His silks, Eton blue and brown, were first introduced here by his grandfather, William C. Whitney.

Box A-33 has been empty part of the season. But its owners, the Alfred Gwynne Vanderbilts, spent at least one afternoon with their elbows propped on the railing. Mr. Vanderbilt, who had *The Racing Form* delivered to him in plain envelopes at St. Paul's School, is the great-great-grandson of Commodore Cornelius Vanderbilt.

The owners of thoroughbreds love parties almost as much as racing, according to Mrs. Elizabeth N. Graham (Elizabeth Arden of the cosmetics empire). She is a "new" member of turf society because she did not buy her first yearling until 1931. She sits in Row B and wears high-styled clothes and small hats. Her silks, which turn up regularly in the winner's circle, are a feminine cerise, white and blue. She once had her horses rubbed down with face cream.

"Saratoga wouldn't be any good without the horses," Mrs. Graham said one afternoon, shortly before her Gun Glory pranced out onto the track. "I think everyone likes the social end of things, too. I know I do."

At last count, close to twenty major parties had either been given or scheduled by the racing set. They range from brunches and luncheons, none of which is permitted to run too close to post time, to after-the-races cocktail parties and supper dances. The C. V. Whitneys were to give a supper dance at a restaurant near the track. Admiral and Mrs. Gene Markey of Calumet Farm invited friends in for giant rum drinks served in what appeared to be beer mugs. Colonel and Mrs. Cloyce J. Tippett and Eddie Arcaro, the jockey, were hosts at another party. The Paysons have entertained one houseguest after another. And Mr. and Mrs. Sanford have mailed engraved and crested invitations for cocktails at Ideal View. They named their Saratoga house for a horse rather than the view of the golf course nearby. "Most entertaining is at home," Mrs. Sanford said. "It's like Washington, I suppose—very dignified. It's eights and tens for lunch and twenties for dinner." Her husband, heir to a carpet mills fortune, is another third-generation Saratogian. If he had his way, he would spend more time here and less at the couple's other homes. His grandfather and namesake ran horses here starting in 1880.

"Saratoga is wonderfully old-fashioned," Mrs. Sanford said. "It's undergoing a renaissance. There's nothing like it anywhere."

"It's always been this way," said Mrs. Payson. "Thirty years ago, the night life was sensational. We went out every night. Now the old gambling places are closed. The night life's quiet. It's very gay in people's homes."

Racing society cherishes tradition and old things; it gets defensive when anyone suggests that the town is only a dingy shadow of its former self. There are a parking lot and shops where the United States Hotel used to be, and the Grand Union has been replaced by a shopping center. Broadway is a neon-lit hodgepodge of drugstores, shops and lunch counters. Bootblack stands still dot the sidewalks. There is a rocking chair brigade on the porches of some of the older hostelries, masses of bunting and racing colors above the main street and a giant arbor of old elms. But there is little except the track and a few big houses to suggest the grandeur and opulence Saratoga represented at the turn of the century.

These changes elude the horse lovers, none of whom frequent the downtown area anyway. They think of Saratoga as it used to be, and the track is pretty much intact.

"The houses out here haven't changed a bit," said Mrs. Payson, waving an arm to indicate the gabled homes, neat lawns and pine trees.

"Well, the trees and shrubbery haven't changed," said Nelson R. Asiel, who has been coming here since 1892. "And it's still the mainspring and center board of racing in the whole country."

Mrs. Winston F. C. Guest is here for the races, and so are Mrs. Richard du Pont, owner of Kelso; John Galbreath, owner of Chateaugay, who won the Kentucky Derby, and Miss Eleonora R. Sears, a horse owner who scandalized turf society when she rode cross saddle instead of side saddle in the early 1900s.

Not all visitors are racing enthusiasts, however. One, Mario Braggiotti, a guest of the Sanfords, sat in a front-row box composing a symphony while everyone else was watching Kelso win the $55,800 Whitney Stakes.

THE NINTH AT SARATOGA IS NOT ALWAYS A RACE

August 1966

As Alfred Gwynne Vanderbilt put it shortly before the Philadelphia Orchestra played the first of fourteen August concerts here in thoroughbred racing country, "We're all in some cultural interchange." But he was putting it mildly. Both the musicians, whose summer home is the new Saratoga Performing Arts Center, and the aristocratic multimillionaires who race horses are in a state of culture shock.

Such singers as Martina Arroyo, Lili Chookasian, John Alexander and Justino Diaz are finding out what fun it is to make a $10 bet. Eugene Ormandy, the orchestra's director, is expected at the race track any moment now. And the horse owners, many of whose families have been spending August here for two or three generations without benefit of concerts, are running around quietly boning up on such compositions as Beethoven's Ninth.

"You take the Ninth," said Mr. Vanderbilt, who knows about such things, "and there goes 80 percent of your evening."

Mr. Vanderbilt and his wife, the former Jean Harvey of Chicago, love music so much that they pop out to the music festival in Aspen, Colorado, every summer before the Saratoga race season begins. But they are exceptions.

A lot of the other horsemen dutifully attended the opening-night Beethoven performance (and gave generously to the center's building fund). But nobody expects them to show up for all the concerts. They have too many other things to do. Invitations to scores of cocktail parties and dinners are out, and during the day anybody who doesn't get to the track by the third race just isn't officially in town.

The elegant Cornelius Vanderbilt Whitneys were among those most

64

seriously affected by the Philadelphians' arrival. Mr. Whitney, whose grandfather founded the family stable after cleaning up with New York's first street railways, agreed to serve on the new center's board of directors, although he and his wife are not actually regular concert-goers in New York. And Mrs. Whitney promptly invited Mr. Ormandy to her Cady Hill House to lunch, found him wonderfully acceptable and rescheduled her big supperdance to coincide with his opening-night performance.

"We usually give this thing after the yearling sales," Mrs. Whitney said, well aware that she had shattered tradition. "But everything about the opening is gala."

It was so gala, in fact, that Governor and Mrs. Nelson Rockefeller flew in for the occasion, made a brief visit at the track, went to Mr. and Mrs. John Hay Whitney's for dinner and then led the cheering that welcomed the orchestra.

"I just have to say," said the governor, who is running for reelection, "that this is the most exciting moment in the eight years it has been my privilege to be governor."

Mr. Ormandy called Mrs. C. V. Whitney at the last minute to say he was too exhausted to attend her dance, but the party, with the Rockefellers in attendance, got the social season rolling anyway. Edward John Stanley, the eighteenth Earl of Derby, banker and president of the British Cotton Growing Association, whirled the diminutive Mrs. McDonnell Ford around Siro's dance floor while Cliff Hall, imported from Newport to supply the music, played "Strangers in the Night." Mrs. Ford, the former wife of Henry Ford 2nd, was never at a loss for partners. She has her own Water Mill Farm racing stable, named for her address on Long Island, and her own coral and turquoise racing silks. General John Coulter, husband of the late Constance Bennett, was her escort.

When Lord Derby wasn't swooping about with Mrs. Ford he was hopping up and down "Bye-Bye, Blackbird" style with Mrs. Cloyce Tippett, who has stables in Florida, New York and Ireland. "This is the first time I've ever done anything like this," said Colonel Tippett, whose frug looked as if it was getting a little out of hand. "I'm much better at the rhumba."

"But he's good," said Mrs. C. V. Whitney, who wasn't sure how many guests she'd invited. "He is very professional."

Despite the concert, what conversation there was above the music at the party centered on racing, horses and the people involved. The C. V. Whitneys' Swiss Cheese beat the John Hay Whitneys' Rosetta Stone in the fourth race, and virtually everybody of consequence said they missed Mr. and Mrs. Stephen Sanford. They had to stay in Palm Beach because of Mr. Sanford's health.

"I don't know what we're going to do without them," said Mrs. C. V. Whitney. "It just won't be the same."

It won't be the same with thirteen more nights of concerts either, but somehow Saratoga regulars will struggle along. Mrs. Payson will go whizzing around in the Rolls-Royce with the MET license plate. Mrs. Gene Markey will continue to dazzle the community with her diamonds. Paul Mellon, owner of Rokeby Stables and a descendant of the Philadelphia bankers, will turn up unexpectedly for a single race and then quickly disappear. And when all else fails, Mrs. Tippett probably will land her purple helicopter in somebody's petunia bed. She always does.

TEA DANCING AFTER THE RACES

August 1967

Mrs. Cornelius Vanderbilt Whitney, who is still hoping somebody will return her $780,000 jewel collection which mysteriously disappeared last week from her Cady Hill House bedroom, tonight gave this 104-year-old shockproof resort something new to talk about. It was what she called a teadance after the races.

"There are so many cocktail parties it's dull to say, 'Come to another one,'" she explained. "This is for the Belmont Ball committee, and I wanted to do something just a little different."

The hostess, who'd spent the earlier part of the day supervising the arrangements for her party ("I can't just drop things. It would be very rude") and meeting with the insurance men and police about her missing jewel collection, was in only reasonably good spirits. But she did manage to hold a gathering that was different all right.

The aristocratic multimillionaires who bring their thoroughbred horses here for the month can remember their parents or grandparents talking about how Diamond Jim Brady loved to strut down Broadway wearing 2,548 of his favorite gems or the time E. Berry Wall, "the King of the Dudes," changed his clothes forty times in one day to win a wager. The second and third generations still remember the elegant carryings-on in such pre-World War II gambling palaces as the Canfield Casino and the day Mrs. Cloyce J. Tippett arrived at the track in a ball gown with her dogs. And everybody who is anybody is used to dancing at the balls or parties regularly held in people's homes.

But tea—and tea combined with dancing when the sun was still shining brightly—is something else.

"I don't remember anybody's ever serving lots of tea," said Mrs. Stephen M. Sanford. "But you can never tell about Saratoga. Somebody must have drunk some tea sometime."

Mrs. Sanford wore a white lace Galanos minidress with white net stockings, white shoes, her usual generous amount of pearls and diamonds and a smile. She was among the nearly two hundred racing notables of one sort or another who turned up at the Saratoga Golf Club for Mr. and Mrs. Whitney's party. She had been at the track earlier for the running of the Sanford Stakes.

Once they got to the clubhouse, the guests, most of whom came straight from the track, found themselves streaming into two flowered tents set up on the crisp green front lawn. The larger tent, which had been decorated with garlands of laurel leaves, potted palms, yellow and white gladiola blossoms, fresh gardenias, strawberry trees, miniature maypoles and masses of twinkling little Italian lights, was for eating the hors d'oeuvre, drinking the tea and other substantially stronger (and more popular) beverages and milling around. The smaller one, with a Cliff Hall quintet fenced off with pots of yellow and white crysanthemums, was for dancing.

Mrs. Cortwright Wetherill and the elegant George D. Widener were among the first guests to arrive. Mrs. Wetherill is chairman of the Belmont Ball, which will be held next spring when the new Belmont track opens on Long Island. "I just got into town," Mrs. Wetherill said as she walked around to see who else was at the party. "I'm only going to be here overnight."

Mrs. Wetherill left in Philadelphia the Romanoff emeralds her grandfather gave her. Instead, she had decorated her raspberry silk dress with three strands of pearls and a diamond, gold, ruby, platinum and emerald pin called "the tree of life." It looked like one.

Mrs. D. Asiel Blight, a ball vice-chairman whose father, the late Nelson I. Asiel, was a stockbroker, told some people her Scotch and water was iced tea.

"The whole idea of tea is fun," she said.

Mr. and Mrs. Leslie Combs 2nd of Lexington drove here in their luxurious new land cruiser, the Blue Goose. It was named for a private railroad car once owned by Mrs. Combs's father.

Mrs. Whitney was gowned in a long-sleeved pale blue Jean Louis silk dress with white polka dots, a massive pearl necklace, pearl earrings, a pearl and diamond dinner ring and her diamond and platinum wedding ring. "They took my engagement ring," she said sadly. "The other pearls would have been too much today." But she changed her mind and she did wear the "other pearls." The pearl set, valued at $500,000, first belonged to Empress Eugénie of France. They were not removed from a bedroom dresser drawer where they were at the time of what the police are calling "a theft by a professional who knew what he was after." Mrs. Whitney also has the elaborate diamond, platinum and gold tiara that belonged to Empress Elisabeth of Austria. It is in a New York vault. She was glad, she said, that she had some of her jewels, but she was still upset.

"I'll have to go around in nothing but my pearls and my tiara," she moaned shortly after news of the theft got around the town. "I don't know what I'll do."

But after a sleepless night Sunday, Mrs. Whitney was making plans to do something positive about her jewel shortage. "I've got to get some of that Kenneth Lane stuff fast," she said. "It looks like I'm going to be a big fan of his. I never felt I needed him before. Now I do."

Mr. Lane is a New York designer of frankly fake jewels that sometimes resemble real ones. In the meantime, Mrs. Whitney also can fall back on an ornate gold and diamond floral spray brooch and matching earrings. She has worn them on several occasions since the theft. "I think some perfectly innocent person in our house must have said something they didn't know they were saying," Mrs. Whitney said, theorizing about the theft. "I'm sure none of our servants are involved."

The Whitneys, whose Cady Hill House was once a stagecoach stop on the route from Albany to St. George, have six servants with them—a valet, a cook, a kitchen maid, a chambermaid, a parlor maid and a laundress. The laundress was the only person in the house between 8:30 and 10:30 P.M. last Wednesday, when the jewels are thought to have disappeared. She has said she heard Mrs. Whitney's French poodle and Mr. Whitney's retriever bark, but didn't think anything about it. The other servants had taken the night off.

The missing jewelry is the talk of Saratoga's social set. But now there's the tea-dance and, by week's end, Marlon Brando is expected to make his first visit here. In the meantime, the Tippetts are flying a new turquoise and white jet helicopter around town. The old purple one seems to have worn out.

"We haven't had a chance to paint the outside of the new one purple yet," Colonel Tippett said of his new airborne toy. "But it's going to be purple and fuchsia. The inside is purple already."

The new helicopter, which goes 150 miles an hour, already has been at the golf club, hovering up and away over the ninth tee, and before long the Tippetts will probably take it to the track. Their immediate problem, however, was a chili and corn-on-the-cob party tonight for Cary Grant. He didn't arrive and they didn't serve tea.

II

Their
Social Capitals

New York, the money capital as well as the social capital, is still where the pickle, haircurler, rental-car, hamburger, real-estate and oil magnates often feel they have to go to prove to themselves that they have indeed arrived financially and socially. And after welcoming and sorting out immigrants for centuries, New York receives these new-comers with varying degrees of enthusiasm. Washington and Los Angeles are also immigrant cities—the former in awe of political power and the latter a pushover for big money.

In Washington, the President is the guest who counts most at dinner parties, and engraved invitations to the White House are still something special. But in this day of global diplomacy, détente and SALT, the demands put upon the aspiring hostess have increased. "All you do to keep up," a prominent hostess confided in 1976, "is read Foreign Policy magazine and invite Henry Kissinger to dinner."

Los Angeles, which goes out of its way to duplicate New York's excesses, often surpasses them. The swimming pool, the movie projection theater at home, the push-button Picasso and the sauna are as essential to the proper house as indoor plumbing. Money is an incentive to change and whether it's a change for the better or the worse is an entirely separate issue. Society, as played in the social capitals of America, is as transient and fickle as the latest invitation.

Jacqueline Onassis is still the guest who matters socially in New York, but it never hurts to include Norman Mailer, either. Between them are Lee Radziwill, John Mack Carter and Elizabeth Cromwell, all of whom are celebrating an article Lee wrote for the *Ladies' Home Journal*. Somebody had it drawn up into a cake.
Tyrone Dukes, *The New York Times* (1972)

New York

For many years, *the* New York social season took place in the fall, beginning with the National Horse Show in Madison Square Garden and running until New Year's. But after World War II, charity balls began to crowd the September schedule ahead of the Horse Show, and the more nearly official opening evening, if there ever was just one, increasingly became the start of the Metropolitan Opera's new season.

For more than a hundred years, the Metropolitan Opera drew everybody who was anybody in New York society, which meant that it also attracted an increasing number of those newly rich who would like to be somebody. Socially, it was always more important to see and be seen at the Opera than to know what was happening on stage, and fashion, as always, was one way almost anybody could attract attention.

At the turn of the century, *the* Mrs. Astor who dominated New York society was Mrs. William Backhouse Astor, Jr., the former Caroline Webster Schermerhorn, and what this tall, commanding brunette wore was more important than what all the other women wore. In the 1890s Mrs. Astor was given to elaborate gowns by Worth, the English designer, and she rarely ventured into the evening in anything less resplendent than a complicated and majestic *robe de style* involving velvet and lace as well as satin.

In those days, her neckline was wide—the better to display her diamond

73

collection. The bodice was wreathed with a draped bertha that covered her ample shoulders or was high-necked with huge puffed sleeves, sometimes fattened by the insertion of small pillows. There was an extensive train.

Her jewels—particularly the diamond stomacher that resembled a string of electric light bulbs, the diamond tiara she wore with other diamonds in her pompadour and a triple-strand diamond necklace—were prominent among the genuine glitter cited as a reason for calling the lower tier of box seats the Diamond Horseshoe.

Mrs. Frederick W. Vanderbilt, whose father-in-law, William H. Vanderbilt, used part of his $94-million inheritance to found and build the Met, also contributed to the splendor. She liked the idea of Venetian beauties of the Renaissance who toyed with a single jewel at the end of a chain, and decided to do likewise. She had a huge uncut ruby or sapphire suspended from her waist to her hemline on a rope of pearls, and, as she walked to her box, she kicked the stone. Neither this ornament nor stomachers and tiaras ever really caught on in fashion. Few women could afford such extravagances.

The Mrs. Vanderbilt, the former Grace Orme Wilson, who married Cornelius Vanderbilt 3rd, had a stomacher and a tiara, too. But before she died in 1952, secure in the knowledge that her brother had married *the* Mrs. Astor's daughter Caroline, she and her lamé headache bands and wide jewel chokers had already been eclipsed on Met opening nights by a beer industrialist's widow who later married a cotton converter. Mrs. George Washington Kavanaugh could have weighed her diamonds by the pound.

In 1944, one of Mrs. Kavanaugh's vintage years, the seventy-seven-year-old platinum blonde did herself up in slim crepe with little curls for a hairdo. Her eyebrows were thin black lines that gave her a surprised look, and her lips, like a lot of lips in the late thirties and forties, were painted into a bright red sweetheart bow. Her jewels that night included a diamond tiara, a diamond necklace with a pendant the size of a baseball and an assortment of oversized diamond rings. She wore four diamond and emerald bracelets on one arm and a big platinum and diamond spray on the other. She would have worn more jewels, the dowager said later, but there was a war going on.

Mrs. Kavanaugh, whose name was as firmly entrenched in the *Social Register* as those of Drexels, Belmonts, Fishes, and Morgans, rotated her furs (a chinchilla cape, a white ermine cape and a white fox cape) from Met opening to Met opening. But her corsage was almost inevitably the same. She liked big purple orchids, preferably in corsages of three or more.

During intermission in 1944, Mrs. Kavanaugh was joined for champagne by Lily Pons, the opera singer—another woman whose clothes inevitably set fashion reporters (and in earlier days, seamstresses and tailors) to scribbling in their notebooks. Miss Pons was addicted to strapless dresses with tiny

Dixie-cup white hats that sat on the top of her head. And at this opening, she wore a gold bib necklace given to her by the Empress of Persia.

Until World War II, it was not uncommon for women to wear white kid gloves long enough to cover their elbows, and the history of big nights at the Met is dotted with the fads of the times. Muffs, fans, toques and aigrette feathers gradually gave way to the orchid corsages, wisps of tulle in the hair and boxy fur jackets of later years. Upswept hair was first bobbed in the twenties and then allowed to drip all over the shoulders in the thirties. And the hemlines, to look back on their movement from 1883 to the present, seemed to go up and down with the regularity of an express elevator.

NEW METROPOLITAN OPERA HOUSE OPENS

September 1966

The premiere of Samuel Barber's *Antony and Cleopatra* was only one of the diversions at the super-gala opening of the new $45.7-million Metropolitan Opera House in Lincoln Center. The great arched house, a brightly lighted architectural toy that is expected to dominate salon conversations for weeks, was under as much scrutiny as the new opera. But neither the opera nor the house could outshine Mrs. Lyndon B. Johnson and an audience that included virtually every member of New York's predictably elegant diamond brigade.

Hundreds of formally dressed tycoons, aristocrats, nabobs, bankers, moguls, diplomats, potentates, fashion plates, grande dames and other assorted Great Society overachievers were among the 3,800 persons who produced a record $400,000 gross—more than twelve times what the Met usually gets for a sellout—and the kind of glamour the nation has come to associate with New York on a good day. The festive air was heightened at the second intermission, when Rudolf Bing, the Met's general manager, came onstage to announce that the strike of the opera's orchestra had been settled.

When the first-nighters found their way into the new building—and a lot of them had trouble deciding where to make their grand entrance—they found themselves surrounded by a mob of early birds who had stationed themselves in the foyers and along the stairway. Men in white ties and tailcoats found themselves pushing and shoving and being pushed and shoved, and at one point the crush was so thick nobody could go forward or backward. The women had no fashionable alternative to hitching up their evening gowns to climb the grand staircase leading to the twenty-nine parterre boxes. It was either that or the obscurity of the elevators.

The three center boxes in the new Diamond Horseshoe had been combined to form a state box for Mrs. Johnson, Ferdinand E. Marcos, President of the Philippines, Mrs. Marcos and their party. And by the time the First Lady slipped into a George Stavropoulos alabaster-white chiffon gown for the opening, she had already characterized the evening and cemented relations with two of the Met's leading lights. She sent roses to Leontyne Price, who played Cleopatra, and a letter to Anthony A. Bliss, president of the Metropolitan Opera Association.

"The gaiety, the splendor, the excitement of the evening are really overwhelming," she wrote. "One cannot help but feel that it is the beginning of another 'Golden Age' in the history of the Metropolitan Opera." And in many ways, it was.

The best red-plush seats in the boxes and orchestra went for $250, and dinner and champagne were extra. For $16, and the sense to have made advance reservations, guests could have filet of beef in either the Canteen Corporation's Grand Tier Restaurant or the Top of the Met. The same dinner was served to members of the exclusive Metropolitan Opera Club, and varied only slightly for Mrs. Johnson and her party in the board room. Across the plaza in Philharmonic Hall, Sherry's was offering a filet of beef dinner for $12. And all the restaurants and bars were well stocked with champagne—250 cases (3,000 bottles) in the new Met alone.

"We'll never run out," said James Rogers, vice-president of the Canteen Corporation. "It would be unthinkable."

By 6:30 P.M.—an hour and fifty-seven minutes before the curtain finally went up—most of the dinner guests had abandoned their Rolls-Royces and Cadillacs, pushed their way through thousands of spectators near the Broadway entrance, discovered that it was fun to stroll across the plaza past the fountain, and were on their way to the various dining spots. The Met's general manager was outside his new building shaking hands with his friends. Governor and Mrs. Nelson Rockefeller were among the first to speak to him.

"Mr. Harrison really outdid himself," the governor told Mr. Bing, referring to Wallace K. Harrison, the architect. Mrs. Rockefeller said she thought the building was beautiful.

Mrs. Lewis W. Douglas, wife of the former United States Ambassador to the Court of St. James's, had a special greeting for Mr. Bing. She called him Rudy and kissed him on the cheek. He later met Mrs. James Price, Leontyne Price's mother, and Mrs. Price, seeing him for the first time, was surprised at how tall and slim he was.

"Mr. Bing," she said, looking him over, "I've always envisioned you as a heavier man."

"Until a week ago I was," he answered.

When Mr. Bing was not shaking hands, he was inspecting the lines of spectators behind police barriers or making neat little courtly bows to such luminaries as Secretary of Defense Robert S. McNamara, Roger L. Stevens, the White House cultural adviser, and Arthur J. Goldberg, United States delegate to the United Nations. Periodically, Mr. Bing was assisted by Lauder Greenway, chairman of the Met's board of directors.

"I've never seen such a lot of flashes," Mr. Greenway said, shading eyes against the popping of photographers' lights.

Mr. Bing, who has never been known as an easygoing executive, had to leave his hospitality post at one point because the scenery had not been fireproofed. He was gone long enough to see that everything that needed it had been properly sprayed.

Mrs. Johnson had been expected at 6:30 P.M. but she was delayed by the busy schedule of President Marcos. They did not arrive until 7:15, which gave them just forty-five minutes for dinner, and she and President and Mrs. Marcos walked the length of a red carpet that stretched 150 feet from the fountain to the main entrance. Once inside, she looked up to the balconies, where thousands cheered, and then she saw the crystal chandeliers the Austrian government had given the Met.

"I looked up at the chandeliers," she said later, "and they just looked like stars."

From the foyer, Mrs. Johnson and her party climbed up the south curve of the grand staircase, passing onlookers who immediately attempted to follow her. And from there the party took an elevator up to the board room for dinner. Mrs. Marcos, a diminutive brunette, wore a pale pink and white dress with a diamond and pearl tiara.

Such stalwarts as Alfred Gwynne Vanderbilt, Cornelius Vanderbilt Whitney and John Hay Whitney, whose families raised the money to found and build the old Met eighty-three years ago, were there along with Mrs. John Barry Ryan, whose father, Otto Kahn, started looking for a new home for the Met in 1908. "It's a dream come true," said Mrs. Ryan, whose guests included Senator J. W. Fulbright and Mrs. Fulbright. "It was sad leaving the old house, but I really like everything about this one. It's a very, very beautiful house."

Mr. Vanderbilt and his wife are not much for New York openings. But, apparently, they thought the Met opening was more than a run-of-the-mill extravaganza. They were there with Pauline Trigère, the dress designer, who kept saying, "This city's never, never going to be the same . . ." Both women wore gowns by Miss Trigère. It was a great night for furs, *haute couture* and enormous jewels. Mrs. C. V. Whitney, who can be depended upon to come up with something significant for the occasion, wore a gold and diamond tiara that had belonged to the Empress Elisabeth of Austria.

This bauble, involving 1,900 diamonds and 75 rubies, was coordinated with chandelier diamond earrings, a diamond necklace and a dress that looked as if it were made of silver-foil ribbons. It wasn't.

"Just a lot of silver lace," said Mrs. Whitney. "Sarmi did it."

For a while, it looked as if Mrs. Joseph Lauder, the cosmetics queen, was going to appear without a tiara. She didn't like the idea of wearing her ruby and diamond tiara with a turquoise crepe dress. But in the end, she found something better—a gold and diamond crown suitable for Queen Elizabeth II.

"You know how it is," she said. "You have to wear something."

Mrs. F. Raymond Johnson, widow of the merchandising executive, also had a moment of indecision. She couldn't decide between "the old Dior I wore to the April in Paris Ball" and "my new Galanos that looks divine with diamonds." The Galanos, all red and green jersey, won, and she had emeralds and diamonds on her arms, fingers, in her hair, around her neck and hanging from her ears.

Mrs. Polk Guest, the former wife of Raymond Guest, United States Ambassador to Ireland, who flew from Washington to attend the opening, was one of the few women who coped with the crowds without disturbing the police or her hairdo. When she wanted to speak to a friend, she simply ducked under the police barriers in her green chiffon ball gown and edged around corners. Her jewels, she said, were not real.

"Call them peridots and topazes," she said, speaking of a necklace of seventeen major stones. "They aren't."

Mrs. Jess Thomas, wife of the Met tenor, wore neither diamonds, peridots nor topazes. But there was no missing her. She had what her press agent said were fifteen pounds of floor-length gold chains hanging over her black dress. And the press agent followed her, handing out mimeographed releases.

Cecil Beaton, the British photographer and designer, left the wearing of big jewels to the women. But his cufflinks were white rock crystal set with emeralds. "The audiences aren't as freakish these days," he said before joining Mrs. Joseph P. Kennedy for dinner. "They don't make such fools of themselves."

At 8:10, the orchestra, under the direction of Thomas Schippers, played "The Star-Spangled Banner." John D. Rockefeller 3rd, chairman of Lincoln Center's board, welcomed everyone from the stage and introduced Mr. Bliss. And at 8:27, just before the opera began, sixty-five photographers came out from behind the curtain, lined up and shot pictures of the auditorium. They received a sitting ovation.

"I've never seen this in Europe—Vienna, Berlin—never," said Mrs. Fritz Reiner, widow of the Chicago Symphony conductor, who was not pleased by the photographers. "Did you ever hear of it in your life?"

May 1965

El Morocco, the supper club that has never been accused of being anything more serious than a zebra-striped playpen for rich adults, has had better nights. But the activities there recently will do for 1965.

Princess Grace of Monaco, the former Grace Kelly of Philadelphia, inadvertently upstaged Princess Benedikte of Denmark and then both met in the confusion of upper-echelon glamour that continues to make old Elmo a proper place to see and be seen. Shortly before midnight, one could see Mrs. Winston F. C. (CeeZee) Guest sitting under a fake white palm tree, twisting her short blond hair back over her left ear. Or Mrs. Samuel P. Peabody, for whom the band played "Happy Birthday" ("I'm not going to say which one"). Or Baby Jane (Mrs. Leonard) Holzer in a white dress with more front than back to it. Or lots of others, all of whom seemed to be taking turns looking at one another over their champagne glasses. And then Princess Benedikte arrived.

The tall, shy Dane whose background ("I love horses. I like to sew") suggests no particular enthusiasm for nightclubs, was the guest of the City of New York. Edward F. Cavanagh, Jr., the Deputy Mayor, and his wife were supper hosts to the twenty-six guests, including friends of their daughter, Nanette. But the bills were to be sent to Richard C. Patterson, Jr., Commissioner of the Public Events Department. Originally, the supper was to have been held upstairs in the privacy of the Champagne Room. But at the last minute it was switched to the wide-open spaces downstairs—Elmo's main drag. This meant that the princess, an authentic member of an old and distinguished royal family, immediately became the most important person present.

Mrs. F. Raymond Johnson made the royal visitor's status quite clear. She swished off in her black lace dress to meet her and ended up, at the Cavanaghs' invitation, sitting with her. Even Mrs. Wyatt Cooper, the former Gloria Vanderbilt, glanced in the princess's direction. And then it was Grace of Monaco's turn.

The former actress swept in, was seated on a banquette in the middle of the room facing the princess's table and proceeded to order some chicken chow mein. Everyone in the room turned around to look. The consuls general of Denmark and Monaco, who accompanied their respective princesses, effected the ensuing meeting. It took place in a minuscule aisle between the tables. The Danish princess made the first move, and the princess born in the United States rose out of her seat and stepped away from her table. The Marquesa de Cuevas, settled on the banquette next to Princess Grace, hardly noticed. But she is the former Margaret Strong, granddaughter and heir of John D. Rockefeller. She is used to kings and queens.

It was much the same with the Maharanee of Baroda, who did not budge from her dimly lit corner. She went right on sipping champagne with such pals as Mrs. Joseph Lauder and Achille Brusoni, a stockbroker who regularly wears sunglasses in darkened nightclubs. And although James Mitchell, a spokesman for the thirty-four-year-old club, said Thursday was one of the "great nights" in Elmo's history, it wasn't really. It is true that nearly everybody who is or was anybody was there, and that the list included Cynthia Phipps, the Carnegie steel heiress; Mrs. John R. Drexel 3rd, the former Noreen Stonor; Pamela Zauderer, whose sister is married to Peter Duchin; Raymundo de Larrain, who designs ballets and directs operas; Robert Romulo, son of Carlos P. Romulo; Christopher B. Cerf, whose father runs Random House, and all those handsome Danes. But some of the key figures were missing.

In the old days, Humphrey Bogart fought a young millionaire over a lady and a pair of stuffed pandas, Aly Khan was a regular, and Arlene Judge walked in to find several of her former husbands sitting at various tables.

THE APRIL IN PARIS BALL
AND ALL THOSE FAMILIAR DIAMONDS

October 1965

The April in Paris Ball has an international reputation for being bigger, flashier, more expensive and less visibly organized than any other charity ball in the world, and it lived up to expectations for the fourteenth successive season.

There were all those familiar faces, all those familiar diamonds and that unbelievably glamorous crush. The extravaganza, a nine-hour siege that laid claim to half a dozen rooms at the Waldorf, including the ballroom, involved 1,300 persons—1,200 tycoons, moguls, magnates and fashion plates who belong to what is loosely known as "American society" and one hundred of their elegant French counterparts. The event was billed this year as

80

"Deauville, Ville du Cheval," and in its own inimitable way it was one of the horsiest events ever held in a pseudo-Norman setting.

Twenty rearing white chickenwire horses had been draped with bright silks representing the racing colors of French and American stables, and there were smaller horses at the centers of the 120 tables. The stage setting, a wilderness of apple trees, fountains and chrysanthemums, and Mrs. Alfred S. Levitt, the decorations chairman, were also supposed to suggest Deauville.

"My hair it is a mane the color of three horses," said Mrs. Levitt, French-born wife of the builder. "It is chestnut, bay and palomino. It's glued with glue. It's two pounds but it feels like four." Mrs. Levitt, who'd spent the afternoon supervising the installation of her elaborate creations, put on her three-foot-high wig after first zipping herself into a new Jacques Griffe dress.

"It's turf green and white," she said, aware of the green velvet she had hung behind each of her horses. "I wanted to match."

Guests began to arrive at seven, but nobody who is anybody appeared at his ballroom table until 8:45. A guard, representing the committee, watched the head table to make sure no one rearranged the place cards. The Duke and Duchess of Windsor were the last to arrive.

"Where is Mary?" the duke said plaintively, looking around for Mrs. Stephen M. Sanford, the ball chairman, "Where is Laddie?"

The Sanfords were there, greeting Mrs. Joseph P. Kennedy. She was in pink satin with diamonds and Joseph Timility, a former Boston police commissioner.

"Ah, Mary," said the duke, spotting his hostess through his dark glasses. "At last."

The duke wore white tie and tails although the invitation had said black tie. The duchess was gowned in hot pink with a beaded wrap banded in mink. And Mrs. Sanford was shoulder to toes in bright purple paillettes, feathers and roses, and diamonds.

"If anyone says I look like Sophie Tucker I'll be very angry," Mrs. Sanford said. "And I'm not Texas Guinan either."

The dinner, in keeping with the Deauville theme, was decidedly Norman. And by the time the 170 waiters (seventy fewer than last year) and fifteen captains got around to clearing the green-velvet-covered tables, the ball-goers had consumed a thousand bottles of wine and champagne, five hundred pounds of chickens cooked in calvados, eight hundred pounds of filet of beef, three hundred pounds of cheese and six hundred heads of Boston lettuce.

"The young kind with the very white leaves," the chef said of the lettuce. "We ordered it special two months ago."

Killer Tippett, the only dog at the party, did not have dinner. But she was dressed for the ball. Mrs. Cloyce Tippett had dressed her pet in gold brocade and pink ribbons. "She's going to be in the fashion show," Mrs. Tippett said. "She's having fun."

Furs from Georges Kaplan, clothes Jacques Heim designed in French and American racing colors, and dresses from the Elizabeth Arden collection were shown during the dinner. And afterward there was dancing to the music of Meyer Davis and his orchestra.

But the maestro, like Cinderella, disappeared at midnight to go to the Americana, where the National Horse Show set—never, never to be confused with America's thoroughbred racing establishment—was having its own ball.

It was a big night all around for emerald and diamond earrings. Mrs. Sanford wore them, and so did the duchess, Lady Peel (Bea Lillie), and Mrs. Tippett. Mrs. Cornelius Vanderbilt Whitney, however, stuck by diamonds that had belonged to Mr. Whitney's mother. With the necklace and earrings she wore Sarmi's scarlet and white dress with little silver ribbons down the skirt.

"I think this ball is entirely too big," Mrs. Whitney said, although she was a vice-chairman of the New York committee and is usually one of its major attractions. "We should treat it the way we'd treat a horse race. When there are too many horses, we add an extra race."

New Yorkers at the ball included Robert David Lion Gardiner of Gardiners Island and the red-haired Mrs. Gardiner; Mrs. Alfred Strelsin, wife of the industrialist; Mrs. John F. C. Bryce, the former Jo Hartford of the Atlantic & Pacific fortune; Vidal Sassoon, the hairdresser; Miss Cynthia Phipps and Arnold Scaasi, the dress designer.

Mrs. Wall Breer, daughter of the late Canadian financier, and the Ralph C. Wilsons (he owns the Buffalo Bills football team) represented Detroit. And the Guilford Dudleys (insurance) of Nashville and Palm Beach were the Tennessee contingent.

The Duc de Montesquiou-Fezensac, a proper French aristocrat who stuck by his white tie and tails in a world full of black ties, headed the French contingent. Its women members, including Regine, "queen of the Paris nightclubs," were dressed by the French *haute couture*. The Baronne de Cabrol, the former Marguerite (Daisy) d'Harcourt, settled for Lanvin's green and gold brocade. The Comtesse d'Eudeville, the former Adelaide Bradish Johnson of New York and New Orleans, chose Dior's red organza with a train.

Ball tickets cost $150 a person, and the committee expects to make more than $200,000 even though 1,300 times $150 comes to only $195,000. Additional funds will come from donations ("One man gave me $5,000," Mrs. Sanford said) and the sale of advertising in the glossy souvenir program. The profits will be divided among French and American charities. Air France, Charles of the Ritz and Van Cleef & Arpels were the sponsors.

The New Frontiersmen have gathered and regathered in New York off and on for years, and not the least of their hostesses has been Lee Radziwill, the late President Kennedy's sister-in-law.

As of 1976, after trying acting, writing and television interviewing, Lee has announced herself as an interior decorator with the Americana Hotels as her account. She and her husband had parted company, and she was often seen with Peter Tufo. But then, a lot of the old Camelot group had changed.

The President's widow went on to marry Aristotle Onassis and was again widowed. She, too, went to work as a consultant for Viking Press while simultaneously lending her name to such community projects as the saving of Grand Central Station.

Pierre Salinger and Arthur Schlesinger, Jr., had new wives. Patricia Kennedy Lawford and Jean Stein vanden Heuvel were divorced. Louise Liberman Savitt went on to become Mrs. Frederick A. Melhado. Adlai E. Stevenson and Maurice Chevalier were dead. The Leonard Bernsteins, Mr. and Mrs. Martin Gabel and the Paul Mellons carried on.

Prince and Princess Stanislas Radziwill gave what the princess called "a teeny, tiny dance for less than a hundred" in their Fifth Avenue duplex. And although the gathering was "not for anyone or anything—just a little thing we're giving before we go back to London," it was well supplied with New Frontiersmen, some of whom have graduated into the Great Society, and other notables. The furniture in the Radziwill dining room, with its apricot moiré walls, had been cleared away for the dancing. A five-piece Lester Lanin ensemble was at one end, beside the windows. There were big bouquets of multicolored spring flowers, some of which had been imported, and lots of champagne. And the princess, who had had trouble deciding which of two Yves St. Laurent gowns she would wear, strolled about the airy, white-walled drawing room greeting friends.

"I'm not sure Dame Margot and Nureyev will be able to come," the former Lee Bouvier said before the dance got under way. "He has to rehearse from six to midnight, or something dreadful."

Even without Dame Margot Fonteyn and Rudolf Nureyev, dancers with the Royal Ballet, the Radziwills had a stellar cast.

Pierre Salinger, press secretary in the Kennedy administration and a former Senator, winged in from California. Adlai E. Stevenson, Chief United

States delegate to the United Nations, arrived after dedicating the new Prudential Center in Boston, addressing a joint session of the Massachusetts Legislature and, in New York, attending a Latin American reception. The Broadway contingent, which included Maurice Chevalier and Sammy Davis, Jr., simply drove uptown after serving the paying customers.

For twenty of the elect, the evening began with cocktails and dinner at Mrs. John F. Kennedy's Fifth Avenue duplex. The princess, who is Mrs. Kennedy's sister, and her husband were in this group along with Mr. and Mrs. Leonard Bernstein, Leopold Stokowski, Franklin D. Roosevelt, Jr., Mrs. Paul Mellon, Mike Nichols, accompanied by Mrs. Sybil Burton, J. Kenneth Galbraith, former United States Ambassador to India and author of *The Affluent Society,* Senator Robert F. Kennedy, looking tan and debonair, Sam Spiegel, the producer, and Mrs. Martin Gabel.

Mrs. Gabel, who is Arlene Francis, the actress, wore Arnold Scaasi's white silk peau-de-soie gown with a beaded strapless top and a matching silk coat. She would have been accompanied by Mr. Gabel, but he was performing in *Baker Street* and could not join the party until it reached the Radziwills'. Mrs. Bernstein settled for a pencil-slim black and white lace gown ("It's my very favorite") by James Galanos, and a matching jacket. And her pearls were tucked in beneath the neckline—a custom that first attracted widespread attention when Mrs. Kennedy lived in the White House.

Another batch of guests went to Mr. and Mrs. A. Ronald Tree's Upper East Side town house for the preliminaries. Guests at this dinner included Roswell L. Gilpatric, a consultant on international problems to President Johnson and former Deputy Secretary of Defense, Mrs. Gilpatric and Mrs. Moss Hart. Mrs. Tree, United States delegate to the Trusteeship Council of the United Nations, was wearing what she referred to as "an old friend" —a draped white chiffon dress. Mrs. Gilpatric wore crinkly blue silk with one shoulder bared. And Mrs. Hart, who as Kitty Carlisle plays "To Tell the Truth" on television, wore Count Ferdinando Sarmi's strapless green chiffon with a necklace of gold, turquoise and diamonds.

In the end, however, the hostess and Mrs. William J. vanden Heuvel made the fashion news. They wore similar gowns designed by St. Laurent. At one point, Princess Radziwill had toyed with the idea of wearing his long, white satin gown. But at the last minute she decided instead upon his new lime green silk crepe with slit-from-the-shoulder drapery edged with gold and emerald embroidery. Mrs. vanden Heuvel's was the same, but in a slightly different color—blue green. It was made in New York by Sam Moore. Mrs. vanden Heuvel was with her husband, who is at work with Sargent Shriver on the antipoverty program, and among the other guests were Mrs. Peter Lawford (Patricia Kennedy) in green; Mr. and Mrs. Stephen E. Smith (Jean Kennedy), Philip C. Johnson, the architect who designed the Museum of Modern Art's annex and sculpture court and the New York State Theater at Lincoln Center; Mr. and Mrs. Adolph Green; Mrs. Liberman Savitt, a former editor at *Vogue* magazine; and Marisol, the artist.

Mrs. Kennedy made the trip from her apartment to her sister's with Mr. Harriman and Mr. Roosevelt. She wore a white silk crepe dress with a white mink jacket.

FORBES ANNIVERSARY A V.I.P. CAUCUS

September 1967

Malcolm S. Forbes, a prosperous Republican of Scottish descent, celebrated the fiftieth anniversary of his family's *Forbes* business magazine by giving a party that may be described as one of the country's largest single assemblies of working tycoons. The gathering, an elaborate dinner-dance at the country house of Mr. and Mrs. Forbes, was so loaded with board chairmen and presidents of major United States corporations that even Hubert H. Humphrey was startled.

"I may be the only Vice President around," he said.

Mr. Humphrey said Mr. Forbes had invited him by saying, "I'm having a little birthday party up at my place—just the members of my family and a few friends." But the Vice President was prepared. He had armed himself for this social confrontation with the very rich with a serious text dealing with what industry and the government should be doing together to combat poverty. But before he could deliver his message, he had other duties. The first, and by no means the least, was on a two-hour receiving line that began at 7:30 P.M.

Among the first of the big moguls to arrive were Roy L. Ash, president of Litton Industries, Inc., Gene C. Brewer, president of U.S. Plywood-Champion Papers, Inc., and James Davant, senior partner in Paine, Webber, Jackson and Curtis.

"I'm a Litton man myself," the Vice President jovially assured Mr. Ash, who looked a little nonplused. Mr. Davant got one of several of Mr. Humphrey's "long time no see's." And when M. J. Warnock, president of the Armstrong Cork Company, appeared, Mr. Forbes introduced him as "the fella who gets under everybody's feet."

Mr. Humphrey thought that was funny. He seemed pleased when Lucien Hooper of E. F. Hutton and Company announced that he, too, was a Democrat. And he laughed when Mr. Forbes answered, "Yes, I know. Unfortunately there are a lot of you around."

By this time, Edmund F. Martin, chairman of Bethlehem Steel, was shaking hands all around. And then came Zenon C. R. Hansen, president of Mack Trucks, Inc., General David Sarnoff, chairman of the Radio Corporation of America, and Donald C. Power, chairman of the General Telephone and Electronics Corporation. Mrs. Power, a motherly-looking woman with upswept hair, hugged Mr. Forbes. And her husband, who was walking with a cane, said he had broken his leg three weeks ago.

"But I'm all right now," he said.

Mr. Power, a former trustee of Ohio State University who has missed only three home football games in Columbus since 1920, studied his colleagues later and decided most of them were Middle Westerners. "I don't know why it is," he said, putting the figure at roughly 60 to 70 percent. "I guess there are more of us."

It wasn't long before the Vice President was on familiar terms with Lammot du Pont Copeland, president of E. I. du Pont de Nemours and Company, Inc. And he reminded Mrs. Copeland that the last time he had seen her, they had had what he called "a nice dance" together.

"I remember," said Mrs. Copeland, who was done up in white satin with two strands of pearls, simple twisted gold earrings and several slim bracelets of diamonds. "It was nice."

Mr. Copeland, an excellent dancer himself, was equally understated. He wore a black satin waistcoat with his dinner clothes, the Crown of Oaks gold and green rosette of Belgium in his lapel and gold and emerald studs.

"My wife gave me the studs," he said.

The Copelands had given their pilot the day off, so they drove up from their Greenville, Delaware, estate. William P. Lear, chairman of Lear Jet Industries, Inc., had one of his planes with him. But he had to ask Mrs. Lear to call the Forbeses and find out where they could land. Mr. Forbes directed all the private planes to the Morristown field.

Mr. Forbes, whom the Vice President later described as "the Jim Farley of the G.O.P. and the Bob Hope of business publications," said something in the receiving line to identify nearly all of his corporate guests. He called George Lesch, chairman and president of the Colgate-Palmolive Company, "the head of a little soap company." And Winston V. Morrow, president of Avis Rent-A-Car, became "Mr. Avis—No. 2." Mr. Humphrey laughed and said he was No. 2, too. H. I. Romnes, chairman of the American Telephone and Telegraph Company, arrived during this last exchange. And at this stage, there was a line of tycoons and their wives stretching from the Forbeses' driveway through their front door to the living room receiving line and out a side door through a maze of massive party tents.

The cocktail tent, an outdoor ballroom more than big enough for the 740 formally clad guests, was blue, green and white—the colors of the Forbes family's tartan. It was carpeted in blue-green, curtained with yards and yards of tartan and ornamented with family flags and arrangements of thistles, heather and candles. To get to the dinner tent, couples had to walk down what may well be the most spectacular passageway ever devised for a single night. It was a 430-foot green tent with a scalloped overhang, tartan curtains, the carpeting overlaid with more tartan and the ceiling aglitter with thousands of little Italian lights.

"Magnificent!" exclaimed Mrs. Power, who has been to more parties than she cared to remember. "Glorious," said Mrs. Copeland. "Lovely," added Mrs. Robert Sarnoff, whose husband is president of the Radio Corporation of America.

None of the women could do their exclaiming until they were well inside the dinner tent because four bands of kilted bagpipers had been assigned to add a final touch. Sixty-three pipers were placed at intervals along the passageway. And throughout the procession, they skirled up the deafening whine that is "Scotland the Brave."

The dinner tent, as enormous as anything Barnum and Bailey ever put up in the old days, also was ornate and Scottish. It was all medieval gold, yellow, blue and gray stone inside, like a castle. Lester Lanin and his orchestra were there for the dancing. During the dessert, a grape ice with spun sugar, fresh grapes and cookies, the Forbeses' sons, Malcolm, Robert, Christopher and Timothy, skirled more bagpipe selections. Then out came the Westminster Choir, with such songs as "It's a Grand Night for Singing" and "Rose Marie."

At about 11:30 P.M., Mr. Forbes, a son of the Scottish immigrant who founded *Forbes* magazine, was paying tribute to nepotism ("I'm here tonight through sheer ability—and 51 percent") and to inheritance ("A lot of us have come up the hard way"). Then he introduced the Vice President.

Mr. Humphrey said, among other things, that in a country afflicted with poverty, wealth is something of which to be ashamed. He also reminded everyone that his family's business, the Humphrey Drug Company of Huron, South Dakota, was founded in 1903—fourteen years before *Forbes* magazine.

The fireworks, which included pinwheels, rockets and things that sounded like bombs, were last. And then virtually everyone got down to some serious dancing.

CAPOTE'S BALL

November 1966

It was hailed as "the party of the century," which it wasn't really, but Truman Capote's masked ball was certainly THE party of the sixties and then some. People who weren't invited did leave town or said they were going. Everyone with even the vaguest pretense of social accomplishment said he and she were invited, whether they were or not, and when the Times *published the entire guest list, the fibbers were caught out.*

As it turned out, the list itself was as much the news the next morning as the coverage of the party, and telephones rang all along the party circuit about who was and who wasn't included. An enterprising businessman took the list, had it printed on toilet paper and gave it to friends. Several people wrote us that they had used the list to paper bathrooms and dens. In journalistic circles, the big question was how the Times *got the list. Suffice it to say that Truman did not give us the list, that we did not steal it, that we had it in type before the party began, and that I copied each and every one of the 540 names down in longhand.*

There is also the matter of cost. Even though the supper was chicken hash and spaghetti, rather than filet mignon and caviar, the price was probably somewhere between $15,000 and $20,000 rather than the $13,000 reported in the story. Truman, who has gone on to star in a movie and write the really gossipy social memoir Answered Prayers, *has always said he did not deduct the cost of the party as a business expense.*

Truman Capote, still stunned by the number of prominent people who begged him to invite them to what he insisted upon calling his "little masked ball for Kay Graham and all my friends," finally gave his much-discussed Black and White Dance at the Plaza last night, and it lived up to nearly all of its extravagant advance notices.

Frank Sinatra let his wife, Mia Farrow, twist most of the fast numbers with Bennett Cerf's son, Christopher. Mrs. Anne McDonnell Ford hugged her good friend, the Maharanee of Jaipur, who was invited at the very last minute, while Mrs. Henry Ford 2nd spoke to some of her partners in her native Italian. Arthur Schlesinger, Jr., and William F. Buckley, neither of whom are short men, kept dancing with taller women. Marianne Moore, the poet, appeared without her tricorn-hat trademark.

There was no main table, but one was exceedingly popular. It was where Mr. Sinatra, Claudette Colbert, John Daly and his wife, the former Virginia Warren, and Mrs. Leland Hayward, wife of the producer, sat.

Mrs. Stavros Niarchos (Charlotte Ford) didn't do badly either. She sat with Lynda Bird Johnson, who was done up in a checkerboard black-and-white top and a full white chiffon skirt, Mrs. Peter Duchin, wife of the orchestra leader, and Wendy Vanderbilt, daughter of Alfred Gwynne Vanderbilt.

The guests, as spectacular a group as has ever been assembled for a private party in New York, were an international *Who's Who* of notables. There were 540 diplomats, politicians, scientists, painters, writers, composers, actors, producers, dress designers, social figures, tycoons and what

Mr. Capote called "international types, lots of beautiful women and ravishing little things." And nobody seemed to be having more fun than the host.

"Oh, it's very pretty, isn't it!" he exclaimed as he and Mrs. Philip L. Graham, guest of honor and president of the *Washington Post* and *Newsweek* magazine, took their places near the scarlet tables in the gold and white, candlelit ballroom. "We're going to have fun." The millionaire author had asked the men to wear dinner jackets with black masks and the women to wear black or white dresses with white masks. And he and Mrs. Graham, in a white wool crepe Balmain, had conformed. Hers was a matching white wool crepe mask sprinkled with jewels, which she had clamped on her nose. And he wore a 39-cent domino from F. A. O. Schwarz. Mr. Duchin's orchestra and the Soul Brothers rock 'n' roll group were required to wear masks while providing the music. The Secret Service men accompanying Miss Johnson were supposed to, and did. President and Mrs. Johnson know and apparently like Mr. Capote, and he would have invited them, he said. But he knew they couldn't attend.

"I asked Mrs. Longworth, Margaret Truman and Lynda Bird," he explained. "I guess that's enough of the White House."

Mrs. Nicholas Longworth, the daughter of President Theodore Roosevelt, is in her eighties. But she made a rare trip from Washington just for the party. She came, she said, because "Truman Capote's one of the most agreeable human beings I know" and the ball sounded "like the most exquisite of spectator sports." Mrs. Longworth's small white mask, which cost her 35 cents and gave her great glee at having beaten Mr. Capote's 39 cents, had the top and bottom cut off. She had fastened it to her temples with adhesive tape.

A lot of the other masks were far more elaborate, and some—those involving quantities of feathers, flowers and rhinestones—were reputed to have cost as much as $600. Mrs. William Woodward's wasn't that expensive, and Mrs. Joseph P. Kennedy, who had several masks in case she changed her mind at the last minute, is said to have spent only $85. "Arlene Francis got me mine," said Mrs. Woodward, the grande dame who has been giving and going to elegant parties since before World War I. "It's all black feathers.

"We used to do this sort of thing in Newport in the old days," she said. "Why, I remember when we all dressed up in lavish costumes and the *Ziegfeld Follies* came up from New York to perform."

Mr. and Mrs. Alfred Gwynne Vanderbilt decided to be black cats for the night—"pool cats," according to Mrs. Vanderbilt. Mr. Vanderbilt wore his black velvet mask under protest.

"It itches and I can't see," said Mr. Vanderbilt, pulling it off and sticking it in a pocket. "That's a lot better."

"He doesn't mind that much," said his wife, who was gowned in black

Leroy Aarons
Charles Addams
Richard Adler
Count Adlerberg
Mr. and Mrs. Gianni Agnelli
Count Umberto Agnelli
Edward Albee
Mr. and Mrs. Archibald
  Albright
Shana Alexander
Nelson Aldrich
Mr. and Mrs. Charles Allen
Mr. and Mrs. Joseph Alsop
Mr. and Mrs. Stewart Alsop
Mr. and Mrs. Cleveland
  Amory
Princess Charles d'Arenberg
Odette Arnaud
Mrs. W. Vincent Astor
Mary Louise Aswell
Mr. and Mrs. William
  Attwood
Mr. and Mrs. Louis
  Auchincloss
Mr. and Mrs. Richard
  Avedon
Mr. and Mrs. George Axelrod
Mr. and Mrs. Harold Arlen

Dan Bachardi
Mr. and Mrs. George Backer
William Baldwin
James Baldwin
Miss Tallulah Bankhead
Benedetta Barzini
Samuel Barber
Trumbull Barton
Charles Baskerville
Mr. and Mrs. Theodore
  Bassett
Cecil Beaton
Mr. and Mrs. Frederick S.
  Beebe
S. N. Behrman
Mr. and Mrs. Harry
  Belafonte
Marisa Berenson
Candice Bergen
Mrs. Seymour Berkson
William Berkson
Mr. and Mrs. Irving Berlin
Sir Isaiah and Lady Berlin
Mr. and Mrs. Leonard
  Bernstein
Mr. and Mrs. Robert
  Bernstein
Lemoyne Billings
Mrs. Pierre Billotte
Carol Bjorkman
Mr. and Mrs. Watson Blair
Mr. and Mrs. Charles Bohlen
Mr. and Mrs. Anthony di
  Bonaventura
Mrs. René Bouché
Anthony Bower
Mr. and Mrs. Thomas Braden
Mr. and Mrs. Benjamin
  Bradlee

Count and Countess
  Brando Brandolini
Henry Brandon
Mr. and Mrs. Frederick
  Brisson
James E. Broadhead
Donald Brooks
Mr. and Mrs. Richard Brooks
Eve Brown
Mr. and Mrs. David K. E.
  Bruce
Mrs. Mellon Bruce
Mr. and Mrs. John Mason
  Brown
Mr. and Mrs. William
  Buckley
Dr. and Mrs. Ralph Bunche
Mr. and Mrs. McGeorge
  Bundy
Susan Burden
Mr. and Mrs. S. Carter
  Burden, Jr.
Mr. and Mrs. Abe Burrows
Robert Burtis
Mr. and Mrs. Richard
  Burton
Mrs. Robin Butler
Mr. and Mrs. J. F. Byers 3rd

Mr. and Mrs. Herb Caen
Mrs. William M. Campbell
Paul Candmus
Mr. and Mrs. Cass Canfield
Prince Carlo Caraciallo
Prince and Princess
  Nicola Caraciallo
Leslie Caron
Margaret Case
Mr. and Mrs. Dan Platt
  Caulkins
Mr. and Mrs. Bennett Cerf
Christopher Cerf
Lord Chalfont
Mr. and Mrs. Hugh J.
  Chisholm, Jr.
Blair Clark
Mr. and Mrs. Richard
  Clurman
Harold Cole
Dr. and Mrs. John Converse
Senator and Mrs. John
  Sherman Cooper
Mr. and Mrs. Wyatt Cooper
General John Coulter
Noel Coward
Chandler Cowles
Mr. and Mrs. Gardner Cowles
Count and Countess
  Rudolfo Crespi
Mr. and Mrs. Walter
  Cronkite
Bessie de Cuevas
Charlotte Curtis
Thomas Quinn Curtiss
Mr. and Mrs. Frederick
  Cushing
Minnie Cushing

Mr. and Mrs. John Daly
Mr. and Mrs. Clifton
  Daniel
Mr. and Mrs. Sammy Davis,
  Jr.
Oscar de la Renta
Françoise de Langlade
Arnaud de Renée
Mr. and Mrs. Robert Delheim
Alan Delynn
Mr. and Mrs. Armand
  Deutsch
Mr. and Mrs. Alvin Dewey
Marlene Dietrich
Mr. and Mrs. Douglas Dillon
Ainslie Dinwiddie
Marquis and Marchioness
  of Dufferin
Mrs. Kingman Douglass
Sharman Douglas
Mrs. Peter Duchin
Drew Dudley
Jack Dumphy
Mr. and Mrs. Robert Dunphy
Mr. and Mrs. F. W. Dupee

Mr. and Mrs. Frederick
  Eberstadt
Mr. and Mrs. Osborn Elliott
Mr. and Mrs. Ralph Ellison
Mr. and Mrs. Charles
  Engelhard
Jean Ennis
Mr. and Mrs. Jason Epstein
Elliott Erwitt
Mr. and Mrs. Rowland
  Evans, Jr.

Douglas Fairbanks, Jr.
William Farenga
Mrs. John R. Fell
Mr. and Mrs. Mel Ferrer
Jason Biddle Fishbein
Mrs. Marshall Field
Frances Fitzgerald
Janet Flanner
Mr. and Mrs. Henry Fonda
Joan Fontaine
Mr. and Mrs. Henry Ford 2nd
Mrs. McDonnell Ford
Michael Forrestal
Mr. and Mrs. James
  Fosburgh
Gray Foy
Mrs. Jared French
Lawrence Fried
Mrs. Donald Friede
Clayton Fritchey
Mr. and Mrs. Winston Frost

Mr. and Mrs. Martin Gabel
Mr. and Mrs. John Kenneth
  Galbraith
Greta Garbo
John Galliher
Geoffrey Gates
Henry Geldzhaller
Mr. and Mrs. Brendan Gill

Genevieve Gillaizeau
Mr. and Mrs. Roswell
  Gilpatric
Peter Gimbel
Bernard Giquel
Peter Glenville
Mr. and Mrs. William Goetz
Tony Godwin
Ambassador and Mrs. Arthur
  J. Goldberg
Mr. and Mrs. Samuel
  Goldwyn
Henry Golightly
Mr. and Mrs. Richard
  Goodwin
Mr. and Mrs. Stefan Groueff
Mrs. Philip Graham
Mr. and Mrs. Adolph Green
Lauder Greenway
Mark Goodson
Mrs. Bailey Gimbel
Mr. and Mrs. Winston F. C.
  Guest
Mrs. Polk Guest
Mrs. Loel Guinness
Thomas Guinzburg
Mr. and Mrs. John Gunther
Baron de Gunzberg
David Guthrie

Mr. and Mrs. Leland
  Hayward
Ambassador and Mrs. W.
  Averell Harriman
Mrs. Moss Hart
Mr. and Mrs. Lennie Hayton
Mr. and Mrs. Richard
  Halliday
Jean Hannon
Mr. and Mrs. Harold Hayes
Mr. and Mrs. William
  Haddad
Ashton Hawkins
Hamish Hamilton
Kitty Hawks
Lord Hardwicke
Mr. and Mrs. Henry J.
  Heinz 2nd
Princess Domiella Herculani
Miss Lillian Hellman
Mr. and Mrs. John Hersey
Mr. and Mrs. William
  Randolph Hearst, Jr.
Mr. and Mrs. Andrew
  Heiskell
John H. Heminway
Helene Hersent
Elizabeth Hilton
Jane Howard
Horsl P. Horst
Jean Howard
Milton Holden
Mr. and Mrs. Arthur
  Hornblow
Emmett John Hughes

Christopher Isherwood

Maharajah and Maharanee
  of Jaipur
Senator and Mrs. Jacob K.
  Javits
Lynda Bird Johnson
Philip Johnson
Alan Pryce-Jones
Mr. and Mrs. Garson Kanin
Mr. and Mrs. Warren Kask

Mr. and Mrs. Alfred Kazin
Mr. and Mrs. Nicholas
  deB. Katzenbach
Senator and Mrs. Edward M.
  Kennedy
Mrs. John F. Kennedy
Mrs. Joseph P. Kennedy
Senator and Mrs. Robert F.
  Kennedy
Mrs. Kenneth Keith
Horace Kelland
Mr. and Mrs. Walter Kerr
Dr. Benjamin Kean
Prince Amyn Khan
David King
Mr. and Mrs. Donald Klopfer
Alfred Knopf
John Knowles
Mr. and Mrs. Joseph Kraft
Jack Kroll
Harry Kurnitz
Mr. and Mrs. Steven Kyle

Melissa Laird
Baron Leon Lambert
Kenneth Lane
Mr. and Mrs. Kermit
  Langner
Lewis Lapham
Marquis Raimundo de
  Larrain
Mrs. Mary Lasker
Mrs. Patricia Lawford
Valentine Lawford
Barbara Lawrence
Mr. and Mrs. Irving Lazar
Harper Lee
Mrs. Oates Leiter
Mr. and Mrs. Jack Lemmon
Leo Lerman
Mr. and Mrs. Alan Jay
  Lerner
Herman Levin
Mr. and Mrs. Alexander
  Liberman
Mr. and Mrs. Goddard
  Lieberson
Vivien Leigh
Mayor and Mrs. John V.
  Lindsay
Mr. and Mrs. Walter
  Lippmann
Mr. and Mrs. Joshua Logan
Mrs. Nicholas Longworth
Anita Loos
Mr. and Mrs. Robert Lowell
Mr. and Mrs. Henry Luce
Andrew Lyndon

Shirley MacLaine
Mr. and Mrs. Norman Mailer
Mr. and Mrs. Joseph
  Mankiewicz
Marya Mannes
Mr. and Mrs. Stanley Marcus
Mr. and Mrs. William
  Marshall
Mr. and Mrs. Paul Masoner
Mr. and Mrs. Walter
  Matthau
Mr. and Mrs. Peter
  Matthieson
Paul Matthias
Mr. and Mrs. Graham
  Mattison
Dr. and Mrs. Russell
  Maxfield

Albert Maysles
Ken McCormick
Roddy McDowall
John McHugh
Mr. and Mrs. Robert
  McNamara
Mr. and Mrs. Joseph A.
  Meehan
Marcia Meehan
Aileen Mehle
Frederick Melhado
Mr. and Mrs. Paul Mellon
Gian Carlo Menotti
David Merrick
Robert Merrill
David Metcalfe
Mrs. Agnes E. Meyer
André Meyer
Mr. and Mrs. James
  Michener
Mr. and Mrs. Arthur Miller
Mr. and Mrs. Gilbert Miller
Mrs. Walter Millis
Caterine Milinaire
Mr. and Mrs. Vincent
  Minnelli
John Moore
Marianne Moore
Mr. and Mrs. Thomas Moore
Mr. and Mrs. William S.
  Moorhead
Mr. and Mrs. Walthes
  Moreira-Salles
Edward P. Morgan
Stanley Mortimer
Ann Mudge
Mrs. Natalia Murray

Mr. and Mrs. Samuel I.
  Newhouse, Sr.
Mrs. Stavros Niarchos
Mike Nichols
Eric Nielsen
Norman Norell

Serge Obolensky
Lord and Lady David Ogilvy
John O'Hara
Patrick O'Higgins

Mr. and Mrs. Bruno Pagliai
Mr. and Mrs. William S.
  Paley
Mr. and Mrs. Gordon Parks
Mr. and Mrs. Iva S. V.
  Patcévitch
Mr. and Mrs. Samuel
  Peabody
Mr. and Mrs. Drew Pearson
Mr. and Mrs. Gregory Peck
William Pennington
Mr. and Mrs. Frank Perry
Mr. and Mrs. Michael Phipps
Mr. and Mrs. Ogden Phipps
Mr. and Mrs. Thomas W.
  Phipps
Princess Luciana Pignatelli
Duarte Coelho Pinto
George Plimpton
Mr. and Mrs. Norman
  Podhoretz
Katherine Anne Porter
Dr. and Mrs. Joel Pressman
Mr. and Mrs. Harold Prince

Prince and Princess Stanislas
  Radziwill

91

Count Vega del Ren
Mr. and Mrs. James Reston
Vicomtesse Jacqueline de
Ribes
Mr. and Mrs. Larry Rivers
Mr. and Mrs. Jason Robards,
Jr.
Jerome Robbins
Governor and Mrs. Nelson
A. Rockefeller
Mr. and Mrs. Richard
Rodgers
Mr. and Mrs. William P.
Rogers
Philip Roth
Baroness Cecile de
Rothschild
Baron and Baroness Guy de
Rothschild
Theodore Rousseau
Mr. and Mrs. John Barry
Ryan 3rd
Mrs. John Barry Ryan, Jr.

Herbert Sargent
John Sargent
Mr. and Mrs. Robert Sarnoff,
Jr.
Mr. and Mrs. Frank Schiff
Mr. and Mrs. Thomas
Schippers
Mrs. George Schlee
Mr. and Mrs. Arthur
Schlesinger, Jr.
Jean Schlumberger
Mr. and Mrs. Mark Schorer
Mrs. Zachary Scott
Peggy Scott Duff
Nelson Seabra
Daniel Selznick
Mrs. David O. Selznick
Mrs. Irene Selznick
Mr. and Mrs. Irwin Shaw
Mrs. Robert E. Sherwood
Mr. and Mrs. Sargent Shriver
Robert Silvers
Agnes Sims
Mr. and Mrs. Frank Sinatra
Richard Sircre
Earl E. T. Smith

Oliver Smith
Preston Smith
Mr. and Mrs. Stephen Smith
David Somerset
Steve Sondheim
Theodore Sorensen
Charles F. Spalding
Sam Spiegel
Mr. and Mrs. Jules Stein
Mr. and Mrs. Robert Stein
Susan Stein
Mr. and Mrs. John Steinbeck
Gloria Steinem
Mr. and Mrs. George C.
Stevens, Jr.
Marli Stevens
Mrs. William Rhinelander
Stewart
Monica Stirling
Mr. and Mrs. William Styron
Arnold Saint-Subber
Mr. and Mrs. Arthur Ochs
Sulzberger

Harold E. Talbott
Mrs. Roland Tate
Mr. and Mrs. Walter Thayer
Ambassador and Mrs.
Llewellyn E. Thompson
Virgil Thomson
Alfredo Todisco
Alvin Topping
Mr. and Mrs. Warren
Topping
Mr. and Mrs. Michael Tree
Penelope Tree
Mr. and Mrs. Ronald Tree
Mr. and Mrs. Lionel Trilling
Van Day Truex

Mr. and Mrs. Giancarlo
Uzielli

Mr. and Mrs. Jack Valenti
Baron and Baroness Van
Zuylen
Mr. and Mrs. William vanden
Heuvel
Mr. and Mrs. Alfred Gwynne
Vanderbilt

Mrs. Murray Vanderbilt
Wendy Vanderbilt
Duke di Verdura
Mrs. Doris Vidor
Marquis and Marquesa
Cristobal Villaverde
Mrs. T. Reed Vreeland

Gillian Walker
Mr. and Mrs. John Walker
3rd
William Walton
Walter Wanger
Mr. and Mrs. Edward
Warburg
Andy Warhol
Mr. and Mrs. Robert Penn
Warren
Whitney Warren
David Webb
Mr. and Mrs. Robert Wells
Glenway Wescott
Mr. and Mrs. Anthony West
Mr. and Mrs. Yann
Weymouth
Monroe Wheeler
Robert Whitehead
Mr. and Mrs. John Hay
Whitney
Mr. and Mrs. Billy Wilder
Thornton Wilder
Mr. and Mrs. Odd Williams
Tennessee Williams
Edward Bennett Williams
Jean Sprain Wilson
Mr. and Mrs. Edmund
Wilson
Donald Windham
Duke and Duchess of
Windsor
Frederick M. Winship
Mr. and Mrs. Norman K.
Winston
Mrs. Frank Wisner
Mrs. William Woodward
Alfred Wright, Jr.
Mr. and Mrs. Charles
Wrightsman

Darryl Zanuck

velvet with a black and white feathered jacket. "But we'll certainly be glad to get them off."

Henry J. Heinz 2nd, the pickle king from Pittsburgh, wore nothing more complicated than a wedge from a paper plate with a nose cut through the center for his nose. Mrs. René Bouché, widow of the artist, managed to have a hairdo half of which was blond, the other half black. And Mrs. Richard M. Clurman, whose husband is chief of Time-Life's correspondents, ended up with a feathered mask on a stick.

"I was going to wear my son's Popeye mask," Mrs. Clurman said. "But then I went to Kenneth [the hairdresser] and I got intimidated."

Mrs. George Backer, who did Mr. Capote's apartment at the United Nations Plaza, planned the décor for the ballroom. ("Red tablecloths, white tapers, miles of smilax—the people are the flowers"). She also gave one of the prefatory dinners ("I'm frantic, I tell you") after first having slipped into a white satin shift, and then appeared at the ball as if she'd done nothing more exhausting than powdering her nose. Like all the guests, Mrs. Backer had to show her little red-and-white admission card. No recent party in New York has been so well secured.

The guest cards weren't printed until late last week and were then held until the last minute so nobody could copy one and get into the ball on a forgery. And when guests arrived, starting at 10:00 P.M., they found that the only way to get to the ballroom was on one of two elevators. The stairways and doors to other parts of the hotel were blocked off and guarded. Ten New York policemen and a sergeant, who'd been told to expect "thousands," patroled the three entrances to the hotel. Five security men were placed at strategic intervals. And the Secret Service saw virtually everyone who got off the elevators.

Mr. Capote spent the early part of the evening in a Plaza suite he had rented for the day. He and Mrs. Graham went to Mr. and Mrs. William S. Paley's for cocktails and then returned to the hotel for something to eat.

The hotel's banquet officials figured that each guest who liked champagne probably would drink half a bottle. But they went up to four hundred bottles of vintage Taittinger and set up two bars. The midnight supper (chicken hash with sherry, spaghetti bolognaise, pastries and coffee), the beverages, taxes and gratuities cost Mr. Capote about $13,000.

"I wanted it at the Plaza," he said, "because I think it's the only really beautiful ballroom left in the United States."

Mr. Capote, who as a boy in Louisiana sent homemade fruitcakes to such "friends" as President Franklin D. Roosevelt, denied that he'd always dreamed of giving such a ball.

"That's not true," he said. "Kay gave a party for me last year in Washington. I promised her I'd give one for her in return."

He got the idea for the black, white and red theme not from his own *In Cold Blood, Other Voices, Other Rooms* or *Breakfast at Tiffany's* but from Cecil Beaton's Ascot scenes in *My Fair Lady*. He wanted masks because he thought they were "romantic."

"The whole point," he said happily, "is to ask anyone you want to dance and sit wherever you want and then when the masks come off at midnight, you can find your own chums or stay with your new ones."

Mr. Capote and Mrs. Graham stood in a receiving line until nearly midnight. They could recognize some of their guests despite the masks, but it didn't matter. They had a man announce the guests' names. And when they weren't greeting people, they watched the dancing. Mr. Capote had a word for everyone.

"Oh, my dear, you look fabulous," he told Mrs. Bouché.

"Oh, Billy, that's fantastic," he said when Billy Baldwin, the decorator, walked by in a unicorn headdress of black and gold curls.

David Merrick had such a good time at Truman Capote's recent masked ball that next year he's going to give a private little extravaganza of his own.

"I was inspired," the Broadway producer said simply. "It was the most interesting guest list I've ever encountered. I thought, 'What a wonderful thing to have a party not for any reason.' I'll get Truman to help me."

Mr. Merrick, an offstage impresario who regularly gives elaborate opening-night parties in connection with his plays and musicals, hasn't decided what form his ball will take. But he thinks he'll have to have it in a hotel ("You need that kind of space") and he's pretty sure the men won't have to wear costumes.

"They wouldn't want to get all dressed up," he said. "They never do, but the ladies love it."

Besides Mr. Capote's guest list, which struck Mr. Merrick as being composed of "everybody from young Holly Golightlys to the millionaires in our land—quite representative," Mr. Merrick was impressed with the party's ambience.

"It was always shimmering," he said admiringly. "It was never still, nor was there a static moment. I guess you'd call this a rave review."

While Mr. Merrick is drawing up his own guest list of diplomats, politicians, painters, writers, composers, actors, producers, dress designers, social figures, tycoons and young things, Mr. Capote is recovering from his. His New York apartment looked like a florist shop for days after the last of the lacy green smilax had been ripped off the Plaza ballroom's candelabra. And when the grateful guests' flowers had faded, he was left with an inundation of thank-you notes, enough Dom Perignon champagne to last him two or three years, and some memorable impressions of the ball.

"I remember Lynda Bird Johnson," he said. "I remember she was wandering from table to table in the most forlorn way. She said she'd lost her mask. I think the Secret Service found it for her."

Mr. Capote, who was thinking back on the elegant black and white masks, the music that never stopped, the kaleidoscope of dancers and the red, black and white color scheme, also remembered John Kenneth Galbraith. When he wasn't dancing with diminutive Mrs. Ralph Ellison, whose husband wrote *The Invisible Man,* lanky Mr. Galbraith was catching napkins thrown by George Plimpton, editor of *The Paris Review,* or dancing around with a candelabra in his arms.

"I remember seeing him dancing alone," said Mr. Capote. "I think he had a good time."

Shortly before midnight, Mr. Capote and Kay Graham, his guest of honor, abandoned the receiving line they'd established in the candlelit entranceway and made their way around the ballroom.

Mr. Capote danced with Mrs. Graham and only two of his other guests: Princess Lee Radziwill and Lauren Bacall, whom he's known since she was married to the late Humphrey Bogart. And he spent a lot of time in the shadows at the back of the ballroom, just watching his party go.

"I stood there thinking how marvelous it was that these people had made such an extraordinary effort," he said. "I thought how cozy it was."

He had thought at first that there wasn't enough red—that the red tablecloths against the baroque gold and white of the ballroom were not enough. But Mrs. William S. Paley, who planned his supper menu, had warned him against lining the walls with red draperies and, in the end, he was glad he didn't. He thought it would have been too much.

While Mr. Capote made the rounds, Philip Roth, author of *Goodbye, Columbus,* whirled either Ann Mudge, his date, Mrs. Norman Mailer, or Mrs. Joseph Fox, wife of Mr. Capote's editor at Random House, around the dance floor. And Mrs. Loel Guinness, wife of the international banker, was having trouble with her necklaces—one rubies, the other diamonds. They were so heavy, she said, that she thought she'd have to stay in bed all the next day to recover. When Mr. Capote heard about this, he burst out laughing.

At 11 P.M., Arthur M. Schlesinger, Jr., noted that "History's made after midnight." But the historian-author went on to forget just what history—if any—was finally made. He did remember dancing with such women as Mrs. Ronald Tree, U Thant's representative to the United Nations International School Development Fund, and Princess Luciana Pignatelli, a radiant Roman who designs dresses.

"We had two crashers and I caught them both," Mr. Capote said later. "When I heard their names announced, I knew I didn't know them, and I said, 'I'm sorry, I don't know you,' and the woman said, 'Oh, we just wanted to come in for five or ten minutes.' Can you imagine that?"

Mr. Capote had hoped to share "a bird and a bottle" with Mrs. Graham before the party began, but neither of them had the time or interest. They were late getting back to his hotel suite after cocktails with Mr. and Mrs. Paley, so they settled for some caviar. "That's all I had all night," he said, admitting he never had any of his own champagne. "I started on Scotch and didn't bother to have supper. I was weak the next morning." Now that his party belongs to the past, Mr. Capote attributes its success to his special advisers (Mrs. George Backer, who helped him with the decorations, Mrs. Paley and others he will not name) and his guests.

He said he thought "the pretty girls contributed just by being there," that the music was good "because it didn't stop," and that "well-planned dinner parties helped a lot."

Three hundred of his five hundred-plus guests went to dinner parties he had asked the hosts and hostesses to give for him. Jason Epstein, an editor at Random House, gave what Mr. Capote called "one of the intellectual dinner parties."

Mr. Ellison, who left a Boston meeting of the Carnegie Commission on Educational Television especially for the party, said Mrs. Mary Bailey Gimbel's dinner was intellectual, too. She is the former Mrs. Peter Gimbel, an associate of United Artists and one of Mr. Capote's neighbors in the country.

"Norman Mailer was telling stories meant to tease and shock," Mr. Ellison said. "I was interested in meeting Roddy McDowall. I didn't recognize him until he took his glasses off."

Mrs. Gimbel's guests also included Alvin and Warren Topping, Long Island potato farmers Mrs. Gimbel and Mr. Capote regularly see in the country, and Patricia Kennedy Lawford, sister of the late President Kennedy.

The Paleys' party was "elegant," with the Gianni Agnellis, who manufacture Fiats; Philip Johnson, the architect; Prince and Princess Radziwill; Charles Wrightsman, the oil man and art patron, and Cecil Beaton, the photographer and designer. Mr. and Mrs. Henry J. Heinz 2nd were supposed to have had Lynda Bird Johnson at their table. But she changed her mind and backed out at the last minute.

Gardner Cowles, publisher of *Look* magazine and newspapers, gave what one guest called a dinner "newspapery" with publishers. And Glenway Wescott, author of *The Pilgrim Hawk*, got Virgil Thomson, the critic and composer, and the irrepressible Anita Loos, who invented Lorelei Lee. Mr. Wescott would have had Katherine Anne Porter, but the writer (*Ship of Fools*) was in a hospital and couldn't attend.

"I put the dinners together myself," Mr. Capote said. "That was the *real* game. I'd call up and take a person from one dinner and put him at another. I did my best."

Mr. Capote began his guest list early last June. He sat in the studio of his Long Island beach-country house staring first into the fire in his fireplace and then out over the dunes. He had a schoolchild's small black-and-white notebook with lined paper and pencil. He doesn't remember which illustrious name came first. "I filled all the right-hand pages and when it was full I turned it upside down and went through it again," he said. "I had that list with me day and night—never out of my hands from June until I gave it to my secretary October 1. I remember the date. I'd carry the notebook around to restaurants in case I saw somebody. I went on a cruise with the Agnellis and finished it—oh, I don't know—off the coast of Yugoslavia, I think. I let two or three people see the list and they made suggestions."

Miss Elizabeth Davies, who is associated with Irving Lazar, Mr. Capote's agent (both later attended his party), got the list in its raw form. It was her job to do the typing.

"Monroe Wheeler came out Morris Wheelan," Mr. Capote said, acknowledging that his handwriting is difficult to read. "I don't know what happened to David Susskind. I don't think he ever received his invitation. I think others may have gone astray, too. I hope my addresses were right."

To this day, Mr. Capote is not sure exactly how many of those invited actually attended his ball, and the list of regrets is as hazy as it is impressive.

Mrs. John F. Kennedy wrote a note saying she would be in Newport, and there were regrets from her Kennedy brothers-in-law—the United States Senators from New York and Massachusetts—the Leonard Bernsteins, Dr. and Mrs. Ralph Bunche, Irving Berlin, Noël Coward (who was ill), Marlene Dietrich, Arthur J. Goldberg, Samuel Goldwyn, Samuel Barber, Harry Belafonte, Mrs. Murray Vanderbilt, Thornton Wilder, Irwin Shaw, Mr. and Mrs. Henry Luce, Jack Lemmon, Paul Mellon, Mary Martin and Governor and Mrs. Rockefeller. Mayor Lindsay and his wife declined because the Lotos Club had already invited him to a dinner in his honor. He had intended to drop by later, and would have if William C. Mattison, the City Commissioner of Public Works, hadn't died the same night. Virtually everyone else who regretted couldn't be in New York.

Elizabeth Taylor and Richard Burton were in Italy, filming *Reflections in a Golden Eye*. Leslie Caron was in the Netherlands for a showing of *Is Paris Burning?* Walter Cronkite had to go to Europe. Clayton Fritchie, the political analyst, was in Hong Kong. Mel Ferrer and his wife, Audrey Hepburn, were in Switzerland. Shirley MacLaine was in Paris. Gian-Carlo Menotti accepted but later refused because he was called to Rome on operatic business. And Mr. Capote is about to finish his own recuperation by doing a little traveling himself.

"Lee Radziwill and I are going to the Sahara in January for two weeks," he said. "I'm working on a new book and I'm going to find out what it's like working on an oasis."

In the meantime, Mr. Capote is paying his party bills (the total is expected to come to about $16,000, about half what a reasonably elaborate New York debut costs) and coming and going about town as he usually does —a social and literary darling who is often alone.

"You can't write with people around you," he said. "I spend a lot of time alone. Maybe that's why when I'm social, I'm very, very social."

A WEEK OF GALAS—EVEN METROPOLITAN
MUSEUM HAD ONE
November 1968

It was gala week in New York with big galas and little galas, and as Charlotte Ford Niarchos said toward the end, "You'd be dead if you'd gone to everything. I didn't."

Mrs. Niarchos, a former wife of one of the bigger Greek shipping magnates, is an elegant blonde with a big, deep Middle Western voice, which she regularly uses on behalf of the Police Athletic League. And it was P.A.L. that got her into orange harem pants last night and out of her Sutton Place apartment. Like the other 399 guests at P.A.L.'s benefit performance of *Zorbá*, Mrs. Niarchos went first to the musical at the Imperial Theater and then on to the Rainbow Room for supper, dancing and a fashion show. It was by no means the only extravaganza in town.

United Cerebral Palsy was having its eighth annual Evening in Vegas in a cellophane ice palace at the New York Hilton. And at the Pierre, which had a certain serenity about it before President-elect Richard M. Nixon and Aristotle Socrates Onassis set up their very separate headquarters there, Pearl S. Buck and her admirers were raising money for orphaned children.

That party began with a Japanese tea ceremony and music from what was billed as a Chinese butterfly harp. Before the evening ended, there were Korean and Chinese dancers, and little children circulating among the guests with fortune cookies. Nothing else this week was nearly so Oriental.

At the Metropolitan Museum of Art, where Mr. and Mrs. Joseph Lauder gave their dinner Monday for the bejeweled Mrs. Frank Jay Gould, everything was medieval in a modern manner. Mrs. Gould's husband was the youngest son of Jay Gould, the railroad tycoon whose yacht had a piano built into its music room, and she is no slouch either. Her house in Cannes is a mini-museum of Renaissance art, tapestries and furniture. She gave one of her medieval tapestries to the museum along with a Bonnard painting. And she showed up for the dinner in a white Givenchy dress, her usual dark glasses and emeralds and diamonds the size of robin's eggs. The pendant sapphire that hung from her necklace was even larger.

"We are both medievalists," Thomas P. F. Hoving, director of the Metropolitan, said of Mrs. Gould. "Whenever I saw her in the South of France, I'd invite her to visit the museum and she couldn't manage it, so this was one way to get her here, and we are delighted."

Mrs. Lauder was delighted, too. The cosmetics empress, who'd seen to it that an array of her soaps, hair spray, hand lotion and Youth Dew perfume was installed for the occasion in the Met's ladies' room, had wanted to do something spectacular for Mrs. Gould. She said she had suggested the idea of the dinner in the museum to Mr. Hoving and that he had been most enthusiastic. "He told me it is the first time and the last time," she said, obviously pleased.

What Mrs. Lauder meant, of course, was that Mr. Hoving doesn't let just anyone have a dinner party in his museum. But this probably won't be the last such party. The Met has never been a regular place for social events, and yet someday it might be. In the meantime, back to the Pierre, where Tuesday's Bal de Tête was one of the liveliest gatherings all week.

Colonel Serge Obolensky, the Russian prince about town, took over the ballroom for a giddy dinner-dance for Bekim Feymu, an actor who may or may not be the Dustin Hoffman of Yugoslavia. Mr. Feymu appears in something called *The Adventurers,* a Paramount film and, naturally enough, Paramount picked up the check. Colonel Obolensky rounded up the guests and somehow cajoled the ladies into wearing elaborate hairdos or headdresses—which is where the tête part came in.

Mrs. M. Montt Balmaceda, wife of a Chilean multimillionaire, didn't bother with little curls, a wig or a special trip to the hairdresser. She simply stuffed her hair up under an enormous gold hat trimmed with masses of brown and white feathers. The front of the hat was hung with diamonds and sapphires, and so were Mrs. Balmaceda's ears.

It was also a night for pants suits and pajamas of one sort or another. Mrs. Ernest Byfield, wife of the McCann Erickson executive, wore a Christian Dior jump suit of black velvet and sheer see-through organza.

"At home, I don't wear any body stocking," she said in her mostly Russian accent, "but it is a little bit too much to go out that way."

Mrs. Lytle Hull looked interesting, too, but in an entirely different way. The music patron who was once married to Vincent Astor wore the simplest of off-white dresses with nothing more than a little glitter in her hair. And then there was Cathy Macauley, the Corn Products heiress. Her tan suede tunic with scrolls and wooden knobs went with tights and thigh-high boots.

"I don't like to go backward in time," she said of her clothes. "I like to go forward."

While the Bal de Tête went roaring onward, another contingent of partygoers was over at the Plaza, dinner-dancing on behalf of the New York Association for the Blind. And it was here, beneath seagull mobiles and a setting vaguely like a waterfront, that Mrs. Edgar W. Leonard, white-haired widow of the investment banker, explained why she had had to have her diamond necklace reset. Years ago, when her first husband, a Dutch banker, gave her the jewels, they were set in silver. But the silver oxidized and kept getting her neck dirty. She has had no such problems since she switched to platinum.

DEBUTANTES BOW IN A WORLD OF PINK AND SILVER

December 1969

The International Debutante Ball, inevitably the most overstated of the season's massive coming-out parties, was held in the Waldorf-Astoria's mammoth Grand Ballroom last night, and the evening was as spectacular as usual.

The ballroom, whose decorators likened it to Versailles itself, was a cotton-candy world of pink and silver. The tables were covered with pink linens and centered with pink tapers in sterling candelabra entwined with real orchids and pink ribbons.

The boxes encircling the room were garlanded with thousands of twinkling pink lights accented with gold, silver and white. The stage, as much the focal point of the evening as the runway at the Miss America Pageant, was hung with pink satin, silver mesh and more blinking lights.

The curtains didn't just hang there, but were held back on both sides by huge twelve-arm brackets draped with silver and pink marabou feathers and more flickering lights. If the blinking lights didn't get you, the silver moon above the stage did. It had a big American flag draped over one side.

The moon was made of silver that picked up the light and scattered it out over the thousand guests, their roast beef dinners and the dance floor, which wasn't pink. Neither were the sixty-two debutantes' floor-length dresses nor their elbow-length kid gloves. But the girls in white did carry pink carnations interspersed with greenery and silver glitter.

"It's very exciting," cooed Suzanne L. Warren, the Florida debutante, "but the receiving line was sheer hell. My feet hurt the whole time." Miss Warren was wandering around among the tables, hunting for her place. But her problems were nothing compared with those of Miss Carolyn Anne McKenzie, the English debutante. She had arrived in a white lace see-through dress with pants, and the committee made her change her clothes.

"I'm not ready for pajamas at a debutante ball," said Miss Beatrice Joyce, the ball's founder. "I don't think we ought to do that."

"They're far more liberal in London," Miss McKenzie said prettily. "It isn't as though I'd done anything indecent."

Dinner in the debutante room off the ballroom was hectic and noisy with Michael Dunn's rock version of such now music as "Funky Broadway" and, according to Miss Leslie A. Becker of New Jersey, "absolutely great."

"I came out once before," Miss Becker said, looking around the room, "and it wasn't as commercial as this is."

One of the chief activities at debutantes' Table A was getting the champagne bottle open. The cork finally popped, and Stephen Rosenthal, whose sister, Miss Nancy Beth Rosenthal, was about to be presented, poured. He was also drinking Pepsi-Cola.

"We're thirsty," Mr. Rosenthal explained. "We only drink champagne on special occasions."

"Yes," said his sister. "At weddings and anniversaries and birthdays and things like that."

"We allowed two bottles of champagne for each table," Miss Joyce explained of her debutante flock. "That's enough."

Miss Joyce was also impressed with the number of bearded escorts in the crowd, the lace jabots on some of the male guests and the amount of hair.

"The times," she said, "are changing, I guess."

The climactic and consciously patriotic presentation ceremonies began after dinner. Skitch Henderson's orchestra swung into "The Star and Stripes Forever," and four midshipmen from the United States Naval Academy at Annapolis marched into the center of the ballroom carrying flags. It was a red white and blue moment, and everybody scrambled to his feet.

From there, the color guard moved to positions flanking the stage and began what for them was a long evening of standing and waiting at semi-attention. Miss Maureen Finch, daughter of Robert H. Finch, Secretary of Health, Education and Welfare, and Mrs. Finch, was the first debutante to appear. She represented the United States.

Miss Finch materialized into the spotlight from the darkness beneath the center box where her parents alternately sat and stood. At her right was Christopher Taylor, son of Mr. and Mrs. John Taylor of Sacramento—a Harvard undergraduate in white tie and tails. And at her left was John W. Forrester, midshipman first class from Annapolis, her honorary escort. He carried the American flag. Mr. Taylor held her hand. The band played "America the Beautiful."

Miss Finch curtsied much as had such other young Republican representatives of the United States as Patricia Nixon, Mrs. Dwight David Eisenhower 2nd (Julie Nixon) and the former Barbara Anne Eisenhower when they were the No. 1 debutantes at previous balls. Miss Nixon was among the onlookers and was accompanied as usual by Edward F. Cox. Besides being one of Miss Nixon's steadier beaux, Mr. Cox is the son of Mrs. Howard Ellis Cox, one of the ball's perennial co-chairmen. He escorted the President's daughter when she made her debut at the ball in 1964.

Like Miss Finch, each of the debutantes who followed her into the spotlight had her name boomed out over the public address system. And each was flanked by a white-tied civilian of her choice and a flag-bearing military escort from either Annapolis, the United States Military Academy at West Point or the United States Air Force Academy. Each debutante also had her own special presentation music. Miss Robin Lee McNair, daughter of Governor and Mrs. Robert E. McNair of South Carolina, appeared to "Carolina Moon." Mrs. Cox's niece, Miss Elizabeth Lathrop Finch, curtsied to "Manhattan."

Before the ceremonies ended, the guests had heard bits and pieces of "Volare," "Lady of Spain," "East Side, West Side" and "April in Portugal." "Winter Wonderland," incidentally, was for Alaska, not Switzerland. And "Tumbling Tumbleweed" and "Wagon Wheels" were for Arizona. After each curtsy, some of which were a lot deeper and longer than the others, the debutantes and their escorts proceeded to the tiered platform at the stage to stand and face hundreds of guests, including families, friends and the WPIX television cameras, which recorded the event for a telecast.

Virginia's Miss Rosenthal was the last but by no means the least of the debutantes to bow, and after she had joined the gang onstage and after applause for everyone, Miss Finch and Mr. Taylor began the dancing.

"It's a very powerful occasion," Bruce Boyke, Jr., said, "but I get tired if I sit down too long. I have to move around."

Eleven-year-old Bruce, who was strolling around studying the other guests, wore the gray-blue Florida Air Academy uniform. He was pleased when someone mistook him for an older man of the military escort.

"I'm just here with my sister," he said. "She's one of those girls."

And indeed she was. Miss Laura M. Boyke represented Illinois. Their father, Bruce Boyke, is in the construction business.

After the ball, which raised nearly $50,000, the debutantes and their various escorts went to Voisin restaurant for breakfast. The evening cost each of the American girls' parents about $1,000, although some parents contribute more than others. The figure does not include the dresses, the travel or hotel expenses. The foreign girls were guests, as were the military escorts.

"One of the nice things about the ball is that the Soldiers, Sailors and Airmen's Club gets its deficit paid," Mrs. Cox, co-chairman of the ball, said. "It's sort of an educational experiment in international living, too. The girls from Europe get to see how the same sort of families live in this country."

HE PARTIES, HE'S IN DEMAND, HE'S THE LITTLEST MAN ABOUT TOWN

March 1963

He has been introduced to the marinated beef at Trader Vic's, Broadway musicals and suits from Brooks Brothers. And although he cries sometimes, likes to sit on laps and has to be spanked occasionally, he usually gets more invitations than his parents. He is the product of an affluent society that is divided into groups, not individuals. He is the littlest man about town.

Shortly after his fourth birthday, the little boy is inducted into this social whirl. It starts with nursery school and goes on to include birthday parties, afternoon visits, dancing school, nights spent at a friend's home, miniature charity balls, membership in clubs and all manner of excursions.

By the time he is nine, he can say, as one little boy said recently, "I'm terribly, terribly busy." It is a phrase he learned from his mother.

"I know it sounds ridiculous, but little boys are actually rushed," said Mrs. Kurt S. Dietrich. "Everyone seems to want a sort of extra man or two at parties for four-year-olds."

On a recent Saturday, Mrs. Dietrich's children went to three afternoon birthday parties. Gregg, who is six, was invited to one; Mark, his four-year-old brother, went to two.

"I spent the whole day running back and forth, dumping one off, then picking the other one up," Mrs. Dietrich said. "It's getting completely out of hand."

A boy's social life begins to get out of hand when a mother sees to it that her child invites everyone in his nursery school class to his birthday party. Other mothers follow suit. If there are fifteen children, there are fifteen parties. Even if a child's birthday is in August, the party is held during the school year. If just one of these mothers also hires an entertainer—magicians, clowns and puppeteers are popular this season—some of the other mothers feel obliged to do likewise.

"My son is invited to parties for forty, fifty, even sixty all the time," the mother of a Collegiate School student said. "We felt it was too much so we turned down some of the invitations. You have to draw the line somewhere."

One of the lines boys' mothers tend to draw is at dancing school for the very young. Although six-year-olds in Mrs. Henry Duncan Wood's mixed classes are learning the cha-cha, many boys do not start such lessons until they are nine—much to the distress of the little girls and their mothers.

"There always seems to be a shortage of boys," said Mrs. Vernon H. Brown, Jr., whose sons are nine, ten and a half and twelve. "Girls like boys, and want to go to dancing school. Boys just aren't as interested in girls."

The extent to which little boys are involved in the social whirl obviously depends on the size of their parents' pocketbooks. Not every parent can afford $70-a-season dancing lessons, $5 luncheons at the Gotham Hotel, $6 seats at an ice hockey game and suits that cost $35 apiece. It also depends upon the goals parents have for their sons or, as a psychologist put it, "the parents' own strivings for status." It is called "a lack of emphasis upon uniqueness." If he is enrolled at one of the so-called "socially acceptable" private schools, a boy has a chance of being selected for membership in the Knickerbocker Greys, an exclusive military drilling club for eight- to fourteen-year-olds. These invitations are rarely refused. Mothers of members describe the club as "a group activity" in which a boy learns "to get along with his peers" and "take orders."

The high point of the Greys' year is a Christmas review in full uniform (black and white with impressive epaulets, sashes and swords) followed by a dance. Lester Lanin's orchestra will play at this year's dance and all boys with the rank of sergeant and up must bring girls. Some sergeants are only ten years old.

Goddard Gaieties is the most widely known of the miniature charity balls. Subscriptions to this series of dances, sponsored by parents of some private school children, benefit the Goddard-Community Center. This year, the Gaieties program includes Square Dance with a Twist for sixth graders and Paris in April Fete for eighth graders. A spokesman for the center denied that the eighth-grade party was a take-off on the April in Paris Ball, a charity affair for adults. Ten more boys than girls are accepted for each of these gatherings. Each dance in the series is $10.

"It's this fear in the city that the child isn't going to have any social life," one mother said, trying to explain the social maelstrom that surrounds her seven-year-old. "It's going to be even worse with my youngest. Every time he hears that the seven-year-old is going to a party, he wants to go, too. He's only three."

TURN OF THE CENTURY IS TOASTED IN STYLE

December 1969

The Nine O'Clocks dance club had its highly publicized "Turn of the Century Party" complete with tiaras, upswept hairdos, enormous hats and extravagant costumes at the Plaza last night, and as Sam LeTulle observed somewhat wryly, "It's clothes, clothes and more clothes—more for the women than the men." Mr. LeTulle, the Texas-born architect, was absolutely right. He designed the decorations, which involved adding potted palms and candles to the Plaza's already palm-fringed Palm Court and giant hanging baskets of red and pink roses to the Terrace Room beyond.

Then, after double-checking to make sure the Terrace Room's fountain was working ("It's so very Edwardian"), he went out and rented a flashy antique military uniform with lots of gold braid. Several other men rented similar costumes, and the men in white tie and tails looked perfectly marvelous, too. But it was still very much ladies' night.

What mattered was who was impersonating which elegant courtesan, dance-hall queen or social lioness of the years between 1890 and 1910, and the time, effort and money that had gone into these preparations was not inconsiderable.

Mrs. Wyatt Cooper set out to look like her cousin the late Consuelo Vanderbilt, and in her ruffled, corseted way she succeeded. Consuelo married the ninth Duke of Marlborough, immediately became the toast of America's robber baron society and starred as a beauty at Ascot in the days of King Edward VII.

It took Adolfo and his staff of three two days to put Mrs. Cooper's bouffant costume and giant hat together, and when they (and the hairdresser who came to her house at the last minute) had finished, she was mauve from head to toe, and Adolfo, ordinarily a talkative man, was virtually speechless.

"She is too beautiful," he moaned.

Mrs. Cooper was by no means the only beauty among the 275 club members and guests. Margaret, Duchess of Argyll, wore a fitted black velvet dress with a low neckline, a pearl and diamond choker and a diamond tiara, and although she insisted she wasn't dressed to represent anybody ("I'm nobody, that's who"), she could have been the Duchess of Marlborough in the Boldini portrait.

"I crossed the Atlantic for this party," the duchess said. "I like this sort of thing."

Mrs. John R. Drexel 3rd, whose mother and father became engaged under one of the Plaza's palms, wore a white ruffled lace dress, a Victorian wig and the diamonds her father gave her mother in 1911 when they were married.

"But the pearls are from Bonwit's," she said. "I didn't really go to a lot of trouble. I wore this dress last summer in Newport."

Mrs. Ernest L. Byfield, Jr., settled for black velvet and taffeta, a hat with ostrich feathers and masses of diamonds. "I am Cleo de Merode," she explained. "She was an actress or an opera singer—one of those great French beauties."

Then there was Mrs. Giancarlo Uzielli, who didn't get around to consulting with her designer (Chester Weinberg) until yesterday morning, and Mrs. Lawrence Copley Thaw in white lace reembroidered with pink and pink ostrich feathers in her hair ("I'm Lady Windermere's fan without the fan").

Mrs. Joshua Logan had problems, too. Her black feathered hat was so high she couldn't get herself into her car sitting up.

"So I stretched out in the back of the station wagon," she said, "on one elbow."

Mr. Logan was rather pleased with the way he looked, particularly with his bushy auburn eyebrows, his bushy mustache and his bushy bangs.

"I've got hair for the first time in my life," he said happily. "I've got eyebrows just like other people."

"He looks just like Howard Lindsay in *Life with Father*," Mrs. Logan said, and there were those who agreed—mostly because they hadn't the vaguest idea what Howard Lindsay looked like.

"I said to Adolfo, 'What've you got?' and he said, 'Something very romantic.' It's like one of the Wyndham sisters out of a Sargent portrait with my hair up *à la belle époque* with tendrils. I certainly hope it stays up."

Neither Mr. and Mrs. Gil Shiva (Susan Stein) nor Mrs. Cornelius Vanderbilt Whitney were inelegant either. Mr. Shiva glued on a lavish nineteenth-century mustache and sideburns for the night, and his dinner jacket resembled those worn in earlier times. Mrs. Shiva's costume was flown in from Universal Studios, her father's film company.

"I'm a green-velvet redhead with a parasol," she said, and indeed she was—her naturally dark brown hair tucked up under an ornate wig. Mrs. Whitney wore Oscar de la Renta's gold lace gown with the high ruffled gold lace collar and long sleeves, a gold veil like one shown with the dress in a recent *Vogue* magazine and her very own, very old diamond tiara.

"Trying to look like someone else is a little silly," she said. "It's all so pseudo-looking. I could say that I'm my own great-grandmother having tea at the Plaza in 1899, but my great-grandmother didn't have tea there. I think I'll just be me—Mary Lou Whitney."

Mrs. Charles Revson had pretty much the same idea. She was herself in a Pierre Balmain gown of apricot satin with a multicolored sequin top, butterfly sleeves and a rather spectacular ruby and diamond tiara.

"Harry Winston wired four necklaces together," Mrs. Revson said, "and that's my bodyguard over there."

She pointed to a man in street clothes who stood a discreet ten feet away from her, and when she moved off to talk with other guests, he followed her.

The party began with a long list of multicourse dinner parties at people's homes and didn't actually get around to the Plaza until nearly 10:30 P.M. At that point, there was a champagne reception (in case anyone was thirsty) in the Palm Court around a tiered table decorated with palms, grapes, ferns and stemmed glasses. It was during this interval that Mme. Elsa Schiaparelli, one of Paris's most successful couturiers, explained that her dress was a 1969 brocade from St. Laurent, that she really didn't want anything to drink and that she never wore costumes. While she was talking, Colonel Serge Obolensky made his entrance. He wore a Cossack uniform with a red tunic, blue pantaloons in boots, and all manner of military paraphernalia, including a jeweled dagger set with coral. The ladies were ecstatic, and there were little shrieks of "Serge, darling" all over the room.

"I didn't know it would be that successful," Colonel Obolensky said, when he wasn't kissing and being kissed by his admirers. "It was made for me for a 1911 party in London. I wasn't sure I could get into it."

By 11 P.M. everyone was beginning to wonder when the dancing was going to begin, and it finally did after the mirrored doors to the Terrace Room had become stuck and then forced open and Meyer Davis and his orchestra had played "Frankie and Johnny" at least twice to an empty room.

Mrs. Revson, her husband and her bodyguard were among the first to cross the threshold, and after them came such other guests as Ray Stark, the producer, and his wife; Earl Blackwell, the club's founder and party organizer; Donald Brooks, the dress designer; Iva S. V. Patcévitch, the publisher, and Mrs. Patcévitch, and scores of others.

Before long, the guests were dancing to such typically bouncy turn-of-the-century music as "In the Good Old Summertime," "Sweet Adeline," "My Gal Sal" and "Let Me Call You Sweetheart," and by 12:30 it was time for crepes and creamed chicken (in case anyone was still hungry), and yet another chorus of "Shine on Harvest Moon."

THE BERNSTEINS AND THE BLACK PANTHERS

January 1970

Editorially, the New York Times *denounced the Leonard Bernsteins' gathering for the Panther 21 as "elegant slumming" but this the most controversial of the "radical chic" fund-raisers served to dramatize an important division within the society: the contrast between the lives and hopes of the rich white élite in America and the poor ghetto blacks.*

That representatives of these dissimilar groups met, mostly for the first time, talked, and attempted to understand each other—regardless of the simplistics of the rhetoric—was an educational experience for them both.

If anything, Mrs. Bernstein, who brought the two groups together, should have been a heroine. Her quiet and determined commitment to civil rights is well known among those who consistently care what happens to blacks.

"What do Negroes feel? What do Negroes feel?" Mr. Bernstein kept asking at the onset of the discussions.

"I'll tell you," his wife answered, quoting from a Richard Harris article in The New Yorker *quoting Roger Wilkins to the effect that the United States had betrayed its black people for three hundred years.*

After the party, Mr. Bernstein went on to deny that he made the statements attributed to him in the news story, although there were many witnesses to his comments who said he had made them. Some of the Bernsteins' "friends" denied they were ever at the party, and in the weeks that followed, the party people who change their views with the prevailing winds of fashion joined in denouncing the party and the other guests.

In any event, the money for the defense fund was raised. The Panthers were tried and found innocent. And Mrs. Bernstein still gives generously of her time and money on behalf of the nation's poor blacks and a wide range of other decent causes.

Leonard Bernstein and a Black Panther leader argued the merits of the Black Panther party's philosophy before nearly ninety guests at a cocktail party last night in the Bernsteins' elegant Park Avenue duplex. The conductor laureate of the New York Philharmonic did most of the questioning. Donald Cox, the Panther field marshal and a member of the party's central committee, did most of the answering, and there were even moments when both men were not talking at the same time.

"Now about your goals," Mr. Bernstein said from the depths of an armchair. "I'm not sure I understand how you're going to achieve them. I mean, what are your tactics?"

Mr. Cox, a tall, handsome man in a black turtleneck sweater and gray pants, nodded his head.

"If business won't give us full employment," he said slowly, "then we must take the means of production and put them in the hands of the people."

"I dig absolutely," Mr. Bernstein said.

"I can't blueprint social change for you," Mr. Cox said. "The resistance put up against us dictates strategy."

"You mean you've got to wing it?" Mr. Bernstein asked.

"If the wealth were redistributed so the poor people had power we might have peace," Mr. Cox continued. "We want peace. We have families, too, and we want to enjoy life."

Mr. Bernstein agreed with that too, fended off several other guests who wanted to ask Mr. Cox questions, interrupted Mr. Cox and apologized, and then allowed the Panther leader, who was standing by one of the Bernsteins' two grand pianos, to go on.

"But if they," he said, meaning representatives of what the Panthers call the oppressive establishment, "attack us in our homes—and we have been attacked in our homes and murdered in our beds—we have the right to defend ourselves."

"I agree 100 percent," Mr. Bernstein said. "But you are presenting everything in defensive terms. You must mean something offensive."

"No, no, no," Mr. Cox said, shaking his head. "You're using the language of the terrorist. After all, who is attacked? You know the system."

Mr. Cox and Mr. Bernstein, who was wearing Black Watch tartan slacks, a turtleneck shirt and a blue blazer, were sometimes aided by such other guests as Otto Preminger, the producer-director, who complained bitterly when Mr. Cox suggested that "the United States is the most oppressive country in the world," and it went on in this vein for nearly an hour.

But before they finished the discussion by hugging one another, agreeing that they were brothers and having dinner together, Mr. Cox had attempted to assure a white woman that she would not be killed even if she is a rich member of the middle class with a self-avowed capitalist for a husband.

"No, no," he said when she raised the question.

"Oh, no," said Mrs. Lee Berry, turning around to comfort the woman. "You sound as if you're afraid. Now there's no reason for that."

Mrs. Berry is the wife of one of the New York Panther 21, which is what the Bernsteins' party was about. The case, which comes to trial February 2, involves twenty-one blacks, including two women, indicted April 2, 1969, on charges of plotting to kill policemen and conspiring to dynamite midtown department stores, police precinct houses, railroad facilities and the New York Botanical Garden. For nine months, thirteen of the defendants, all of whom are paupers, have been held in jail—ten on $100,000 bail, two on $50,000 and one on $25,000. Arson and possession of dangerous weapons have been added to the charges.

It's not the sort of cause that ordinarily produces social gatherings in the Bernsteins' living room (although Mrs. Bernstein did found the women's division of the New York Civil Liberties Union) and the party itself began somewhat stiffly. There they were, the Black Panthers from the ghetto and the black and white liberals from the middle, upper-middle and upper classes studying one another cautiously over the expensive furnishings, the elaborate flower arrangements, the cocktails and the silver trays of canapés.

Upon meeting Miss Cynthia Phipps, whom he had no way of knowing is a member of one of the country's wealthier aristocratic families, Henry Mitchell, a Harlem Panther defense captain, smiled and put out his hand.

"I hope we can do something to help," Miss Phipps said.

"What do you do?" Mr. Mitchell asked.

"I work at the Metropolitan Museum," she answered, going on to discuss last year's "Harlem on My Mind" exhibition, which drew the wrath of black and white liberals alike.

Mr. Mitchell listened. Miss Phipps then tentatively raised the subject of Nigeria, which Mr. Mitchell said he really didn't know too much about. She asked if there were any good capitalists and Mr. Mitchell said he didn't think so. And from there they went into a discussion of their problems with the telephone.

"The F.B.I. would pay the bill to keep our phones going so they'll know what we're saying," Mr. Mitchell explained.

"Oh, really," said Miss Phipps.

"Sometimes we have to wait six or seven minutes for a dial tone," Mr. Mitchell said.

"I have the same problem," Miss Phipps answered. "They really ought to do something about it."

After perhaps an hour of what may or may not have been the social hour, a bell was rung and the party moved into another room for the meeting. Mrs. Bernstein thanked everyone for coming and introduced Leon Quat, a lawyer.

"I'm assuming we're an élite corps of effete snobs and intellectuals," he said as people settled themselves. "I suppose you know I'm referring to our Vice President."

Then, calling this one of the gravest periods in American history, Mr. Quat introduced Mr. Cox. He discussed party goals, which include blacks having power over their own destiny, full employment, an end to police brutality and to exploitation by whites, housing, education and peace. He also described what he called the government conspiracy against the Panthers. Mr. Cox was accompanied by several defendants' wives and Panthers and by attorneys for the defense, including Gerald B. Lefcourt. Mr. Lefcourt also discussed the case. And then Mr. Quat asked for contributions.

The first was an anonymous donation of $7,500. Mr. Bernstein pledged the fee from his next concert, saying he was sure it would be "four figures." Mr. Preminger gave $1,000 and Mr. Cox shook his hand.

From there it was Sheldon Harnick, the lyricist, $250; Burton Lane, the composer, and his wife, $200, and Mrs. Harry Belafonte, $300. The grand total for the evening was nearly $10,000.

"I grew up in France during the rise of Nazism," said Mrs. August Heckscher, wife of the city's Administrator of Parks, Recreation and Cultural Affairs, "and I think the one thing we must always support is justice." She gave $100.

LOOKING AHEAD TO SPAGHETTI PARTIES FOR EIGHT . . .

November 1970

For a while, it looked as if what New York's chic upper echelons call "this new mood" might have been nothing more than a variation of the old Marie Antoinette game: the rich tiring of their diamonds and—strictly for the fun of it—casting them aside and dressing like the poor. But it goes a lot further than that.

Whether because of the recession, inflation, Vietnam, campus unrest, the desire to get closer to nature, a new introspection or simply boredom with the old extravagances, a new life style is emerging, and emerging quickly.

Spaghetti parties for eight are replacing formal black-tie dinners for twenty-four. Ladies are effusive about the "coziness" of luncheons in casual clothes at home rather than dressed up in elegant French restaurants. Charity balls are disappearing or losing the once-glittering names that attracted the crowds. At the same time, people aren't getting dressed up as often as they used to. Some of the city's most publicized party-goers have taken to bridge suppers or quiet evenings at the neighborhood movies. And after years of being visibly out on the town, it's suddenly terribly chic to stay home.

"It's more like a small town," Mrs. Joseph A. Meehan said enthusiastically. "People are more serious, more down to earth. I think we got caught up in a lot of trivia and we're not going to be bothered anymore." Mrs. Meehan, wife of a stockbroker, is typical of the new life style. Instead of lunching out and shopping, she and her friends are wearing mostly last year's clothes and taking up speed reading or visiting the art museums that they couldn't fit into last year's frantic party schedule. She says she feels "more serious," that she's concerned with the election, and that "the whole wardrobe thing is different, to say the least.

"Nobody's spending money—especially on clothes," said Mrs. Meehan, who isn't exactly wild about the midi. "Prices are so exorbitantly high everybody's being careful, even if they don't have to be. I suppose the recession has something to do with it, but I see it more as a mood than an economic thing—a resistance to trivia."

Mrs. T. Suffern Tailer, wife of the independently wealthy golfer, agrees.

110

She said last year seemed like "one big thing after another" and that this season "people just don't want great big snarling parties."

"I can't tell you why it is," she said. "We're all talking about how quiet it is. Let's hope it's not because we're too old. Maybe it's that I'm just not in the mood for big things."

Aside from fashion shows (she regularly wears midis), a Nine O'Clocks gala and a charity ball or two, Mrs. Tailer's party schedule consists mostly of intimate dinners for four, six or eight. She remembers only one dinner this fall where there were as many as fourteen guests. She likes the new mood.

"I'm having a wonderful time with my husband and my dogs," she said. "I keep thinking I'll start my eggnog parties again, but the last one went to ninety people, and I can't face that."

While charming, Mrs. Tailer's eggnog parties were hardly the kind of gathering that made previous seasons brilliant. Yet it looks as if that's just what this and future seasons may hold.

Harold Prince, the producer-director, and Mrs. Prince had one of their usual informal buffet suppers not long ago. Stephen Sondheim was the *pièce de résistance,* playing and singing the score of his new musical, *Follies.* But what one guest remembered with particular pleasure was the ambience ("It was comfortable and we sat on the floor") and the food. The Princes served "solid Italian stuff" instead of "that vapid French food."

"It makes perfect sense," said Mrs. Anne Slater, a woman who used to sally forth in sequins and satin. "I've been having chili parties in my new kitchen. We all gather around the stove and take things to the table—you know, very casual."

When Mrs. Slater says, "We all" she means six people. In the old days before the new mood, "small" meant at least forty people. Even Mrs. Joseph H. Lauder, the indefatigable party-giver and -goer, has a new idea of small. Her parties, which ran to fifty for dinner (and probably still will during the Palm Beach winter season), are down to eight—"never more than fourteen."

Mrs. Lauder also concedes that "diamonds aren't fashionable." She says she has to specify "black tie and long dress" on invitations because nobody seems to know what to wear, and that although the midiskirt is not the most flattering look to emerge from Seventh Avenue, "it's fun to wear all those sweaters and skirts and leather things." So much for brocade and gold lamé.

Mrs. Slater isn't as enthusiastic. She's boycotting the midi and the stores, "until something pretty comes along." Mrs. John Fell, widow of the investment banker, isn't quite so reluctant. She was at La Côte Basque for luncheon the other day in a short black turtleneck dress with a fur belt. But she does have two midiskirts she doesn't like very much.

"I don't need clothes anyway," she said. "Nothing's coming up, so I don't feel forced to buy."

Yet clothes are very much a part of the new life style, whether last year's or this year's—regardless of length. Pastels and bright colors have all but vanished. And the midi, whether sportsy, outdoorsy skirts and sweaters or sinuously clinging dresses, comes mostly in somber colors.

"Bittersweet chocolate, raisin, plum, navy blue, carbon, dark murky seaweedy greens and very graphite grays," according to Donald Brooks. "Very wartime—like 1944 or 1945, when it was bad taste to do anything opulent."

Mr. Brooks, like his Seventh Avenue colleagues, thinks such clothes look better with dark stockings or boots, and although some women are resisting the long skirts, they already had the stockings and boots. As a result, virtually everybody looks vaguely like an Italian war widow.

"It's a down time," he said. "It's time for shopworn, not razzmatazz. People are thinking about serious things—Mr. Nixon's state-by-state endorsements, the latest massacre in California. Everybody's less jazzy, less giggly, less drunk."

Such is the rhetoric of fashion (and of what passes for society, for that matter). In home furnishings, the thinking is almost as "introspective."

The den of architect Philip Johnson's new guest house has dark walls. Blacks and browns are becoming increasingly popular wall colors. And Billy Baldwin, the decorator who has never been accused of anything less than elegance, likes dark walls, small "cozy" parties and the increasing informality.

"The psychological reaction is to the stock market," Mr. Baldwin said. "It has to be. But I don't think people are letting their houses run down. I still see lots of expensive flowers and the food is still good."

Mr. Baldwin says he can't help noticing the clothes at the little parties. Besides being casual ("I mean you know they went home and had a bath before they came to dinner, but the clothes are the same they might have worn earlier in the day"), he, too, finds them more somber.

"If the women wear those dark colors against dark walls they're going to be lost like a lot of moles," he said.

The new introspection apparently doesn't preclude conversation, and if there's one thing rich New Yorkers insist they're having these days (after years of thanking God for those loud charity ball orchestras that kept them from having to talk), it's lots of interesting, "meaningful" conversations.

Mrs. Fell remembers more analytical political discussions than usual for an off-year election. Mrs. Samuel Peabody, who dropped out of the social hubbub three years ago to work in a Harlem drug program, says that when she does see friends socially, the talk often concerns the urban crisis. And Mrs. William Rayner, the decorator, is hearing more about the young and the drug problem.

"We've all changed," said Mrs. Rayner, whose face has appeared on countless fashion pages. "That giddy racing around is gone. It's a reaction to what's happening. If you're giddy now, you're insensitive to the world's problems."

Aside from the informality, the self-proclaimed seriousness and the rejection of a lot of the old glamour, the most significant addition to virtually everybody's agenda is the movies. Mrs. Slater watches late shows. When Richard Feigen and his fashion-plate wife aren't giving gala parties, they are grabbing corned beef sandwiches and going to West Side double features.

"Last year's movies," said Mrs. Feigen, a regular at last year's big parties. "We have a lot of catching up to do."

And for contrast? Well, Raffles and Le Club still get their share of what's left of the city's diamond brigade. The New York City Cultural Council's theater benefit and supper, which had to turn away would-be patrons, was hardly understated. And nearly a thousand people managed to ditch the informality thing long enough to attend the April in Paris Ball.

HARLEM: IN ERMINE, PEARLS AND JEANS

November 1972

The invitation to the Dance Theatre of Harlem's gala benefit at the newly refurbished Loew's Victoria Theater on West 125th Street said, "Come on back in ermine, pearls and jeans," and that's what rich and elegant blacks and whites by the hundreds did last night. But not without some soul searching.

After all, everybody who is anybody remembers the 1937 Richard Rodgers-Lorenz Hart song: the one that clearly established who did and who didn't like crap games with barons and earls, to say nothing of going to Harlem in ermine and pearls. And the one thing nobody wanted to do was either offend somebody or seem tacky. But after many a white liberal discussion about what one should or should not wear to Harlem in 1972 (let alone whether one should go or not), the party-goers finally got themselves together. They first stopped at one of the scores of quickie buffet suppers, there to reiterate the cultural significance of the nation's first all-black ballet company and the importance of projects that cross racial lines.

And then finally, blacks and whites together, they climbed into rented buses or limousines, locked the doors, joked about whether or not they were safe and were off to what for most was as foreign a place as Timbuktu.

When they arrived at the brightly lighted theater, Harlem was waiting for them behind police barriers. Black children in bell bottoms, teen-agers in faded corduroys and adults in the worn cloth coats of the poor stood six rows deep to stare, whistle, cheer and comment as black and white women in minks, sables and even chinchilla climbed out in the middle of 125th Street.

Brock Peters, Rod Steiger, Mrs. Alfred Gwynne Vanderbilt, a man who called himself Chanteclair, Raymond St. Jacques and Mayor Lindsay caused the most excitement. Cheers went up when Mr. Peters and Mr. Steiger hugged each other under the marquee. There were whistles for Mrs. Vanderbilt's very short black mushroom-shaped skirt and red feather jacket.

Two little boys, who had been standing on an automobile, dived into the crowd when Mr. St. Jacques, tall in a fur cape, waved at the crowd.

Chanteclair, whose turban was white ermine with a red feather on top, removed his white ermine cape and blew kisses. And the mayor, no newcomer to politics, shook people's hands, first on one side, then the other, on his way into the theater.

"What's happening! What's happening!" cried Mrs. Adam Gimbel, the dress designer, as children darted straight at her, bumping and pushing to get at the mayor.

Scores of uniformed police, including six black women, kept Harlem from the invading force. But the children were permitted to break through the lines for autographs or, in the case of Sidney Poitier, the last big name to arrive, to hug and kiss him and then squeal with delight.

"I got him," one young black girl shrieked after grabbing Mr. Poitier. "I got him! I got him! It's the best moment of my whole life!"

The clothes were spectacular, of course, with dashikis next to fur coats, young white women in blue jeans and sweaters next to black and white women in diamonds or African necklaces and a background of men and women—black and white—who were not exhibitionists.

"I think we should pay Harlem the compliment of dressing nicely, but not overdoing it," said Mrs. Oscar Hammerstein 2nd. "We must go with respect for the people, not with a lot of whoopee." Mrs. Hammerstein, whose late husband—like Richard Rodgers—was born in Harlem, was true to her word. She wore a simple long black dress with pearls. Only one prospective $100 ticket buyer had turned her down. "She said the newspapers would make it sound as if we were patronizing Harlem," Mrs. Hammerstein said. "She said if she went, somebody might think she was a Democrat. Frankly, I think she was just a little frightened." If either black or white guests were afraid of what might happen to them on 125th Street, nobody, including Mrs. Hammerstein, admitted it. It was always the nameless stay-at-homes who were described as frightened.

"Someone asked me, 'Aren't you afraid of muggers?' and I said, 'Good heavens, no,'" said Mrs. Harold Reed, the art dealer's wife. "I said, 'I'm wearing my best fur coat and my best pearls. Harlem is not a jungle.'"

Mrs. Reed, who is not known for blue jeans, had wanted to take the ermine and pearls part of the invitation literally. But her ermine, which had belonged to her great-grandmother, was yellow with age. She settled instead for white satin pants, a white satin halter top, masses of pearls and a white mink coat with a fox collar.

Mrs. Peters, noting that her role in this day of women's liberation was to be "the very Mrs. Brock Peters" as well as benefit co-chairman, was draped in black matte jersey, Norwegian fox and silver.

"I'm not an ermine and pearls person," she explained.

"Harlem was a cultural center in the late twenties and early thirties," said Mrs. Henry Moon, founder of the Urban League Guild and a native. "I think we're seeing a revival in the arts, the black arts. The trouble, of course, is that not many of us live there anymore."

For the successful blacks, especially those who were born and raised in Harlem only to depart for better neighborhoods after World War II, the gathering was a homecoming, a return to what Arthur Mitchell, executive director and founder of the Dance Theatre, called "the black Mecca."

"When my husband was a boy, his teachers included Countee Cullen and Langston Hughes," said Mrs. Peters, referring to the poets of Harlem's prewar heyday. "Now we're having another renaissance."

Even Mrs. William B. Jaffe, who admitted to a somewhat sheltered life, said she'd been to Harlem once, but that that was beside the point. "Everybody from Harlem comes down here now," she said, meaning the Upper East Side. "We go to the same parties. We're all going back because they're going back, too."

Harlem to Mrs. Carol Weil Haussamen, the real-estate heiress, is familiar territory. She went back in black satin pants, a white satin shirt, ermine and pearls.

"I went as a kid and I had a ball," she recalled. "I even campaigned there with Mrs. Roosevelt. She stood on a wooden chair. My job was to hold the chair for her."

The theater itself was a blaze of lights. Inside, the marble floors had been restored. The chandeliers were lowered to make the vast, 2,270-seat hall more intimate. A team of Harlem housewives had finished covering the chairs with red velvet.

The buses and limousines all seemed to arrive at once, and the lobby was jammed. Eventually, guests took their seats, the house lights dimmed and the giant production, *Harlem Homecoming,* with Lena Horne, Leontyne Price and Mr. Peters at the helm, began.

RITA HAYWORTH—OR MARION JAVITS?

December 1970

The resemblance is there—around the eyes, maybe, or the cheekbones and the generous mouth. And Marion Javits doesn't mind at all. In fact, Rita

Hayworth is not somebody with whom almost anybody loathes being compared. And, as Marion Javits herself said, "It's nice."

It's also a new Marion Javits in a succession of Marion Javitses, starting not so much with the bright little girl who was forever president of her class, but the fifteen-year-old who entered a Ginger Rogers look-alike contest at a "Loew's something-or-other theater," and almost won.

Ginger Rogers?

"Oh, yes," said Marion Javits. "Nobody ever mistook me for Ginger Rogers, although I did feel romantic about her. Ginger Rogers was the Doris Day of her time, but I was never ever Doris Day. Then I guess I graduated to Rita Hayworth."

The Rita Hayworth thing began in the fifties, when people were forever telling Marion how much she resembled her. By the sixties, the Rita image was gone, and there was Eunice Kennedy Shriver and her sleek bouffant bob. In 1968, Marion and Anne Bancroft looked so much alike they could have been sisters. And the reason Rita's back (and she is, she is) is that Marion Javits has been to the hairdresser.

Like a lot of fashion sisters, Marion has one of those slightly tousled new hairdos that are all the rage, and eureka! Rita Hayworth. Not necessarily the slinky, sensuous, long-haired Rita Hayworth whose photographs seem to have sustained virtually every American male involved in World War II, although there is some of that, too.

But certainly the tempestuous, sultry, curly-haired Rita Hayworth of *The Loves of Carmen,* a 1948 gypsy type whose whole appearance (voluminous maxi-length tiered skirts, wide lace-up belt, fringed shawl and plunging neckline) might have been the very model for what passes for contemporary fashion.

Yet a woman isn't always what she appears to be, and the question of who Marion Javits really is persists—if only for Marion Javits. If not Ginger, Rita, Eunice or Anne, then who? A question that inevitably plagues bright wives of famous men and mothers whose children are almost grown.

"Who am I?" she asks. "I'm my husband's wife and I'm striving to be my own person."

There was a time, mostly when she was a lot younger, when she aspired to be an actress. Even in 1962, fifteen years after her marriage to Jacob K. Javits, United States Senator from New York, she was still saying the theater was what mattered.

By that time, she'd played a small part in the Tony Curtis-Dean Martin comedy film, *Who Was That Lady?*

"I'm still known as 'Marion Javits, the producer,'" she said somewhat wryly. "I produced one play—just one play—*Hang Down Your Head and Die.* I *was* going to become a lady producer but it was just too tough. I had to deal with the unions and such things."

Since then, and sometimes simultaneously, there has been Marion Javits, the community worker; Marion Javits, the social butterfly; Marion Javits, the political campaigner; Marion Javits, the idea lady; Marion Javits, friend of the arts and artists; and, of course, Marion Javits, wife and the mother of three. She's in Washington more often than she used to be, helping to reorganize her husband's office, dutifully standing by his side and entertaining now and then at their Watergate apartment, which replaced the house they used to have. But mostly, she's in New York.

"I'm uncertain about who I am," she said. "I'm a creative person and a functionary. I do things that are me and things I have to do. I don't do the writing or the painting but I can put it together. I'm a catalyst."

At the moment, the Marion Javits who matters to Marion Javits is a writer of sorts and a would-be author. She's working on "a book about where things are—my places—where I've been and things I've done." Like *her* florist, or *her* trip to Europe, or *her* psychoanalysis. Very personal.

"It will be me related to my life," she said. "I'll be sharing with people."

At the same time, there's Marion Javits, the combination catalyst and friend of the arts. One project is the Experimental Center in the Arts, which, she says, would have brought "a whole other ambience" to the waterfront piers if it had been done properly. Her role with the Experimental Center is somewhat tenuous, which apparently is where "Marion Javits, the catalyst" comes in. But there is nothing ambiguous about her relationship with Broadside Art, Inc. She describes it as "my business." Broadside's chief product is Robert Rauschenberg's giant, three-panel lithograph entitled "Rauschenberg Autobiography," which retails for $150. Whether art or not, the "Rauschenberg Autobiography" was a marketable idea, and Marion Javits has thousands of ideas. Not long ago, she did a study that showed an airline what it could do to make airports, airline personnel and airplanes more interesting.

"I was always thinking of environment," she said. "One of my ideas was to put a Dial-a-Poem stanchion in an airport or on a plane. You put in a dime and get out all these poems read by poets. It's distracting."

The "me" Marion talks about regularly apparently is not Marion Javits, the functionary—committee member, political campaigner or social butterfly—or so she says. "The lady on boards and committees isn't me," she said. "My 'work' has consisted of submitting twenty-five names, having my picture taken, going to a meeting and appearing at a function if there is one."

Nor is it "me" to attend charity balls, parties or movie openings ("theater openings went out five years ago") either, "except sometimes," and, of course, she's a regular at such gatherings. "I wonder why people are there," she says of massive social functions. "Aren't people hiding in a crowd? Aren't they allowing you to hide? You rarely get to talk in any interesting way. You're really there to avoid being alone. Aren't they getting me away from what I really want to do?"

Besides projects and ideas, the real "me" seems to come out in other "creative" ways. As Marion Javits, fashionable hostess, she has taken up a black maxi-length skirt, a wide belt and a clingy blouse with plunging neckline as her "uniform."

She considers her interest in astrology "me" too. "Every year I have my horoscope read," she said. "I used to send away to a Greek lady. But last year, I went to the astrology machine in Grand Central Station. You pay $5 and answer a few questions and the machine gobbles up the information and tells you what you'll be all year. It doesn't tell me who I am but it tells me where I'm going."

The evolving Marion Javits continues to evolve. As of 1976, she had registered as a foreign agent despite the Senator's sensitive job on the Senate Foreign Relations Committee and was touting Iran for big money until the question of conflict of interest was raised.

Insisting that she, a woman and a feminist, had a right to her own life and career, she refused to give up the public relations job, but finally did. Shortly thereafter, it was learned that she was also working for the Mexican government in an effort to help resolve the Jewish boycott of that nation after Mexico voted for the United Nations resolution classifying Zionism as a form of racism.

Mrs. Javits had also changed her hairstyle. Some people even thought she resembled Audrey Hepburn.

ARTIE SHAW AT SIXTY-TWO

February 1973

"Happiness, I've found, isn't a state you arrive in, like Rhode Island or Vermont."—Artie Shaw

Artie Shaw used to poke fun at marriage in the 1950s, but after seven tries and six divorces he attempted an explanation.

"I made an unholy botch of every last one of them," he conceded. "Of course, I believe I can state, equally accurately and with complete dispassion and objectivity, that I had a good deal of help in making those unholy botches."

It's now twenty years, another divorce and another marriage later, and Mr. Shaw, once the world's most celebrated clarinet player, is even more philosophical. Despite the Cassandras, the advocates of group sex, the new permissiveness, the radical feminists, the guilt-ridden machismo-conscious males and even the latest batch of would-be marriage experts, he thinks old-fashioned romantic marriage is not just possible but a goal worth the pursuit.

"It's conceivable," he said in his rather wry way, "that two people can live together happily, if they are remarkable. They can live together if they're willing to adapt and change. It *is* conceivable."

Which, in Mr. Shaw's case, is real optimism. That he has seen few such marriages in his going-on-sixty-three years bothers him little because, as he says, such bliss is possible.

"One and one," he said, "should add up to three. If she makes me more than I am and I make her more than she is, that's better than two people. That's great. That's what it should be. I don't care how it's achieved."

The trouble, in Mr. Shaw's view, is that one and one usually add up to "less than two," which is how he sees most marriages. "How long will they last? That depends on each person's tolerance."

Until recently, Mr. Shaw hasn't been enormously tolerant. His first six marriages, including those to Ava Gardner and Kathleen Winsor, rarely lasted more than two years. He and Lana Turner split after only five months.

Miss Turner (who later confided, "Artie was my entire college education") explained they couldn't live together without fighting. Miss Gardner, still a good friend, said, "He told me to leave . . . so I left." And after two and a half years with Jerome Kern's daughter, Elizabeth, he suddenly announced they'd better separate.

"Right now?" she asked.

"Yes," he said.

So they did.

"Many people marry the same kind of people over and over again," Mr. Shaw said. "Either that or they zigzag from one type to another. I zigzagged—from a nurse to a big movie star to a homebody to Ava to a housewife-turned-writer to an actress."

Let's see, now. That's only six, starting with wife No. 2. Somehow, he hasn't included his first one—June Carns of Ashtabula, Ohio, nor his last, also an actress. Oh, well. Try as he would, the Shaw system obviously didn't work.

"I behaved the way I had to," he said. "Looking back, a lot of it was nonsense. Our big mistake in every case was in getting married."

Yet he is still the romantic.

"A lasting marriage can be nothing more than two people living together and somehow managing to get past the problems," he said. "The marriages I know like that exist because of long-suffering people who have no better alternatives. Or men who worry about being taken to the cleaners. Or people who have run out of energy." The trials of such marriages, he argued, are exemplified by merely contemplating life with Pablo Picasso.

"He's a man of perfect order," he said. "Just try moving a peacock feather, just one feather. Picasso can get away with that. Society reinforces him. Would anyone put up with that if he wasn't a great artist?"

The implication, of course, is that in most marriages each person has something of Picasso's demands without his ability to have his way, is therefore frustrated and has to tolerate.

Hardly Mr. Shaw's ideal, but all right for people willing to settle for working arrangements. If the question is whether to legalize such an arrangement, Mr. Shaw's answer is a qualified yes. "If you're going to live together anyway you might as well get married," he said, not very enthusiastically. "Just think of it as a tax device."

On the other hand, if the ability to tolerate has worn out, the next step may be divorce. "Divorce always makes people feel less than they were," Mr. Shaw said. "It's painful. Even the worst marriage is hard to break up. It's as tough as kicking cigarettes."

At the moment, Mr. Shaw, now a theatrical producer, is married to the former Evelyn Keyes, wife No. 8. Between 1957 and 1962 they apparently had an ideal marriage.

"We had a one-to-one monogamous relationship," he said. "After 1962, that no longer sufficed, so we fumbled our way into 'open marriage.' Neither of us wanted a divorce so we moved aside to live as we pleased. I like her very much and she likes me, but we've found it about impossible to live together."

Mr. Shaw lives in New York. Miss Keyes doesn't. He has seen her once in the last four months, perhaps three times in the last two years. They have property and tax forms in common.

Yet he is optimistic.

"Lately things that have been happening have given me hope," he said. "I see the possibility of a really good relationship."

He didn't say with whom.

OFF TO BERMUDA—FOR A BITE OF LUNCH

January 1972

David Frost took sixty of his better friends to lunch the other day. In Bermuda.

His guests reported at Kennedy Airport at 9:30 A.M. and were welcomed with coffee, with or without cognac. Carl B. Stokes, former Mayor of Cleveland, was among the first to arrive. Then came Bobby Fischer, the chess champion, Barbara Walters, the television news commentator, John Kenneth Galbraith, James A. Michener, Mrs. Bennett Cerf, Joseph E. Levine and a raft of newspaper and magazine people.

By ten, the host and his cool-eyed overachievers, some of whom had never met each other, were belted down in the chartered front section of a Boeing 747 with regular passengers in the back. The first round of what was to be a day of champagne was served. Frederick Brisson, the producer, described his office's reaction to the event. "When I told everybody I was going to Bermuda for lunch," he said, "they laughed first. When they realized I meant it, they booed."

Once the plane was up, it became a flying cocktail party. Guitarists strolled down the aisles. A palmist and a graphologist, both of whom insisted upon being called "behaviorists," went about their work. The canapés and caviar appeared. It was *de rigueur* to exclaim over the host's borscht-red acrylic seersucker suit.

Mr. Levine, who was elegantly outfitted in black, with a cane and a small black alligator bag for his wife's swimming suit, read *Day of the Dolphin*, which is to be his next film.

Mr. Stokes talked politics, Mr. Fischer huddled with Joseph Kraft, the political columnist. "I don't know much about politics," Mr. Fischer confided. "In fact, I don't know many of these people."

In another corner, Charles Addams, the cartoonist, and Mrs. Jacob K. Javits exchanged gossip. Peter Graves, star of "Mission Impossible," had his palm read.

Two hours and perhaps ten bottles of champagne later, the plane landed in sunny Bermuda. The temperature was 72 degrees. Senator Javits, who'd flown in from London minutes before, rushed to greet his wife and join the party. Buses took them to the Castle Harbour Hotel. A calypso band played for more cocktails, this time on a high terrace overlooking sloping emerald lawns, gardens and the Atlantic Ocean. After a buffet lunch, Richard Roundtree, star of *Shaft*, headed for the golf course. Clive Barnes stretched out on the grass. Mr. Fischer played tennis. Mr. Graves and Mr. Galbraith swam in the hotel's smaller pool while Senator Javits took to the Olympic pool by himself. "I need exercise," he explained. Mr. Brisson went bird-watching.

Theodore W. Kheel, the labor mediator, in a blue blazer with little white stripes, shopped, but couldn't find anything for his wife. Kitty Carlisle, Mrs. Cerf and Wyatt Dickerson, the Washington real-estate man, were luckier. They bought Mr. Frost a red, white and blue scarf with the British flag on it.

The host took Mrs. Javits around in a golf cart. But she was in a hurry to get back.

"I'm going to talk to the palmist again," she said. "She's telling me fascinating things about my future."

The trip back to the airport was by boat. By this time, Mr. Frost, who'd kissed all his female guests at least once, was rubbing lipstick off his face. An associate whispered that after the party he was flying to Bangladesh to interview Sheik Mujibur Rahman for television.

The return flight was a replay with more champagne, more hors d'oeuvre, more caviar, the palmists in the lounge and Billy Taylor at the piano.

Mrs. Henry J. Heinz 2nd, wife of the Pittsburgh food mogul, and Mr. Addams, who snapped pictures of friends with his own camera, scanned the *Reader's Digest* and British *Harper's Bazaar* on the way. Mr. Kheel studied *New York* magazine. Mr. Fischer took out his pocket chess set and gave impromptu lessons. Mr. Galbraith said he'd recently been in Acapulco.

"You stroll along the beach," he said, flicking at a wayward lock of wet gray hair, "and you have the distinct feeling that we must be the only race of people where it looks as if the men bear the babies. All the men looked pregnant. The women were slim."

At 6 P.M., the plane landed and the peaceful eight-and-a-half-hour food and drink marathon came to an end. The guests, raving about what a good day it had been, hugged and kissed Mr. Frost goodbye. New York was dark and overcast. The temperature was 45 degrees.

"It's back to the ordinary things," Mr. Levine said. "Nathan's and plain old '21.'"

PRINCESS GOES TO SOHO ARTISTS' PARTY

October 1972

Robert Rauschenberg's formal dinner for Her Royal Highness Princess Christina of Sweden was perhaps the most unusual interpretation of a black-tie party since somebody dressed a monkey in a dinner jacket and seated it next the hostess. The host, an artist who once created a celebrated *oeuvre* by merely stenciling a box with the words "Art Work," had obviously risen to the occasion. He rejected the idea of wearing a suit made entirely of neckties.

"No," he said thoughtfully. "I think I have something more suitable."

After first settling his wavy, shoulder-length coiffure with a bobby pin over each ear, he did indeed put on a white shirt and a black tie. But his jacket was an American Indian fringed suede relic embroidered with porcupine quills.

The princess, apparently aware that an evening in the SoHo artists' district in 1972 was not the same as a ball at the St. Regis she attended in 1965, dressed differently, too. She wore ruffled tiers of green, black and red chiffon all right. But her neckline plunged daringly and there was no sign of white gloves, her diamond necklace or her tiara.

Before she arrived, Mr. Rauschenberg, whose friends had spent days preparing his house-around-a-chapel for the 309 dinner guests, explained the protocol.

"I've granted everybody immunity," he said. "You don't have to curtsy or bow. Sweden is a very liberated country."

The princess, who'd studied art history at Radcliffe, seemed to agree. At an earlier reception—the unveiling of the New York art collection destined for Sweden's Moderna Museet—she said, "Nobody in Sweden calls me princess anymore."

The host and guest of honor finally met on the fourth floor of Mr. Rauschenberg's house. The princess and such other upper-echelon types as the Swedish Ambassador got there by climbing up eighty steep steps.

"If you don't get your leg muscles developed tonight, you never will," said Mrs. Harold Reed.

Once there, the visiting Swedes were surrounded by artists, including Roy Lichtenstein, Larry Rivers, Alex Hay, James Rosenquist, Oyvind Fahlstrom and Andy Warhol, Mr. Rauschenberg's SoHo friends and a sprinkling of refugees from the Upper East Side.

"I'm Penelope," said a young woman in a mint-green satin nightgown with a lace bodice and train. "I never use my last name."

Penelope was accompanied by her baby daughter, Hummingbird, who sat in the middle of the floor. Then there was a young woman who professed to be Moki or Moki Cherry. She said she hadn't decided whether she had one or two first names.

Moki, or Moki Cherry as the case may be, wore a beaded headdress with a peacock feather and bright red eye shadow. She said she'd spent the afternoon running up her pink and green satin tunic.

"The fabric?" she asked, looking a little puzzled. "Why, that was easy. Some of it was in the garbage or draped over trees. The birds flew some of it in my window."

The princess, who said she was having "a nice time," also met Kevin McCarthy, who had a "Men for Women for McGovern" button on his dinner jacket, and August Hecksher, the Park Administrator. Mr. Hecksher said he might be just a little out of date. "Someone asked me which paintings I liked best and I said the abstract expressionists," he said. "That makes me the fifties, not even the sixties."

While Mr. Hecksher studied newer paintings stored behind the improvised bar (one was all gray with white chalk squiggles), Jeffrey Potter, the writer, sat on a filing cabinet, sipping his drink.

He said his name began J-E-F rather than G-E-O-F "because G-E-O went out with the American Revolution." But he was in black tie.

Mr. Potter was with Mrs. Armand G. Erpf, who has worked long and hard for Experiments in Art and Technology, which assembled the art collection and is raising funds to send it to Sweden. She is the widow of the financier.

"I love parties like this," she explained. "I really believe in supporting the arts."

Eventually, the important guests on the fourth floor went down to join the others for dinner. Tables centered with roses and daisies, and mobs of people were jammed over three floors. Mr. Rauschenberg and the princess sat in the chapel. The meal began with fresh salmon flown from Sweden and served on paper plates. The wine, a Muscadet, was poured into plastic cups. When the entree was slow in arriving, Mrs. Jacob K. Javits left the princess's table to help.

"It's impossible," she said. "There isn't enough space but I did my best."

La Petite Ferme, the Greenwich Village restaurant, prepared the chicken with dill according to Mr. Rauschenberg's own recipe. Eventually it arrived with carrots in butter. By the time the fruit and cheeses were passed, there were no more paper plates or silver.

"It's great," said Robert Scull, the taxi tycoon, reaching across Mrs. Scull for the bread. "Just think of it as a picnic al fresco."

The Marquis Bernard-Alexis Poisson de Menars, Chancellor of the Order of the Grand Occident, thought it was marvelous, too.

"I haven't had fruit in a basket since I left France," he said, helping himself to seven grapes, four strawberries and a banana.

Brief speeches, mostly inaudible tributes to art, the artists, the fund-raisers and the friendship between Sweden and the United States, were delivered on all three floors. Outside the chapel, one exchange turned into something of a debate.

"Women are just as responsible for this collection as men," Jill Johnston shouted during one speech. "Larry Poons drew his ellipses and his wife painted them in and Patty Oldenburg [the former Mrs. Claes Oldenburg] sewed every stitch of those soft typewriters and things herself." Miss Johnston, the self-styled "lesbian nationalist" who rarely goes anywhere these days without a purple-and-white "Dyke" button pinned to her United States Marine Corps jacket, was rewarded with applause, mostly from the women.

Back in the chapel, Billy Kluver, an E.A.T. impresario, was busily presenting the princess with what he called a medal, and she dropped it. Shortly thereafter, Miss Ellen Johnson, an art historian from Oberlin, read Mrs. Lichtenstein's palm. By this time, it was nearly midnight. Most guests didn't stay for coffee.

MAFIA CHIC: THE LAST DELICIOUS DAYS OF JOEY GALLO

June 1972

"People like me are a plague on people like you."—Joey Gallo.

"No, Joey. The reverse is true."—Marta Orbach.

He spilled spaghetti sauce on Thomas H. Guinzburg's shoes. He played pool with Bruce Jay Friedman's sons. He cleared the dinner plates at Marta and Jerry Orbachs' and emptied their ashtrays. He probed "the meaning of life" in a deep discussion with the fashionable Mrs. John Barry ("D.D.") Ryan 3rd.

The he, of course, was Joseph ("Crazy Joey") Gallo, the tough Mafioso, convicted extortionist and suspected murderer, who exuded what his newest friends have described as "refreshing insight and intelligence in a world of clichés."

He didn't make it to Park Avenue, or even El Morocco, but in his final days he unknowingly had become something of a sought-after social pet.

"Everyone talked about it," said Mrs. Richard Clurman, an authority on such matters, who refused to meet him. "It was the thing to do. You'd go somewhere and people would say, 'Have you met Joey Gallo?' and it was like Stravinsky or Yevtushenko. If you hadn't met him, you weren't in."

Eleven years ago, in the pre-lockup days when the Gallos were kidnapping the Profacis to get their way back in the rackets, you could see, if not actually meet, Joey Gallo in Greenwich Village bars. There, often in the company of journalists, he was as likely to cite Céline, Hugo or Kafka as to talk of events of the neighborhood or joke bitterly about what would become of his family.

Then came the nine-year stretch. By 1971, when Mr. Gallo was released, the Village bars were changed or gone. It was another world. In January of 1972, when he telephoned the Orbachs because friends had admiringly described Jerry's movie role in the Mafia spoof, *The Gang That Couldn't Shoot Straight,* he called from Brooklyn.

"We weren't sure what to do at first," Mrs. Orbach said. "We wanted to meet him—more out of curiosity than anything else."

What may have started for them as the tingling excitement of knowing a real live hood quickly turned into what they considered friendship. They accepted his invitation to dinner in a Brooklyn restaurant and were surprised to discover that the notorious Joey Gallo was "only about five feet six or seven." They found him "charming" and "brilliant." It was at that first meeting that he casually asked Mrs. Orbach whether she preferred Camus or Sartre. As she tells it, "I almost fell into a plate of spaghetti."

After that, he'd drop by the Orbachs' late at night, sipping coffee laced with anisette or a brandy, talking mostly with Mr. Orbach.

"He once told me to shut up," Mrs. Orbach said. "I'm Italian and I understand that. We had to make it very clear that in our family and our world women are bright and they talk, too, and he began to understand."

The conversations, hardly evidence of anyone's brilliance, ran to casual discussions, occasionally punctuated by Mr. Gallo's humor. He argued that people who broke the law should expect to go to jail, which rather startled the Orbachs. He said it was tragic that men like von Gogh weren't recognized and rewarded in their lifetime rather than years after death.

"Liberals," he explained, "are the first to dump you if you fail them or get into trouble. Conservatives are better. They never run out on you."

If he had lived in Italy, he once said, he might have been a Fascist. He was interested in power and money. Within weeks of meeting the Orbachs, Mrs. Orbach, herself a writer, was working with him on his memoirs and a "prison comedy." He believed the ventures could be profitable. The friendship had obviously blossomed.

Between January and April 7, when he was gunned down on his forty-third birthday in a Little Italy restaurant, the only way to meet Joey Gallo—unless, of course, you were his parole officer, the cops who followed his violent career or his South Brooklyn business associates—was to know the Orbachs and get invited to one of their regular five o'clock Sunday "brunches." The rub was that the actor and his wife were purposely protective of him. They didn't invite just anybody.

"We knew his background and he knew we knew and nobody pretended it didn't exist," Mrs. Orbach said. For them, it was enough that "he'd read in prison." They believed he was "rehabilitated." "He said he wanted to go straight," Mrs. Orbach added. "I know it sounds outrageous, but he was shy."

Shy? Indeed that does sound outrageous, particularly about a man who jabbed one enemy with an ice pick and broke a protection-money victim's arm. But the Orbachs simply shake their heads, argue that people just don't understand and insist: Joey was shy.

"He'd sit around my kitchen with those sad, sad eyes," Mrs. Orbach recalled. "He wanted to talk about things—everything. He needed people who were as bright as he was. We never invited anyone who wouldn't understand this. Just our closest friends."

Those who did go, and they're now caught somewhere between affection for the man, the horror of what he represented, and the notoriety of being publicly identified as acquaintances—let alone friends—of a gangster, found themselves at a typically informal family gathering.

What with the Orbach youngsters, the family cat and what Mrs. Orbach calls "our rude dog" (he jumps on people), it was pretty much of a do-your-own-thing afternoon.

Everyone wore comfortable clothes (which in that set can include $200 pants suits), sipped red wine or made their own drinks while Mrs. Orbach, often in blue jeans and an old sweater, put the finishing touches on dinner. Then everyone, including the children, gathered around the big dining room table to help themselves to spaghetti and green salad.

"Everybody I know is tired of the dressing up and the sitting down, with the servants waiting on you and the Baccarat crystal," Mrs. Orbach explained. "I was raised on spaghetti. I hadn't had Sundays like this since I was a child and my grandmother cooked. Joey liked it that way."

After dinner, there were lingering political debates over the last of the wine and espresso or somebody off shooting pool at one end of the living room. At the other end, twos and threes clustered on the elegant white brocade sofas to talk.

Comedian David Steinberg went to these parties. So did playwright Neil Simon, Broadway producer Harold S. Prince, actress Joan Hackett (who adored Gallo's calling her a "broad") and Richard Mulligan, her actor-husband, the Friedmans, the Ryans, assorted wives and girl friends, the Guinzburgs and nearly everybody else on the "best friends" list.

"Joey would sit at the poker table with his back to the wall and listen," Mrs. Orbach said. "Sometimes, he headed for the sofas. I'd see him playing host, making sure everybody was included."

What's unusual about these parties and all the conversations is that virtually none of the celebrated guests, not even the literate Mr. Guinzburg, who became his publisher, can remember anything Mr. Gallo said. Try as they will, those who are eager to talk about him (and some friends are not—mostly because of the old notoriety thing) really haven't much to say.

"He was as bright and interesting as people said," according to Mrs. Ryan, with whom he had one of the lengthy brocade sofa talks. "He'd done a lot of thinking. It was nice to talk with somebody who'd had the time to think. I'm sorry I didn't know him better."

We know, Mrs. Ryan, but what did Joey Gallo say?

"Well, I know it's a cliché, but we talked about life. He knew so much about life's value . . ."

Aside from the brunches, Mr. Gallo's last delicious days with the Orbachs have been somewhat exaggerated. If they were, as one report suggested, "part of the theater-going, nightclubbing celebrity set," not many people noticed. In the twelve weeks the friendship lasted, they went to three Broadway shows and two nightclubs. They were twice at Elaine's literary saloon and twice at Sardi's, where Mrs. Peter Stone, the writer's wife, distinctly remembers meeting Mr. Gallo's mother.

"She seemed very nice," Mrs. Stone said.

Like the Orbachs, Mrs. Stone met Mr. Gallo on the telephone. Mrs. Orbach told him the Stones' dog had been stolen. Mr. Gallo offered to help find it. "He called me up," Mrs. Stone said, "and I told him I'd had answers to my ads in the paper, and he said he'd check them out. He thought there might be a dognapping ring. I didn't meet him until he came to the apartment to go to see people who'd answered the ad. He wouldn't let me go alone."

Besides the nights out, the last days included Mr. Gallo's wedding at the Orbachs' town house—with the priest getting his name wrong and Allan Jones singing "The Lord's Prayer"—and two small dinner parties. One was at the Guinzburgs'. The other was at the Ben Gazzaras'.

When the Orbachs asked Mr. Gazzara if they might bring their friend to dinner, he knew precisely who Joey Gallo was, and he agreed.

"He served his time, didn't he," he said rhetorically.

Of such nights out and the brunches was the image of the new Pal Joey legend made. Those who met him liked him. Those who didn't either schemed, fumed privately or declared themselves unalterably opposed to dinner with a gangster. Once again, there was the question of radical chic.

While Mr. Guinzburg says, "Gangsters have always exercised a certain fascination for society," he insists that "somehow this wasn't the same. Each of us who knew him well tried to keep him away from people who would take him up and use him badly."

To a certain extent, they succeeded. Yet the relationships remind Mafiologists of the days when Hollywood stars, including Jean Harlow, lionized "Bugsy" Siegel and Meyer Lansky was something of a wheel in Miami society. They also smack of *naïveté*.

His new friends can say all they want about his "loyalty and sense of honor," his patience with little children at the pool table, his wit, his charm and his obvious intelligence, all of which may well be true—right down to the possibility of his complete rehabilitation. But in the end, one of the fascinations Joey Gallo held for this group of people was that he was a gangster, and nobody seems to have come to grips with that.

THE RICH PREPARE TO GET THROUGH THE ENERGY CRISIS, SOMEHOW

December 1973

Multimillionaire Charles Revson is not exactly down in the dumps, but what with the fuel shortage he honestly doesn't know what to do about *Ultima II*, his luxurious 250-foot, 1,200-ton yacht.

His problem, one he shares with Aristotle Onassis, William Levitt, the King of Norway and the British royal family, is not so much the rising cost, although there is that, but the shortage of diesel power. Does it mean he will really have to scratch his celebrated world cruises for the duration? That, of course, is a delicate question the tight-lipped Mr. Revson is not about to discuss in public. What he will say, however, is, "I have given the matter a lot of thought. I suppose I'll have to stay in one area. Thank goodness I don't have a company plane." Mr. Revson's new immobility, assuming he has to confine *Ultima II* to cruising solely in the Gulf of Mexico or solely in the Caribbean, is hardly the lot of the ordinary citizen. And yet it does say something about the special plight of the rich and famous.

Whether the energy crisis is real, or, as Mrs. Jerry Orbach, Melanie Kahane and Arlene Francis have implied, yet another Nixonian scare tactic, it hits the rich and famous, too, and they're already preparing to cope and fight back.

"I'm not concerned about myself," snapped Mrs. Edwin I. Hilson. "I'm concerned about the poor. Who's going to see that they're warm?"

Mrs. Hilson, a Republican whose charitable contributions border on major philanthropy, is particularly upset about rising gasoline prices. Not for herself, she says, since she just traded her big car for a smaller one that gets more miles to the gallon, but for people on a budget. She's also turning out the masses of lights she loves ("I'm going to miss them terribly") and doing mild battle with her landlord. She wants the heat turned down as the President requested. "I hate the cold," she said, "but I can do without. We will survive. We're not used to being disciplined, but it won't hurt us. We've never really sacrificed—even in World War II. It could be good for us. Anything that's a sacrifice is character-forming. Even so, I don't like it a bit."

Does that really mean that the energy crisis is simultaneously reviving the Puritan ethic of salvation through self-denial as well as memories of World War II? It certainly does, and not just for Mrs. Hilson.

Philip C. Johnson, who's riding the train to the country and counting on the winter sun to warm his glass house, finds "a wartime excitement about all this.

"And don't forget what wonderful friendships we made then," he said, "and how we lost our selfishness."

Ah, yes. Optimism springs eternal.

"New Yorkers are marvelous in a crisis," Miss Francis said. "They'll help each other the way they did in the big blackout."

Or, as Miss Kahane, the decorator, put it, "We're a pampered and indulged society. We're going to have to reset our sights. I have implicit faith in American ingenuity."

Miss Kahane thinks this crisis could be "like the Depression, which was the most galvanizing thing this country ever experienced. It pulled us together." And in that spirit, she has gone about resetting her sights. "I absolutely will not refill the cigarette lighters in my house," she said. "If necessary, I'll go to New Jersey and buy kitchen matches. I think they're illegal in New York. I guess that makes me a smuggler."

Miss Kahane has turned back the heat, removed the plants from her fireplace and ordered wood. "Lowering the thermostat is good for the sinus and fine furniture," she said. "Now my furniture will have the atmosphere it had in Europe."

Mrs. Thomas Kempner has always preferred cool, candlelighted drawing rooms, cold bedrooms and wood-burning fireplaces. Heat, she explained, "is bad for paintings, book bindings, lacquered furniture and middle-aged skins," and for years she has refused to turn it up. When chilly guests complain, Mrs. Kempner, a clotheshorse and fashion consultant, hands them her best sweaters. She would, however, be lost without her electric blanket.

"If worse comes to worse," she said, "we'll wear our long underwear—we have 'his' and 'hers'—and then our ski boots. My best protection is that awful English camisole. You know, with the faggoting and pink ribbon around the edge. And bloomers. And that knitted silk underwear from Grieder's in Zurich. Silk is much warmer than wool."

Enid A. Haupt, former editor of *Seventeen,* is also of the cold-house school, mostly because of her vast orchid and exotic plant collection. Despite the challenge, she says, the energy crisis has produced some good. "It got the Alaska pipeline through," she said. "Furthermore, I've never liked driving fast and I don't like to see planes take off half full. It means that an industry is in trouble, and I don't like that."

The Ford Motor Company, along with the rest of the transportation industry, already is in some trouble, which concerns Charlotte Ford Forstman, the board chairman's daughter.

"Let's face it," she said, "Lincoln Continentals eat gas and we still have ours. When we want to go anywhere, we'll have to go commercial. We can't use the company plane."

To Mrs. William C. Langley, the Newport hostess who ran for Congress last year, the crisis means the first woolen slacks she has ever worn on the city streets, fewer lights, the same fuzzy bathrobes and ankle-high slippers she has always worn in winter, and public transportation. She's putting her Rolls-Royce into storage.

While Mrs. Harold Reed is taping her thermostat at 68 degrees, banishing lights from her Christmas tree and hoping for the best, Mary Hemingway is depending upon her Franklin stove to see her through any heat stoppage that may develop. At the moment, Mrs. Hemingway's fuel is firewood, which costs something like $10 for an afternoon's burning. After that comes the Sunday *Times.* If all else fails, she said, only half facetiously, "I'll just burn up the furniture."

Mrs. Orbach, on the other hand, plans nothing so drastic. She has turned out lights and cut the heat. But that, she says, is as far as she and her actor husband intend to go for a while. "Jerry refuses to go fifty miles an hour because President Nixon really does have gas," she said. "Jerry's ready to be arrested. After gasoline comes milk and I don't know what else. It's all very suspicious. Or isn't it [the crisis] just to get the Alaska pipeline through? Which is a disaster. It will wreck the environment. It's all President Nixon's fault. Could it be some evil plan of his?"

Even the supremely calm Miss Francis has some reservations.

"You don't think Nixon thought this up to take the heat off Watergate, do you?" she said.

No matter who's right, the crisis has replaced Watergate as the talk of the Manhattan party circuit, a situation that has S. Joseph Tankoos, Jr., the real-estate investor, reeling. As far as he's concerned, "the people who don't know much about it are doing the talking" and "the conversation is just about as uninformed as it was about Watergate."

130

One woman, whose name Mr. Tankoos would not divulge, particularly startled him. She told him she had already made reservations for next summer's annual trip from Palm Beach to Newport. She thinks planes will be gone by then, so she's going by train.

"Now that's what I mean by 'a certain hysteria,'" he said with a chuckle. But, of course, the woman actually could have the last laugh.

Alice Roosevelt Longworth was ninety-two in 1976, and still the toast and delight of Washington. "I have no sense of humor, just a sense of irony," she once said. She has decided she is "less wit than mimic, more wit than wise." No matter. Peter Hurd painted her. She sits cross-legged, reads three books at once and knows nearly everybody who's anybody everywhere in the world. But that doesn't mean she likes them.
The New York Times (1967)

Washington

---

*P*olitically, Washington is the nation's capital and an engraved invitation to a White House dinner still counts for something. Mostly, however, it's the smaller, more intimate dinners with the frankly powerful that really matter socially although the embassies and the Georgetown regulars do their best to keep things going.

America's richest party-givers and -goers are in and out of Washington as it suits their purpose, and every four years they pause long enough to notice that the nation is once again having its national election. Their response to the campaigns inevitably requires giving and going to more parties, mostly for pet candidates, contributions of big money and attendance at the national conventions.

Ostensibly, the conventions are serious political meetings, but they are a lot more than strategy sessions in smoke-filled rooms, politicking in darkened corners of cocktail bars and carefully orchestrated television extravaganzas in balloon-hung convention halls.

They are social occasions with parties meant to give everybody—the money moguls, delegates, journalists, spouses, party faithful, convention-city biggies and hangers-on of one sort or another—a good time, a sense of belonging and the will to go out and work on the campaign.

Campaigns around the country are luncheons, receptions and banquets with hand-shaking, chitchat and fund-raising as well as political maneuvering and public speeches on bunting-draped platforms. The candidates' wives and children are involved, and when it's all over in November and the people have once again had their say, it's back to Washington with the plans for the inaugural ceremonies, receptions and a series of balls in honor of the new or reelected President.

The allegedly beautiful people of the Democratic National Convention were playing with Hugh M. Hefner's waterfall button early this morning, sending his waiters to the kitchen for everything from steaks to Scotch, tilting his pinball machine and clustering around the color television set that disappears behind a painting.

The party, which is five days older than the convention itself, began last week when the *Playboy* magazine publisher casually invited everyone who is anyone to drop by, and it has been going on ever since. The busiest hours usually are between 11 P.M. and 3 A.M., but at six this morning after continued violent riots in the streets, guests were still hashing and rehashing politics and the brutality—the clubbing and the tear-gassing—that has marked the police treatment of student demonstrators.

This was after Cleveland's Mayor Carl B. Stokes, making his second visit to the multimillion-dollar mansion in a single day, found Boston's Mayor Kevin White swimming around the underground pool. Mr. White was wearing a borrowed swim suit. Some people, including Mr. Hefner's Bunnies, find suits confining. But apparently they had gone to bed.

Earlier, Ed Pauley, Jr., the California oil industrialist whose father has one of the late John F. Kennedy's rocking chairs in his Beverly Hills house, had worn himself out playing Ping-Pong. "This is a nice place," he said on his way to what could have been either a late supper or early breakfast. "I like it here." In a dining room, Mr. Pauley found himself in the company of Jack Valenti, the movie industry czar, and David Merrick, the Broadway producer. It was 2 A.M. then and Mr. Valenti, in a pin-striped suit with Gucci loafers, said he wasn't a bit tired.

"I'm for Hubert Humphrey," Mr. Valenti announced, although that had been clearly established months ago in far more hallowed halls. "I cherish him. I'm trying to help in my small way."

Mr. Merrick said something, too. It was either inaudible or else Walter Cronkite was tuned up too loud. But it was something rather strong about how he was opposed to freedom of the press. He didn't say why. During a quieter moment, Mr. Merrick said that the convention was "a good show—a lot better than Miami Beach," that he was enjoying himself and that Chicago was a lot like Vietnam.

"Those checkpoints," he said, rolling his eyes toward Mr. Hefner's painted Italian rafters. "The barricades. The soldiers. Everything at gunpoint."

Mr. Merrick arrived with Borden Stevenson, who is still known as the late Adlai E. Stevenson's son.

"All I do is see friends and come here," he said from the depths of a huge orange sofa. "It's my fourth night in a row."

At that point, nearby Lincoln Park was the scene of yet another conflict between the police and the hippies, and Mr. Hefner's television was tuned in on Chet Huntley and David Brinkley. The news commentators were telling how everyone who wanted to get into the hall had to wear a rubberized necklace with a metallic ticket that has to be shoved into an electronic slot before it can be validated. Nobody was listening.

"Yes," said Mr. Stevenson, after a quick tour of the billiards room. "This is a comfortable place. Last night I sat around with Hugh. He's a marvelous man."

Mr. Stevenson could have been thinking of Hugh O'Brien, because the actor was off behind a gigantic chess set, whispering into an unidentified lady's ear. But he wasn't.

The real Hugh, Mr. Hefner himself, was in his blue-and-red-print batik pajamas with an olive green velvet bathrobe. He was up against his oak-paneled wall, dwarfing short Mr. Valenti and being dwarfed by the ten-foot stone fireplace.

"I come and I go," Mr. Hefner said before the last fifty of his guests arrived. "I'm a guest as well as a host." Mr. Hefner, as is his style, was drinking Pepsi-Cola. Before that, he was on Fresca.

At 8 P.M., while several guests were downstairs having shrimp salad at the table beyond the two suits of armor in the main hall, he was upstairs having his nails manicured and his hair washed and cut. It was then that he described what his week-long party has been like.

"I always get new insights from Max," he said. "Warren Beatty's being a little withdrawn."

Max is Max Lerner, the columnist. He and Jules Feiffer, the cartoonist, were with Mr. Hefner early yesterday when the threesome was accosted by the police. According to Mr. Hefner and Mr. Lerner, they were walking in Mr. Hefner's neighborhood when the police approached them. They had drawn guns, Mr. Hefner said, and shouted what he called "unprintable obscenities."

"And then I got hit in the back," Mr. Hefner told a news conference. "What we saw were a number of very uptight guys. I've never looked down the muzzle of a gun at close range before."

Mr. Hefner's party was by no means uptight. And at about 1 A.M. Mr. Beatty, the actor, wasn't being at all withdrawn. That was when somebody dragged him away from the television set long enough to meet a foreign diplomat. Mr. Beatty bowed and said a formal hello.

"I knew Warren when he was just on his way to being a genius," Mr. Valenti said later. "He's from Houston, you know. Houston's my home town."

Edward Day, a former postmaster general, heard this and he didn't want to be reminded of Texas.

"President Johnson did us two favors," he said. "First, by deciding not to run and then by not showing up."

This was followed by a general discussion of other favors the President might have up his sleeve, and the news from Richard Rosenzweig, Mr. Hefner's assistant, that he was holding two important telephone messages (and a spare room in the house) for Frank Sinatra.

"Nobody knows what Sinatra's going to do," Mr. Rosenzweig said.

Perle Mesta had been far more predictable. The Washington hostess, whom Mr. Hefner described as "the other big party-giver of our time," appeared earlier in the week. She admired such furnishings as the apple green and lavender Picasso painting over the fireplace and went away telling friends Mr. Hefner was a charming man.

On another night, Leslie L. Carpenter, the Texas newspaperman whose wife is Mrs. Johnson's press secretary, went swimming with Henry Wallace's grandson. Nobody remembers if that was the same day Terry Southern, the author, showed up or whose visit coincided with that of Mrs. Bess Abell, Mrs. Johnson's social secretary. What everybody does remember, however, is that neither Norman Mailer, the author, nor Walter Reuther, the labor leader, had set foot in the door. Mr. Mailer was out with the hippies, observing the riots for a book. And the Reuther signature in Mr. Hefner's guest book is a forgery.

Guests signed somebody else's name now and then so there would be no record of their ever having been inside what in some quarters is still considered Mr. Hefner's Bunny Hutch.

JUBILANT REPUBLICANS CELEBRATE AT SIX INAUGURATION BALLS

January 1969

Thousands of newly entrenched and obviously jubilant Republicans were out celebrating at six different inaugural balls, but there wasn't very much dancing.

Unless guests had tickets for one of the 540 $1,000 boxes with chairs in them, there was virtually no place to sit. And instead of dancing, the $35 ticket-holders stood around in their formal clothes talking, buying drinks and lining up to get a good look at President and Mrs. Richard M. Nixon.

The President's first stop was at the Smithsonian Institution's Museum of History and Technology, where there were perhaps four Negro couples among the nearly five thousand essentially middle-class persons jammed in front of the big white presidential box. They cheered long and hard when he, Mrs. Nixon and their daughters, Julie Eisenhower and Tricia, arrived.

"I think you've heard me speak enough today," Mr. Nixon said after saying, "Thank you" six times to quiet the crowd. And then, looking around at the sea of faces, he added, "I thought this was supposed to be a ball." Everybody laughed.

The President was in a jovial mood, so jovial that he got just a little confused.

"Our theme is 'Bring us together,'" he said. "Duke Ellington says, 'It don't mean a thing if you don't have that thing . . . er . . . swing.'"

He also had trouble introducing the Cabinet members in the box with him. "I keep forgetting this designate thing. Well, we don't need it anymore," he said. "This is the Secretary of Health . . . no, the Secretary of Housing and Urban Development, Mr. George Romney."

Mr. Nixon's family laughed right along with him. Tricia clapped her hands when Julie was introduced. Julie clapped her tiny gloved hands for Tricia. Then everybody cheered and applauded Mrs. Nixon. Noting that Guy Lombardo's orchestra was playing at the Smithsonian, Mr. Nixon remembered that he and Mrs. Nixon were in New York on V-J Day and had gone to the Roosevelt Hotel, where they celebrated World War II's end by dancing to his music. "Guy Lombardo has lasted this long," the President said, "I hope we're dancing to his music when we end the next war."

The Nixon women were properly radiant. The new First Lady wore a glittery jewel-studded mimosa yellow silk satin gown designed by Karen Stark of Harvey Berin. Her husband reminded the ball-goers that eventually the dress would be given to the Smithsonian's First Lady collection.

Julie, who couldn't seem to stop smiling, was in white silk organza trimmed with pale blue satin flowers and beads. Tricia wore pink and white lace covered with more beads. Tricia's escort was Secretary of State William P. Rogers's son, Douglas. Julie was accompanied by her husband, David Eisenhower.

At past inaugurals, the diplomats, like Cabinet members, were parceled out among the various balls. This year, they and the Justices of the Supreme Court were all elegantly ensconced together in beige-curtained boxes at the Smithsonian. And the astronauts joined them at the last minute. This move resulted in the Joint Chiefs of Staff and two governors being redirected to the Sheraton Park ball—a maneuver that enhanced that party considerably. But, as expected, the Smithsonian had more than its share of cachet despite its improvised flower arrangements.

Guests at yesterday's reception for Vice President Spiro Agnew stripped the Smithsonian of $25,000 worth of carnations and roses. They were to have been ball decorations. And it took volunteers all day to find more flowers and arrange them into what a spokesman called "a token display."

137

The Reverend Dr. Norman Vincent Peale and Mrs. Peale were at the Smithsonian. "Mr. Nixon's very calm about this," Dr. Peale said. "Really very collected. He looks like he is enjoying himself."

The Peales followed Chief Justice and Mrs. Earl Warren into the Smithsonian mob. And by the time they arrived, the escalators were not running. They had been spilling too many people too fast on to the second floor.

"Look what I've got," said Ralph F. Becker, a former national chairman of the Young Republican Club. In his hand, Mr. Becker had ball tickets with some astronauts' autographs on them.

"That's a great souvenir," he said. "All you have to do is go over and ask them."

The atmosphere at the other balls was equally blatant, as well as expectant, enthusiastic and crowded. At the Statler Hilton, where there were icicles hanging from the ceiling and the ladies were wearing their fur coats because the ballroom was so chilly, forty "Nixonaires" were distributing the souvenir scarves and other favors. By 10:30 P.M., the Statler bartenders were saying there was a run on Scotch (at $1.50 a highball). Bob Crosby had played nothing but foxtrots. And everyone was wondering which—if any—of the guests were actually among the 30 members of the Nixon and Eisenhower families expected to attend.

Except for highly perfumed ladies in culottes and plunging necklines, lots of Boy Scouts and Senator Everett McKinley Dirksen reciting patriotic songs from the bandstand, nothing much was happening at the Mayflower except Vice President Agnew. He arrived unannounced and waved to the audience while the orchestra went right on playing. Not many people knew he was there.

At the Shoreham, most guests were as interested in seeing Mrs. Henry Ford 2nd, wife of the motor magnate, as they were in staring at Melvin R. Laird, Secretary of Defense, and Winton M. Blount, the Postmaster General. But Mrs. Ford and her husband were late in arriving.

When the President arrived, the Shoreham took on a much more festive air. But the ballroom was so jammed nobody could have danced, even if he'd wanted to—a situation that seemed to please the President.

"The one thing I was afraid of tonight was that I might have to dance," he said.

He also said he had called former President Dwight D. Eisenhower last night and that Mr. Eisenhower had said he was glad Mr. Nixon called because "tonight is the last time I can call you Dick." Mr. Nixon added that, in the eight years he was Vice President, he had never called General Eisenhower "Ike."

The boxes at the Sheraton Park ball went unoccupied for hours, but Sammy Kaye, whose orchestra had played for a lot of the guests' grandparents, did his best to keep everybody busy. Not a song was played without being announced in a melodious and stentorian fashion. When Mr. Kaye wasn't announcing songs, Art Linkletter, the master of ceremonies, was cracking jokes.

At the Washington Hilton, where the big guns from New York and Pennsylvania were gathered, Mr. Nixon spoke to the crowd for fully ten minutes.

"When Art Linkletter at the Sheraton Park saw the crowd of us come in," the President joked, "he introduced me as General Eisenhower's grandson's father-in-law."

On that note, the President introduced his son-in-law and Julie, then Tricia and finally his wife.

"I just assumed everybody knew the lady I was with," he quipped. "She's been the First Lady in our house for twenty-eight years. Now she's the First Lady in the White House."

He went on to repeat the news of his telephone call to General Eisenhower and then he talked about his new Cabinet.

"Since I announced the Cabinet," he said, "every one of them has called on the General. He thinks it's the finest Cabinet in history."

He also had his say about the Supreme Court Justices whom he had seen at the Smithsonian.

"Believe it or not," he said, "all nine Justices were there. This is one time when all nine were dancing to the same tune."

Which wasn't true, of course. Only a couple of the Justices ventured out on the dance floor. But that didn't matter. Mr. Nixon's line kept his audience laughing. When he was planning his inaugural speech, the President recalled, he found a book that told how other Presidents had gone about the task.

"Only one President was unhappy when he became President," he said. "He thought the honor should have come to him earlier in life. This morning as he went to the inaugural parade—it was James Buchanan—he said to a friend that all the enemies he hated and wanted to punish were now his friends and all his friends were dead."

"Oh, no!" moaned Tricia as the crowd roared sympathetically.

The President was undaunted. He talked on about Jefferson ("He said the Vice Presidency is an easy and honorable position and the Presidency is a splendid misery"), praised Mr. Agnew ("I think he's going to be one of the busiest and one of the best Vice Presidents, and don't you think he married above himself, too?"), and then, as at all the balls, he wondered aloud about the lack of dancing.

Before he left the Washington Hilton, Mr. Nixon said he wished he could meet "each one of you from all over this land." He introduced Lionel Hampton, whose orchestra was assigned to the Hilton.

Mr. Agnew had his say, too.

"The appropriate thing for me to say at this moment," he said, "is 'Thank you, Mr. President.' "

Mrs. Adnan Khashoggi, the wife of a Saudi Arabian industrialist, said she'd have liked Mr. Nixon's speech more if it hadn't been for the man behind her. She had to move because he kept pinching her.

"I think I'm going to pass out when I see him," said a young lady who identified herself as Sally Story. "Two gentlemen put me up on their shoulders so I could see, but it was really quite ladylike, believe it or not."

Mrs. James Ellis of San Antonio heard Mr. Nixon while leaning against a pillar. "We didn't want to spend all the money for a box," she explained. "And I've never spent so much money for one post in all my life, and I'm enjoying it."

SOCIALLY, WATERGATE WAS A BORE

Rolling Stone, November 22, 1973

"I called Providence yesterday to order bunk beds for my farm and gave my address as Watergate, and the saleslady asked me, 'Is that one word or two?' I guess not everybody's reading the papers."
—*Bruce G. Sundlun, business executive,*
June 1973, in the Washington Post

The Sam Ervin T-shirt is passé, the country-lawyer senator a budding recording star city-slickered into an album of homilies, biblical teachings and down-home jokes destined for the Christmas trade. Senator Howard Baker's diminished mail shows a sharp decrease in marriage proposals. Can you honestly remember Senator Gurney's first name? Just about anybody could get a seat beneath the giant chandeliers in the Senate Caucus Room, yet nobody who is anybody did. And those who'd like to pass for chic, politically hip and even literate in Washington those last days went about muttering grandly that Watergate was a bore. It was, of course, predictable.

Americans at heart are neophiliacs. What's new and shocking is more exciting than what's old and shocking. The national attention span is like the marriage of puppies, lasting only a few minutes. Even without the Nixon White House's massive campaign to undermine and trivialize the hearings, Watergate couldn't have survived the new, more thrilling escalation of leaks, threats, charges and countercharges leading to Vice President Agnew's resignation.

At the height of Watergate, when every lawyer in town had a piece

140

of the action and the chic of the week was a Senator for dinner who just might drop a clue as to what was going to explode next, did the Washington cocktail circuit care that the White House lied about the bombing of Cambodia? By then, Vietnam was passé, too. The new thing was movie parties, where nobody had to talk. Or think. Such parties, it is said, were invented by none other than Peter G. Peterson, the former Bell and Howell executive who went on to become Mr. Nixon's Commerce Secretary, and they were floor-sitting blue-jeans affairs with Brie, wine, popcorn and everybody's children.

"Our purpose," Mrs. Peterson has explained, "was a whole long wonderful evening with our kids and then a discussion afterwards with everybody, including the kids, talking current issues. The kids loved it. They had a chance to ask Henry [Kissinger] questions and argue with him."

The Petersons have long since moved on, leaving their party idea to others. Now, the gatherings are more likely to be for adults, include dinner and get everyone home in time for the late show. "How else could you entertain George Shultz," one hostess moaned defensively. "He's not exactly the most exciting person to have around."

New York's Bella Abzug immediately said the Gerald Ford confirmation should be considered in terms of his possible succession to the Presidency. When she mentioned impeachment, she could have been speaking of something as quaint as Maureen Dean's hairdo. You remember, the *new* hairdo Mrs. Dean devised to conceal her identity in the streets. The *same* one she showed off for the millions who watch the Dinah Shore show.

Yes, Mrs. Abzug's voice seemed to come across the centuries that separate us from last summer. You could hear similar voices on educational television and read them in the nation's better publications. But did anybody care?

As it turned out, Mrs. Abzug was merely ahead of her time, which isn't chic, either. She and White House analyst Hugh Sidey, who wrote in the October 22 *Time* magazine that "Richard Nixon stands nearer his own resignation or impeachment than ever before," were harbingers of those new and shocking thrills that came on a quiet World Series Saturday when the Middle East was in flames—the evening when the President fired his Attorney General (because *he* wouldn't fire Archibald Cox, the special prosecutor), his Assistant Attorney General (for the same reason) and, finally, through the efforts of the new Attorney General-designate, Mr. Cox himself.

Since that Saturday Night Massacre the investigations, the judicial process and the political infighting have heated up considerably, but the endless embassy parties, a nightly Greek chorus of hors d'oeuvre, buffet tables centered with uptight bouquets and drinks in short, fat glasses, go on. Everyone is very polite. Despite its bloody battles, Washington, like Congress, is a *family*, and families tend to be forgiving. They are kind to their own freshly decapitated. They'll even go to dinner with the same men who tapped their telephones. After all, the old thinking goes, nobody's perfect, tomorrow it may be me. Now, what's this about that $50,000 Howard Hughes contributed to Senator Hubert Humphrey's campaign?

By the same token, Washington can be as easily titillated by gossip. Asked what the town was *really* talking about two days before the Agnew departure, one by no means innocent bystander quickly answered, "Sally Quinn. It looks as if she's going to marry Ben Bradlee."

Sally Quinn, for those of you still clinging to your Sam Ervin T-shirts, is a CBS newscaster. Ben Bradlee is executive editor of the *Washington Post*. And thereby hangs a romance that could stall the dinner forks between plate and mouth, banishing further debate on the matter of arms for Israel.

And what about columnist Joseph Alsop's separation and impending divorce? Now there's a truly *significant* item, and away goes any chance of reviving a discussion of the Cambodia bombings.

"They've let it be known that you can invite him, her or both of them to parties," a congressman's wife said, describing the very social Alsops. "They're living in the same house, you know."

With these interests and this sense of family, it should come as no surprise that the ever gentle benefit ladies quietly removed H. R. Haldeman's initialed briefcase from among the donations to a school auction rather than further embarrass the deposed presidential chief of staff. Or that the Senate wives rallied during the dark hours of Mr. Agnew's troubles to give poor Judy a highly publicized luncheon. Or that Bess Abell, the social secretary from the Johnson administration, was there with cheese and crackers when Peter Malatesta, Bob Hope's nephew and Mr. Agnew's devoted aide, suddenly became jobless. Or even that Mr. Malatesta refused to point a finger at those he is known to blame privately for his mentor's downfall. He, too, wants to survive, particularly since his recent elevation to "co-hostess with the mostest," a sobriquet he shares with the Iranian Ambassador. Survival depends upon playing the game.

"I'm going on with my parties," Mr. Malatesta said bravely just forty-eight hours after the Agnew deluge. "Buffy Cafritz is bringing the lasagne. I'll make the salad. We'll be maybe thirty people and I'll play the new Sinatra album for them. Then next week, I'm having a little sit-down dinner for Eva Gabor and her new husband. . . ."

Such are the priorities, and they have survival value. Looking back on it all, even Alice Roosevelt Longworth, the doyenne of Washington society, has her regrets. "I was never allowed to meet Haldeman, Ehrlichman and those," she said, somewhat wistfully. "I never laid eyes on them. I asked Bill Rogers to sit in a hall with me once and point them out so I would know who they were, but they didn't pass our way. I was so disappointed . . . I did so want to meet Bebe Rebozo."

A T-shirt perhaps for Bebe Rebozo. With Mr. Rebozo, at least, there's still a chance. While he is hardly the darling of the dinner party set, *his* house is *not* for sale, and he is not yet in exile. He is, however, very much on the Watergate agenda. The next big number.

The Senate investigators are keeping him and Howard Hughes ready for what may yet be the thrilling new round. Presumably, Mr. Rebozo and some stand-in for Mr. Hughes would then be sprung, along with allegations about White House manipulations of the Internal Revenue Service, thus restoring the Sam Ervin T-shirt. Mrs. Longworth, however, is not optimistic about her chances for an introduction.

Her good friend, the President, has other things on his mind. And, as she said, "Dick knows they really weren't my dish." What the President apparently didn't know was that Mr. Rebozo, like Frank Sinatra, has his own rather special appeal. Particularly in Washington, which, unlike New York or Los Angeles, is always a little short on glamour. But then, the President has never really understood radical chic, and since Stewart Alsop devoted an entire *Newsweek* column to the *death* of radical chic, how is the President to find out? Mrs. Longworth knows, of course, but Mrs. Longworth knows everything. "I've met some criminals over the years," she said in a moment of reminiscing, "and I've liked them. Forty or fifty years ago, I had a party for a great friend of ours—Albert Fall. Meanwhile, his pockets were rustling with $100 bills. I'm afraid I keep up my associations whether people are criminals or not. I'm very careless about that."

Carolyn Hagner Shaw, by contrast, is never, ever careless. At thirteen, she sat at her mother's knee, learning the social-arbiting business she has since inherited and the inner workings of its publication, the *Green Book*. The volume is Washington's answer to the *Social Register*. Mrs. Shaw took Watergate as something of a personal affront. "It's been perfectly ghastly," she said. "Watergate was blown up so terrifically by the press and TV; why, people were just bored to death, just sick and darn tired of it, and my poor board! Their work was very difficult. They went off to Florida to sit it all out."

The secret board's secret work, done without benefit of red wigs and face masks, although it was alleged that one woman often wore clean white gloves and a lorgnette, was the elimination of what Mrs. Shaw called "the unpleasantly notorious," which, in this instance, meant almost everybody at the White House.

The frankly scandalized Mr. Nixon, however, was accorded a listing, and so was Mr. Agnew. Neither were considered "unpleasantly notorious" enough. Mrs. Shaw said that although the board made the decision, it was her "personal opinion" that "neither the President of the United States nor the Vice President should be removed until [*sic*] they are proved guilty." So there they are, Mr. Agnew with his $10,000 fine, his three years' probation for income tax evasion and the reek of graft, whereas divorcing couples, including the impeccably civilized Alsops, are out.

The Haldemans and Ehrlichmans, never active on the party circuit, did their friends a favor and left town. So did L. Patrick Gray 3rd, acting director of the F.B.I., but that was a blow to some of the hostesses. They counted on him to be their extra man at dinner. Jeb Stuart Magruder, enjoined from making a living by reciting his Watergate testimony on the lecture circuit (thereby raising yet another civil liberties question), was attempting to organize a research service with the support of a few Republican friends. He and Sally Harmony, his secretary, are still speaking although it was her testimony that damaged him. On a good day, when Mr. Magruder is feeling particularly courageous, he may be seen lunching, some say self-consciously, in some of the better restaurants. When he called Sans Souci, which is to Washington's power elite what Mecca is to the Moslems, the maitre d' assured him of a reservation. "Of course, Mr. Magruder," he said, "you still belong to Sans Souci." He is, of course, awaiting sentencing.

John Dean 3rd, whose testimony seriously implicated the President, has not put his $85,000 house up for sale. But he hasn't used it much in recent weeks. He is presumed by Watergatologists to be hiding out, working on a book, the contents of which might be subpoenaed if it were known he was engaged in such a project. Neither he nor the younger Watergators were much socially, mostly because the President didn't want them out on the town. Perhaps he thought somebody would co-opt them. "Listen," one insider explained, "Pete Peterson would still be Secretary of Commerce if he hadn't gone to the parties. They accepted him in Georgetown and the White House hated it."

Aside from his sociability, Mr. Peterson's trouble seems to have stemmed from his delicious sense of humor coupled with a certain insight into the workings of the White House mind, a perception he was willing to share with Democrats as well as Republicans. He spoke of "the German Mafia" at the White House, joked about the heel-clicking required to get along and, of course, had those nice healthy movie parties with the kiddies pointing out that daddy's leaders were not perfect.

Georgetown, which is capable of rising above the furor of day-to-day politics, understands such humor, applauds it regardless of source, and cherishes it. The White House does not, as was proved one day when Mr. Peterson was *moments* late for a press briefing. Herbert G. Klein, then White House Director of Communications, remarked on the Commerce Secretary's lateness, and when it was Mr. Peterson's turn, he, too, had something to say. "Having been on the White House staff," he said, "and knowing in what low esteem they hold Cabinet officers, I try to exhibit my independence in trivial but symbolic ways—by being ten seconds late." The remark was deleted from official texts of Mr. Peterson's talk, but the White House said the words had not been censored, just "overlooked."

Mr. Peterson is nicely surviving the Nixon cold shoulder. He is chief of Lehman Brothers, the investment bankers, in New York. Now he is the darling of the Upper East Side as well as Georgetown.

Once unreachable, James McCord now seeks reporters' attention, even writing them letters. Mostly, the takers are autograph seekers. One of his letters was recently sold to a collector for $40.

"They are all very free for lunching these days," Maxine Cheshire, the *Washington Post*'s society columnist, said of the Watergate dropouts. "They seem to miss seeing themselves in print."

During Mr. Nixon's first year in office, Mrs. Cheshire told David Frost, "Washington is like Paris during the Nazi occupation." She has since revised her views.

"Now it's like the French Revolution," she said. "I feel like Mme. Dafarge knitting in the names as if the guillotine was out in the square. We sit here waiting for more heads to roll."

BARBARA HOWAR: THE CHANDELIER SWINGER

May 1973
From The New York Times Book Review, *May 20, 1973*

People come and people go. Besides Alice Roosevelt Longworth, only a few go on forever. . . .

During World War II, when Barbara Howar was a girl in Raleigh, North Carolina, she would dress up in the WAC uniform her mother brought her from New York, stand along the main highway that links New York and Miami and watch the convoys coming or going between Quantico and Fort Bragg.

Sometimes, she tells us, she stood rigidly at attention, her rifle over her shoulder, her hand over her heart. Other times, she held up her water canteen in what she called a comradely salute to the truckloads of soldiers. Without knowing it, of course, the girl who was to become the Johnson administration's foremost chandelier swinger was dressed up and waiting for the press and, just as predictably, the press obliged. "A photographer took my picture in full uniform saluting a convoy," she writes. "The day it ran in the Raleigh *Times* was one of my proudest moments and probably the beginning of a deep and abiding love for personal recognition."

Yes, that probably was how it all began, her preoccupation with power developing later, and if *Laughing All the Way*, Mrs. Howar's delightful, gossipy, occasionally hilarious memoirs, has a message, it is not what the

Kennedys, the late President Johnson or Henry Kissinger are *really* like (although there is plenty of that, too), but how she managed to survive her own antics and enough personal recognition to choke a goat. That she succeeded and still succeeds despite the fickle whims of a neophiliac society is as much a testimony to the symbiotic relationship between the press and today's disposable celebrities as it is to her charm, guts and delicious wit. But no matter. The naughty party girl has a telling eye for detail, the ability to keep herself in perspective at least some of the time, a graceful way with a story and enough big-name trivia to keep her laughing all the way to the bank.

She is, she explains, another Scarlett O'Hara, rising from the cashmere sweaters, pearls and familial alcoholism of mildly eccentric Southern over-privilege. She slipped painted turtles into the baptismal font, stuffed an alley cat into the choir organ and edited an underground paper called *Epar News,* which is "rape" (she tells us) spelled backward.

She confesses to drawing mustaches on the movie stars in her elder sister's *Photoplay* magazines and screaming "hubba-hubba" into the extension when her sister's boy friends phoned. In turn, her sister cut the heads off her Dionne Quintuplet paper dolls and painted her Scotty dog's paw-nails with Ultra Violet polish. She obviously needed a larger, more worldly pond.

Her mother (whose social encounters with Arab kings are funnier than anything that happened backstairs at the White House) backed the author's relocation in Washington, which, Mrs. Howar suggests, she expected to conquer immediately although her talents were limited to "a vague but cosmetically encouraged resemblance to Grace Kelly and six years of elocution lessons at Miss Bootsie MacDonald's School of Tap and Toe." It is one of her better lines, the kind she was forever flinging to a press corps stuck mostly with dull, official pronouncements.

She had some Congressional connections, too, and, before long, a temporarily indulgent and willing multimillionaire husband, whom she acquired, she says, because one day she woke up "disposed to do the only thing I had not tried: Marriage."

Upward, upward she climbed, putting up with President Johnson's mashed peas, campaigning for his election, raising money for the right charities, and giving and going to all the right parties. Finally, she was holding hands with the President, shopping for Lynda Bird and Luci Baines and combing out Mrs. Johnson's hair.

That she fell with a thud is common knowledge. That the fall was precipitated not by her public comments ("Did you get this recipe off a Frito bag?") or private love affairs (first with an unnamed United States Senator and then with an unnamed White House aide) comes as one of her campier rationalizations. With a perfectly straight face, Mrs. Howar attributes the mess mostly to a hitherto secret Johnson poll purporting to

146

show that the country disapproved of an exuberant political night life in the middle of the Vietnam war.

In any event, the merrymaking went on, but without its only authentic madcap. She was into a divorce, a nasty business following a love-nest raid she cheerfully describes right down to the detectives who jerked her around "for a full-face photograph after they tore off the strap of my nightgown." Survival became more difficult. For the first time, she needed money and needed money fast.

At this point, the story begins to falter. She blew a Washington television news program, the special ministerings of a would-be writing mentor at the *Washington Post* and a New York talk show. These pages, though hardly as tragic as the self-serving paragraphs imply, are not funny. In each case, she seems to have bitten or misunderstood the hand that fed her. But then, analytical thought was never her forte. What matters now, of course, is whether this latest venture, her book, will sell, and the answer is yes, but probably for all the wrong reasons.

When all else fails, George C. Freylinghuysen may be depended upon to toss a little party for a hundred people in his Beverly Hills house, and before long guests are in the trophy room, patting the tiger he shot in India. Dear George. Dear tiger. He also keeps live dogs.
The New York Times (1969)

Los Angeles

Every time it looks as if there is about to be some semblance of social structure in this pastel empire, a new wave of immigration sweeps in, knocking it to bits. A few institutions and individuals have survived these successive invasions. They have adopted a "the more the merrier" philosophy or withdrawn to such button-down bastions as suburban Pasadena. The rest simply fade into the palm trees. One's bank account has a lot to do with one's status, and so does personal accomplishment and how long one's family has lived in California. But it is not smart to scrutinize other people's ancestors. Somebody might find out about one's own.

The new leaders are a lot like the first Vanderbilts, Mellons and Astors. They have their own ideas about what an establishment should be like. They retain membership in exclusive country clubs but use these facilities infrequently. This is because they have all-purpose do-it-yourself country clubs for homes—backyard swimming pools, tennis courts, spacious lawns, exotic gardens and patios with built-in bars and rotisseries.

They are not much for servants either, but not because help is costly. They simple don't want to be bothered with having to eat at the cook's convenience. And although there are still those who believe there is nothing like an Ivy League education, the vast majority look upon the entire East

149

Coast with some disfavor. "What's the matter?" a prominent oil man asked a graduate of Harvard. "Couldn't you get into Stanford?"

The Autumn Cotillion, which is generally accepted here as having society members, had its annual fall dinner and dance last week, and the guest list included only one or two of the Los Angeles names Easterners might consider kindred blue bloods. When asked about this, a member of the new order bristled: "You don't judge society here by traditional standards. Those old people don't do anything. They don't count. Nobody pays any attention to them."

Before the fraternity rejects Los Angeles (population: 6,500,000) as being beyond the social pale, it had better take another look. The edges may be a little rough, but there are diamonds here, and more in the making. As a group these people could buy and sell Newport and most of Rhode Island. But, as one woman put it, "Who'd want to?"

When they are not flinging epithets at one another's credentials, the various social factions are championing their own leaders. One woman's name crops up again and again. She is Mrs. Norman Chandler, the feared and revered wife of the president of the Times-Mirror Company. Within a few months, she expects to have reached a new plateau.

"I will have all the money I need for my music center," she said. "I have another eight hundred thousand or nine hundred thousand dollars to go." The center, a three-building complex not unlike Manhattan's Lincoln Center, is a $20-million project. Mrs. Chandler raised about half that amount herself. The largest building is for Los Angeles Philharmonic concerts. The completion of the center, the construction of which may be viewed from Mrs. Chandler's Times-Mirror office, will fulfill a tenaciously held dream.

"I wanted my symphony to have a home," she said.

Dorothy Buffum Chandler, Buff to friends, was born in Lafayette, Illinois, and raised in Southern California. She met her husband, who inherited his prosperous newspaper, at Stanford University. She has been active in community affairs since 1935. In 1959, after almost single-handedly saving the foundering Hollywood Bowl concerts, she became president of the Southern California Symphony Association. It rules the Philharmonic.

She is a tall, handsome woman with a freckled tan. She is rarely seen without her trademark, a gold identification bracelet with "Buff" spelled across the top in diamonds.

"It opens up," she said. "I keep a $100 bill inside. Sometimes I forget to take money."

Mrs. Chandler's favorite dress designers are Balenciaga of Paris and Norman Norell of New York. "I plan my clothes just as I plan my music center or my house," she said.

She is not sure what she will tackle when the money for the center has been raised. She is a regent of the University of California and a director of half a dozen other civic groups. None provide the stimulation she says she needs.

"What I'm doing is upgrading the country," she said. "I'd like to do something else in that vein. There's no challenge at the University of California. Where could you go? Chairman of the Board of Regents? I don't want that."

The name of another University of California regent, Edward W. Carter, causes virtually no dissension among would-be social arbiters. He is considered society, although he neither seeks nor likes it. "I have three principal interests," he said solemnly. "Business, education and the arts. I do not play golf." Mr. Carter is educated (U.C.L.A. and the Harvard Graduate School of Business Administration), cultivated (his office contains a collection of seventeenth-century Dutch paintings) and successful in business. He is president of Broadway-Hale, the department-store chain.

He, too, is in the final stages of a fund-raising campaign. His goal is $10-million, the bill for the Los Angeles County Art Museum—the largest to be built since Washington put up its National Gallery in 1941.

Among the hundreds of others who figure in the Los Angeles social disorder are Stuart and John O'Melveny, Mr. and Mrs. Martin Manulis, Mr. and Mrs. Robert Pusey Hastings, members of the copper-rich Mudd family, and the Frank L. Kings. They are not necessarily friends, or even acquaintances. The O'Melvenys are elderly lawyers whose progenitor was an Illinois judge who rode to California on a horse in 1850. Their firm, which represents such celebrities as Bing Crosby and James Arness, is eighty-two years old.

"There have been lots of changes since I was a boy," John O'Melveny said. "I can remember when Wilshire Boulevard was a dirt road." Mr. O'Melveny, a University of California at Berkeley graduate who went on to Harvard Law School wearing a Phi Beta Kappa key, raises cattle, quarter horses and English bulldogs. His 1,500-acre ranch is inside the city limits. At sixty-eight, he still ropes and brands his own cattle.

The Manulises, whose elegant hillside house is in Bel Air, are new Californians. She is Katharine Bard of Chicago, daughter of Ralph Bard, Franklin D. Roosevelt's wartime Under Secretary of the Navy. Her husband, born in Brooklyn, is the television and movie producer. He did *Days of Wine and Roses*. "People out here are lonely on a gala scale," Mr. Manulis said. "They have parties because they don't know what else to do with themselves. The big thing is to put up a tent and invite everybody you know."

"We like a simpler life," said his wife. "We don't have full-time help."

"We have a little woman named Katharine Manulis who comes in and does dinner every night," her husband added.

Mrs. Hastings, whose civic-minded husband is a Yale and a Harvard

151

Law School graduate, is president of Las Madrinas, a children's hospital affiliate. In December, it will present thirty-six debutantes at its twenty-ninth annual ball.

"If we could have Chavez Ravine," Mrs. Hastings said jokingly, "we'd have more room for more debutantes."

The senior Mr. King is chairman of the United California Bank, Los Angeles. His daughter-in-law, Mrs. Frank L. King, Jr., is Janine Brooks, a third-generation Californian who is descended from New England whaling captains. She and her husband live in Pasadena. "There's lots of new money," she said, "and people who are willing to spend it. It's not like San Francisco, which has old families. We're full of new families. They keep coming and coming."

When asked about Hollywood, Mrs. King said: "I don't know why anyone would go there unless it would be to go to a movie or to the Hollywood Bowl."

By November 1, when the San Francisco Opera comes to town, society will be well into what may be one of the busiest seasons in its history. On November 9, the Assembly, a group whose fifty members were born in Southern California, will stage its invitational dinner and ball.

And then, on November 14, virtually anybody who wants to be taken seriously will attend the Los Angeles Philharmonic's first performance of the season.

JULES STEIN AND 600 FASHIONABLE HOUSEGUESTS

March 1969

Dr. and Mrs. Jules Stein ended one of the country's biggest, longest and most opulent social extravaganzas here last night by tossing yet another black-tie gala for their six hundred rich and glittering houseguests. The gathering, a supper dance after the premiere of the movie version of *Sweet Charity*, was held beneath the crystal chandeliers of the new $15-million Sheraton-Universal Hotel's baby blue ballroom.

It was in the same room—before those same extravagantly dressed princesses (including Princess Gina of Liechtenstein), playboys, Irish aristocrats, titled Frenchmen, tycoons, interior decorators from three countries, members of nice but no longer inconspicuous old families, movie stars, and all the other odds and ends of what passes for international society—that Bob Hope, master of ceremonies at the Thursday night dinner dance, attempted to analyze the party for posterity.

"A conglomerate festival?" he said hopefully. "A block party that will

152

do wonders for the neighborhood? A benefit for Jules Stein? A P.T.A. meeting in Liechtenstein?"

The Steins' three-day party was all that and more. Dr. Stein is the ophthalmologist who became chairman of the Music Corporation of America, Inc. MCA owns Universal, which made *Sweet Charity*, and owns the Sheraton-operated hotel. And when he and Mrs. Stein made their plans, they obviously were thinking about what their party and the predictable floods of publicity would do for their investments. The Steins are generous and hospitable people indeed, and they never, never talk about money. But MCA picked up most of the tab and can deduct at least part of it as a business expense. Guests estimated that the event must have cost more than a quarter of a million dollars. Besides a free round-trip flight from either New York or Paris (which inexplicably dazzles men and women for whom $1-million isn't really that much money), the Steins' invitations included rooms and meals in their hotel and a long list of excursions. And by Wednesday night, the planes and most of the guests had arrived.

Mrs. Dorothy (Baby Doll) Laughlin, the Palm Beach steel heiress, booked her own flight from Miami and appeared with her maid and her little dog, a *bichon frisée* named Quick As A Flash. Mrs. Bob Six, who was Audrey Meadows until she married the airlines executive, had her maid and her poodle along, too. But thoroughbred racing's stellar Colonel and Mrs. Cloyce Tippett had to send Gooney, their harlequin Great Dane, back to Llangollen, their horse farm near San Diego. "Gooney didn't know he wasn't allowed," said Mrs. Tippett. "I guess he was too big."

On the New York flight, which was seated as if it were a formal dinner party, Margaret, the Duchess of Argyll, and elegant Mrs. Paul Felix Warburg, widow of the investment banker, rode in what would normally be steerage. Iva S. V. Patcévitch of Condé Nast Publications and Adam Gimbel, former chairman of Saks Fifth Avenue, rode up front. The Patcévitches, Josephine Hughes, Bergdorf Goodman's super-saleslady, and Kenneth J. Lane, the jewel designer, played gin rummy throughout the flight. Oscar de la Renta, the dress designer, kibitzed. And Mrs. Joseph Fields, widow of the playwright, read Philip Roth's *Portnoy's Complaint*. "I took the yellow cover off the book so it wouldn't be so obvious," said Mrs. Fields, who apparently had some reservations about the frankly sexy best seller. "I don't think the navy blue underneath was as noticeable."

An accordionist roamed the New York plane, while the Steins' daughter, Mrs. Gil Shiva—her hair up under a black wig—acted as hostess. And Colonel Serge Obolensky did his best to interest everyone in the view from forty thousand feet. "My God, we have some bleak places," he exclaimed somewhere over the Nevada desert. "It looks like the moon."

The Steins and a kilted band of Scottish bagpipers met the planes, and there were bagpipers on the buses to the hotel. Craig Mitchell, the investment broker, rode most of the way with his fingers in his ears.

After registering, the party reassembled for a buffet supper in the hotel's Circus Room. It has tables on a merry-go-round that moves and a decorative animal wagon Mrs. Stein designed herself. "This is my first hotel," she said. "I've done a lot of things in my life, but I've never tried to open a hotel before."

While Mrs. Nion Tucker, one of the de Young sisters whose father founded the *San Francisco Chronicle*, filled her plate with beef Stroganoff, John Shapiro, owner of Maryland's Laurel race track, and Mrs. Shapiro, sister of United States Senator Joseph D. Tydings, were off with Mr. and Mrs. Joseph Lauder. They were talking about who was and who wasn't there.

"I didn't bring my personal maid," Mrs. Shapiro said.

"I didn't either," said Mrs. Lauder.

It was an early night. Yet by noon Thursday, the Sheraton-Universal's lobby might have been the Plaza-Athenée at the height of the spring season in Paris. Everybody was dressed to the teeth. They hugged and kissed each other, rushed wigs off to be set, asked directions to the swimming pool, hauled their jewels off to the hotel safe (which wasn't built to hold the Hermès cases the rich always carry around with them) and got themselves ready to go in a variety of directions.

Mrs. Ernest L. Byfield, Jr., went off to Disneyland in her fifty-five-carat diamond ring and the kind of pink and white polka-dot silk most women reserve for formal luncheons. But she wouldn't let her husband wear a silk scarf with his yellow T-shirt.

"It's too much," she said.

Neither Mrs. Lauder, in a Courrèges dress and an enormous gold, ruby and diamond Maltese cross, nor Mrs. Byfield rode the Matterhorn roller coaster. Mr. Byfield said it was because they were scared. "It's funny," he added. "They aren't at all scared of the real Matterhorn."

Mrs. Cummins Catherwood, wife of the Philadelphia financier, was so excited about Disneyland she could hardly smoke her little black cigars. She rode everything.

"The Caribbean pirates were divine," she said later. "But they wouldn't let us eat ice cream cones on any of the attractions."

Clare Boothe Luce joined the trip to the Jules Stein Eye Institute. She even stayed around after the tour to have her eyes examined—free.

Another group went to the Universal Studios and had lunch in the commissary. Mr. Mitchell played golf. And Mollie Parnis, who dresses the presidents' wives, had a long lunch in Beverly Hills with Mrs. Kirk Douglas.

"I've never seen such security," Miss Parnis said when she returned. "I had to show my room key to get past the hotel guards."

Several hours later, it was time for the two-hour cocktail reception and the three-hour dinner with dancing. Mrs. Nils Onstad (Sonja Henie) was there with her white fringe and several pounds of rubies and diamonds.

The newly-married Duchess d'Uzès (Peggy Bedford Bancroft d'Arenberg) was there, too, along with her look-alike, the Ohio-born Viscountess Paul de Rosière, wife of the jewel salesman, and such others as Artur Rubinstein (whom Gregory Peck affectionately called "the real glamour boy tonight"), a couple of Bernadottes from the Swedish royal family, Governor Ronald Reagan, Mrs. Frank McMahon, wife of the Canadian industrialist, and Gerald Van Der Kemp, the curator of Versailles.

Then there were people with names like von Thurn und Taxis zu und von Furstenberg, Honeychile, Pucci, Rutherfurd, Bloomingdale and von Pantz. Bob Hope said General de Gaulle wasn't there because "he couldn't find a crown that still fitted him."

"It's the most wonderful weekend in the history of mankind," said Mrs. Albert D. Lasker. "You couldn't ask for a better party."

Which seemed to be what virtually all the guests were thinking—right on up through yesterday afternoon at Santa Anita (when Reinaldo Herrera-Uslar, the Venezuelan real-estate tycoon, won $100 in one race and Mrs. Catherwood lost a wager because she didn't follow her usual system of betting the No. 2 horse across-the-board) and the final gala.

THE "INFORMAL" HOUSE THE OHRBACHS BUILT

April 1969

Mrs. Jerry Ohrbach wanted what she called "an informal country house with antiques" and, after a year and a half and several million dollars she thinks that at long last she has it. Nothing too elegant, mind you. Just one or two large drawing rooms full of silver, marble, vermeil and rock crystal, a brick-lined wine cellar with casks for atmosphere and pewter plates and candelabra for little dinners, a tiled barbecue room filled with blooming orchids, and a dining room with green trellises and flowers painted on all the walls and a white stone floor. That sort of thing.

The upstairs rooms are equally understated. Beyond Mrs. Ohrbach's baby blue boudoir is the blue and white tiled roof garden for her potted pansies, her white marble bathroom with its gilded fixtures and blue and white printed silk draperies, and her baby blue bedroom with a built-in television set. After a long, balmy winter, the bedroom gets just a little boring. So for the long, balmy summer, the silk draperies and the bedspread go into storage and the silk panels come down from the walls. In their places go the lavender, blue and pink printed Porthault linen draperies, the bedspread and the matching linen wall panels. It just couldn't be simpler.

The Ohrbachs also have a sauna. It's in Mr. Ohrbach's gray marble bathroom, with brown wood moldings—back of the sterling silver topped clawfoot table. To get to it, Mr. Ohrbach has only to pass through his dressing room, where the walls and closet doors are faced with a couple of hundred thousand dollars' worth of panels from what was once one of the world's best Coromandel screens. Or, as the divinely blond Mrs. Ohrbach explained it, leading the way, her husband can go straight through his gray and brown velvet bedroom. The bedroom also leads off into his study. There, besides a massive desk topped with the usual gold pens and a gold sword imbedded in a giant chunk of crystal, are some of Mr. Ohrbach's leather-bound books. The volumes of Brontë, Hawthorne, Maugham and Brinton's *The Anatomy of Revolution* are especially interesting. They have been gutted to make a false front for a private elevator.

When the Ohrbachs are alone in their house, they like to spend quiet evenings in the wood-paneled library—in a cuddly soft beige sofa with the antique English boiserie on their left. Black and gold painted wood aborigines stand guard over the library's mirrored doorway, and, if an Ohrbach (or the butler in his black alligator shoes) touches the right switch, the aborigines light up. The false-front bookshelves open into a bar in one corner and a men's room in another. Some of the other books are real.

"We like a quiet life," said Mrs. Ohrbach, a Swedish beauty who skis, plays a good game of tennis and works for charities. "We like to stay home and show movies." Mr. Ohrbach, the graying department store heir who turned to Wall Street for his daily bread, isn't part of the movie industry. But, like most of his Beverly Hills friends, he has his own projection room. It's out across the lawn on the second floor of a party house and bar. Mrs. Ohrbach isn't sure how it works.

"You push a button over here," she said, hunting for it along a dimly lighted chartreuse wall. "The screen comes down over there." She pointed at the opposite chartreuse wall. "And the equipment is over here."

"Movie evenings are nice," she added. "We have eight or twelve for dinner, then a lot of others in afterward. The movie usually starts at nine o'clock. The evening's finished by eleven or eleven-thirty."

On one side, the chartreuse projection room faces the tennis courts. On the other is what looks like a natural pond in a garden of palms, giant ferns, azaleas, calendulas, tulips and calla lilies. That's the swimming pool. Instead of having their pool's walls and bottom painted smooth like everybody else's the Ohrbachs had it lined with earth-colored cement set with polished natural gray and beige pebbles. Valerian Stux Rybar, the Ohrbachs' interior decorator, says the pond would look even better if it had ducks floating on it.

"I don't know about that," Mrs. Ohrbach said. "It might be too much trouble."

And besides, the Ohrbachs don't use the pool very much. Not unless sun-happy Easterners come to visit them in the winter or it's very, very hot.

"You just don't," Mrs. Ohrbach explained. "It's there and you look at it. When you have the sunshine all the time, you take it for granted. We try never to sit in the sun."

Except at the beach house in Malibu, where it's all right to stretch out on the sand. But in Beverly Hills, Mrs. Ohrbach has all she can do to keep from tanning. "You can't help it playing tennis," she said.

Mrs. Ohrbach, whose father was a foreman in a steel factory outside Stockholm, rarely goes anywhere in anything less than a Courrèges or a Dior ornamented with jewels. Her sapphires are only slightly bluer than her eyes. Her rubies are pavé so no chinks appear among them. She has a few emeralds around for contrast. And her diamonds are enormous.

"I love Courrèges," she said happily. "I have two street dresses, two pants suits and a coat." She keeps her Courrèges imports (the luncheon uniform in the best Beverly Hills restaurants) and all her other clothes in the countless baby blue closets near her bedroom. Her wigs are in her hairdressing room. And, like many of her fashionable friends, she refuses to wear the new chunky shoes.

"They don't look right," she said. "They're too heavy on me—not very feminine."

At that point, she was seated on the pale yellow suede sofa in the formal yellow drawing room. Behind her was the tortoise table. Her feet rested on a brown and gold handmade Portuguese rug spotted to resemble leopard. Hanging exquisitely heavy over her head was the crystal chandelier.

"It's a comfortable house," she conceded. "It's what we wanted."

III

Their Home Bases

$\mathcal{E}$ven today, there are those who are under the impression that American society sprang full blown from the Mayflower. Yet it is hard to imagine a group less socially brilliant than the hundred motley Pilgrims who arrived in December of 1620 at Plymouth Harbor. By British definition, and that was the accepted definition, there wasn't a gentleman—a man who didn't have to work for a living—in the lot.

The Puritans of the Massachusetts Bay Colony, the New York Knicker-bockers, and the Pennsylvania Quakers weren't exactly sparkling either, but there were a few aristocrats, particularly among the first families of Virginia, Maryland and what became the Carolinas. What matters, however, is that before very long there were land, mercantile, shipping, tobacco, rice, cotton, indigo, and manufacturing fortunes in the making, and with the fortunes came the beginnings of American society.

Society flourished in such cities as Boston, New York, Philadelphia, Baltimore, and Charleston before the American Revolution as well as in New Orleans, which was French, then Spanish, and finally—to some of its aristocrats' everlasting dismay—American.

"Why, she's pure Creole," said a friend who wanted to pay New Orleans's Mrs. Russell Clark the nicest sort of compliment. "She doesn't have a drop of American blood in her."

Through the centuries, the westward migration and a growing country's needs produced new fortunes and new social orders: Pittsburgh steel; Chicago meatpacking; Detroit automobiles; San Francisco's shipping, banking and mercantile empires; Seattle's logging and fishing; and after the Civil War (which, like all American wars, produced new millionaires), Texas got its share of migratory Southerners, cotton, cattle, and finally—just before World War II—the oil billions for which it has become legendary. At the same time Hawaii, the link with Polynesia and the Orient, was growing pineapples and the newest pioneers were building asphalt highways, hamburger stands and even backyard barbecues across the Alaskan wilderness.

What can be said of all these communities is that once the original fortunes were made and the upper echelon formed, the local social order became entrenched and intentionally closed. Neither big new money nor old money for that matter guarantees an outsider anything more than a place in line. These are the cities in which one must prove himself by doing the good works while wearing the right uniform and reciting the right charming lines.

Proper Bostonians work hard, abhor ostentation and are filled with a sense
of noblesse oblige. Thomas Dudley Cabot, chairman of the Cabot
Corporation, is one of them. He also has a sense of humor. Oh, he does, too.
Jack Manning, *The New York Times* (1965)

Boston

Boston's aristocratic old establishment is still dedicated to hard work, education and the pursuit of perfection and truth, but there are moments along the Charles River when the Puritans are not quite so staid and proper as they once were.

The Cabots, the 335-year-old city's social saints, run their carbon-black empire not from quaint, Dickensian quarters but from new Scandinavian-modern offices equipped with chrome-legged chairs and rubber plants. They are also suspected of having voted Democratic in the last national election.

Samuel Eliot Morison admits to having a relative "who is bringing up his daughter so she will be able to ride in a taxicab without feeling like a fallen woman." And Ralph Lowell, who rarely goes anywhere without wearing his Phi Beta Kappa key on a gold chain across his vest, recently startled his conservative colleagues by backing the intention of the Boston Museum of Fine Arts to buy a Picasso painting and a Brancusi sculpture.

"Now, I don't believe in all this modern stuff myself," Mr. Lowell said frankly. "But I'm not always right."

Despite his lofty position at the top of Boston's social hierarchy, Mr. Lowell never seems to have conformed to all of the establishment's rules. The benign, pink-cheeked banker, whose ancestors included pioneers in the

163

New England textile industry, judges, poets and scholars, steadfastly refuses to eat oatmeal in a world where it has been a breakfast staple for more than a century. His daughters went to Vassar College, which to some Bostonians is a questionable educational outpost. And although he is a virtuoso at making and raising money—particularly for Harvard University—he will take no for an answer.

"I'll take $10 from a man when I know I ought to get a lot more," he said sheepishly. "I'm not very good at pressuring people."

Mr. Lowell, whose bushy mustache and round face cause him to look vaguely like William Howard Taft, is chairman of the board of the venerable Boston Safe Deposit and Trust Company and sole trustee of the Lowell Institute, a nonprofit, family trust devoted to adult education. He has been treasurer of the Harvard class of '12 since he, Robert Benchley, Frederick Lewis Allen and Joseph P. Kennedy were graduated.

"When we say college here, we mean Harvard," he said, adjusting himself in the leather swivel chair behind his simple wooden desk. "I can't think of any Lowells who didn't go."

The Adamses, Cabots, Saltonstalls and Forbeses are Harvard men too, and so are most of the other male members of the establishment. But in recent years, the competition for admission to Harvard has become so stiff that some younger members of the old families have had to settle for Princeton and Yale.

"Boston men do not leave Massachusetts for their education," said Mrs. Richard Sears. "But they do go away for the holidays. At Christmas, there isn't a young man around. They're all off in New York, Baltimore or Philadelphia."

Mrs. Sears and Mrs. Morison, although married to impeccable Bostonians, are not Bostonians themselves. They are "foreigners" from Baltimore.

"We could live here a hundred years and it wouldn't help," Mrs. Sears said over a Bloody Mary she was sipping at that awesome enclave known as the Somerset Club. "I'm not sure anyone ever takes us seriously."

After thirty-eight years at what she has come to recognize as the hub of the universe, Mrs. Sears, the former Frederica Leser, has a fair notion of what the members of the establishment are like.

"Boston men don't age," she said. "They never look old. They live such regular lives. Boston women are generally up and corseted by 8 A.M." The Somerset Club, she said, was built by Mr. Sears's great-grandfather, David Sears—a descendant of Joshua Montgomery Sears. The family founder was a merchant who made his fortune in the West Indies trade. When he died in 1857 his money went into a trust fund that is still very much in existence.

"When I tell my Baltimore friends my husband is a trustee it always sounds as if he were in jail," Mrs. Sears said. "A trustee is someone who deals with trust funds."

164

The Somerset Club is a prim, understated old house with a sedate cream-and-red dining room that was once the laundry. Its regulars include everybody who is anybody in Boston and two women who ask for "dungarees" when what they want are daiquiris. Mrs. Sears likes to lunch there because lamb kidneys are often on the menu.

"No Sears eats entrails," she said, "so I have to eat them when I'm out."

Mr. Sears and his wife, an imposing woman who is given to dresses with sleeves, pearls, heirloom diamond pins, little hats and sensible shoes, live in a typically upper-caste house. The exterior is red brick. Stone steps climb up to the vestibule (where newsboys regularly place copies of *The Christian Science Monitor* now that the *Boston Transcript* is defunct) and into the shadowy hallway. The high-ceilinged, peach-colored drawing room contains such treasures as a huge tapestry, an aging apricot-velvet sofa, a gilded mirror, a crystal chandelier, a carved-marble fireplace flanked by antique jardinières, a baby-grand piano and a painted Oriental coffee table.

Bunko, the Searses' "slightly incorrigible Corgi," prowls about the room periodically, hunting for water. It is in a hand-painted Chinese bowl near the fireplace.

Admiral and Mrs. Morison's house, built in 1870, is similarly arranged. And on New Year's Eve, formally dressed party-goers gather in the drawing room to dance beneath the chandelier attached to a teapaper ceiling—a shiny and cherished vestige of the China trade, which brought Boston a lot of its old money.

"We can never have very many guests," said Mrs. Morison, the former Priscilla Randolph Barton. "Only eighty or ninety at a time. It is very like London with interesting people mixed up together. Until I met the admiral, I thought professors were puny, little pipsqueaky people, but they're not."

Besides being Harvard's official historian, Admiral Morison is the author of such works as *Admiral of the Ocean Sea: A Life of Christopher Columbus,* which won a Pulitzer Prize; the fifteen-volume *History of U.S. Naval Operations in World War II* and *The Oxford History of the American People.* He does not approve of "blowing money the way the European aristocracy does."

"They don't put on any dog here," he said, referring to his lifelong friends. "They try to do something for the community."

Boston's sense of noblesse oblige is ingrained. And although most aristocrats deny that they look down on persons who do not spend a lot of their leisure time working for civic projects or improving their minds, they do. They also have little patience with those whose code of ethics is not absolute. "Moral values do not change," said Thomas Dudley Cabot, chairman of the Cabot Corporation. "I was brought up to have a strong sense of noblesse oblige, and I brought my children up that way." Mr. Cabot, a properly sack-suited Harvard overseer, former president of the United Fruit Company and first director of the Department of State's Office of International Security Affairs, is equally outspoken about his ancestors. He is "tired of being teased about being a Cabot," believes some of his forebears "probably lived in shanties" and acknowledges that he is a descendant of a passenger on the *Mayflower*.

"The Cabots got their money the hard way," he said dryly. "Samuel went to work for T. H. Perkins, a great merchant trader and shipowner. He married the boss's daughter."

EXERCISING AND THE STRENUOUS WALTZ

February 1965

Bostonians are an elegantly athletic lot, and they prove it periodically by swirling, twirling and swooping about in graceful dance patterns until beads of perspiration materialize on their aristocratic brows and they are short of breath.

This particular form of exercise, no more strenuous than touch football, is known as the Viennese Waltz. Boston's devotion explains why there are Waltz Evenings—one of which was held here Friday night in the Sheraton Plaza Hotel's spacious ballroom. "We don't play any of your slow English or American waltzes," Ruby Newman said as he was about to raise his baton for the first set. "We play fast—very fast."

On that note, Mr. Newman and his twelve-piece orchestra began to work their way through a vast repertory that included the waltzes of Johann Strauss (who visited Boston in 1872), Oscar Straus, Franz Lehar, Leroy Anderson, Ravel and Khachaturian. Most of the sheet music was beige with age.

"I collected a lot of it in Salzburg before the war," Mr. Newman said.

During the first set, which began at 9:30 P.M. and lasted twenty minutes, Richard K. Thorndike 3rd, parish-properties administrator for Emmanuel Church (Episcopal), swept Mrs. Thorndike onto the floor. They and scores of others moved down-two-three, around-two-three one side of the ballroom and then crossed-two-three, below-two-three the stage.

They had circled the room and encircled a three-tiered arrangement of more than one hundred pink carnations on a patch of grass in the center of the floor before the music ended. No one, even women in sleeveless ball gowns of chiffon and lightweight silks, seemed to notice that the temperature in the ballroom was only 59 degrees.

166

There was a five-minute rest before the dancers went whizzing off again like a giant cascade of confetti. This interlude was punctuated by the popping of champagne corks, the ladling of fruit punch into cups, the development of a crowd at the bar and the discovery that, despite the falling snow outside, Arthur Drinkwater had decided to come to the party.

"He's eighty-four," a woman at his table whispered. "He's quite amazing."

"I'm eighty-five, and it is not amazing," Mr. Drinkwater replied, brushing at the patch of white silk that is his hair. "I play tennis—singles, mind you—I swim, I figure skate. I don't get out of breath like the other fellows unless I have to carry my partner. But I shan't dance every dance."

Mr. Drinkwater, a lawyer who was graduated from Harvard College in 1900 and from its law school in 1903, thinks waltzing is an art as well as a pleasant diversion.

"You should move along like a cat or a thoroughbred horse," he said, delivering himself of what he meant to be a catlike step or two. "It must not be jumpy."

The Right Reverend Frederic Cunningham Lawrence, Suffragan Bishop of the Episcopal Church in Boston, and his wife were among waltzers whose step did not look jumpy. Mrs. Lawrence is a stately woman who wore green brocade, a pair of dangling earrings and a simple seed-pearl necklace. The bishop, an imposing figure who stands very straight, was graduated from Harvard in 1920. Most of the women wore bouffant gowns, not much makeup and very little jewelry. Orchid corsages have not gone out of style, however, and some of the hairdos looked like those worn by Queen Victoria.

The men, most of whom seemed to be graduates or undergraduates of Harvard, of the Massachusetts Institute of Technology or of Boston University, wore tail coats or dinner jackets. Charles Woodard, a young publishing executive, had a gold chain across his waistcoat, centered by what an observer mistook for a Phi Beta Kappa key. Actually, it was the insignia of the United States Marine Corps. Mr. Woodard also wore classic dancing pumps with faille bows at the arches. He was graduated from Middlebury College. With Mr. Woodard at one point during the evening was Miss Valerie Rough (Radcliffe '66), whose grandmother is credited with saving the Viennese Waltz from extinction. She is Mrs. E. Sohier Welch, a petite, blue-eyed Quaker with a fringe of gray hair across her forehead. And although Mrs. Welch did waltz, she spent most of the time with friends on a large, fenced-in dais opposite the ballroom stage. She does not approve of the saxophones Mr. Newman has in his orchestra.

"It should be all strings," she said.

The waltz was introduced here in 1834, when Mrs. Harrison Gray Otis, Jr., a society belle of the period, and Signor Lorenzo Papanti, Boston's dancing master, performed it in Mrs. Otis's Beacon Hill mansion. Other social leaders, including Mrs. Otis's father-in-law, were aghast at what he called "an indecorous exhibition." But the waltz survived until the Jazz Age.

"My husband and I loved it so much we decided to invite twenty-five couples to a waltz party," Mrs. Welch said. "They came to our house, and we danced to records. The idea became so popular, we had to move to a hotel."

The Welches gave their resuscitation party in 1934 in the high-ceilinged drawing room of their house in Louisburg Square. In 1852, that room had been the setting for Jenny Lind's marriage to her accompanist.

Having saved the waltz, Mrs. Welch now concerns herself with keeping America beautiful. She is an outspoken critic of billboards on highways, of litterbugs and of laws that prevent the sale of birth-control devices in Massachusetts.

There were about three hundred dancers in all, and the younger set included postdebutantes, budding lawyers, physicians, stockbrokers, bankers and a few scholars. Christopher Bay, stepson of C. Michael Paul of New York and Palm Beach, said it was his first "all-waltz evening." He is at Boston University.

"I'd never go to Harvard," he said in an aside calculated to scandalize Boston's upper echelons. "I'd rather see real Americans. I'm not sure Harvard is real."

At 11 p.m., there was a waltz contest. It produced four winning couples who will compete in May for the "tops-of-the-year" award. And shortly before midnight, a procession of young renegades made their way to the bandstand to ask Mr. Newman to play something besides a waltz. One couple asked for the tango (granted). Another requested a foxtrot (granted). And a third said they wanted to twist.

"Not tonight," Mr. Newman said firmly. "But I can't stop you from twisting to the waltz."

Mr. Newman also played a succession of polkas, which have always been permissible at Waltz Evenings, provided they do not start until after midnight. And he introduced "Bluesette," a New York waltz with a touch of jazz.

"You can applaud if you like, and hiss if you don't," he announced.

A third of the party-goers, including Michael Robbins (Williams '49), hissed politely.

"It's not elegant," said Mr. Robbins, one of the waltz-contest winners. "The waltz is supposed to be elegant."

By 12:35 A.M., earrings that had been lost during the evening were being retrieved, and it was time to go home. Mrs. Courtenay Crocker, Jr., director of the Waltz Evenings, said goodbye to the last of the energetic dancers. The temperature in the ballroom had risen to 64 degrees. And the orchestra played "Goodnight, Ladies" as a waltz. Mr. Drinkwater said he thought the whole thing had been as dignified as usual.

Bostonians like to remember the stormy night Mrs. Robert Homans turned up at the Somerset Club asking to be put up for the night. She wanted a room in her husband's club, she said in unmistakably aristocratic tones, because the roads were impassable and she could not get back to her home. But the club, a rigid and supremely awesome establishment, refused her. It had a house rule forbidding a room to a woman alone.

"In that case," said the impeccably correct Mrs. Homans, starting toward the door, "I'll go out and get my taxi driver."

Abigail Adams Homans got her way, of course, which is more than can be said for the Boston Fire Department.

When firemen were hustled to the club to douse a major blaze, the fire had to wait while an overly zealous employee showed them the way to the service entrance—the more accessible front door being for the exclusive use of members, their wives, widows and guests. It is an episode that still enchants Mrs. Homans.

"We always pride ourselves on our sense of humor," she said recently. "But sometimes we're pretty solemn fellows."

Mrs. Homans, a widow in her seventies, is more than a small, vigorously independent and elegantly wrinkled woman who has not changed her hairstyle in forty years. She is like Boston itself—stanchly and superbly there. And like her great-great-grandmother, the Abigail Adams who met George III and hung her laundry in the East Room of the White House, she is an outspoken observer of life as it is lived among what she calls "frightfully nice people."

"When it comes to style, Boston doesn't have much," she said, settling herself on a flowered sofa in her Beacon Hill apartment. "We all have what we call a hat. You know, they cover your head. My daughter makes me burn them now and then."

Mrs. Homans had been reading a biography of Queen Victoria ("I dislike her very much. The late Mr. Justice Holmes is my only 'heroine'"). And every time she wished to make a point absolutely clear, she slammed the palm of her hand against the book, doing heaven knows what kind of damage to her diamond and platinum watch. "My father tried to make a lady out of me by sending me to a convent, but it didn't take," she said.

In Quincy, where she became rampantly apathetic about her clothes, her life revolved around tennis, snowshoes, sailing, fishing and riding. And then along came Mr. Homans, an upper-caste lawyer with a Harvard degree. He was followed by summers on the South Shore of Massachusetts Bay, and the couple's four children.

"I did very well," she said. "I arranged it that our children should not drown."

Her daughters, Mrs. Henry L. Mason and Mrs. Carl Joyce Gilbert, are graduates of Radcliffe, and her sons, George and Robert Homans, like their Adams and Homans ancestors, were graduated from Harvard.

Mrs. Gilbert is chairman of Radcliffe's board of trustees and acting president of the school for the year 1964–65. Robert is a successful San Francisco lawyer, which proves to Mrs. Homans that Adamses-Homanses are not all stay-at-homes. And George is a professor of sociology at Harvard.

"I don't quite know what sociology is," said George's mother, blinking her large brown eyes, "and it's probably just as well."

Mrs. Homans does know that Boston has "a regular society, a regime under which you live and do the things you ought to do," but the existence of such a system does not prevent her from doing what she likes.

"If I stood in the Common on my head, people'd say, 'Oh, that's just Abigail Homans.' They wouldn't pay any attention. We're conventionally independent."

But there is a hitch Mrs. Homans neglected to mention. She would not dream of standing on her head in Boston Common. And although Boston's elderly aristocrats can and do essentially what they want to do, they rarely seem to want to do anything less constructive than working ten hours a day, turning their fortunes over to educational, cultural and philanthropic institutions without much fanfare, and living incredibly quiet, community-minded lives.

"I'm the last of the old Adamses," she said, speaking of her own generation. Charles Francis Adams, a nephew, is chairman of the Raytheon Manufacturing Company. "My mother was a Crowninshield from Salem. They were shipping fellows. My father was John Quincy Adams, named for his grandfather. He was a great raconteur, if that's what you call them. My father never wrote anything—not even a letter, I think."

Her Uncle Brooks left her the Oriental rugs on her apartment floor, and some of her English watercolors. Her Uncle Henry, who took her to Washington and to Europe, was the author of *The Education of Henry Adams,* which she has read several times. An ornate, gilded panel Henry bought in Japan in the 1880s hangs behind her living room sofa. And beside a window is "an inoffensive little table"—the first Abigail Adams's desk.

Mrs. Homans is not sure Boston is as wonderful as some Bostonians would have the world believe. "It doesn't look the way it used to," she said, "and no one's made a formal call on me for thirty years."

On the whole, Philadelphians, including (left to right) Franklin Watkins, Mrs. Alexander Biddle and Samuel Chew, would rather be in Philadelphia. In Boston they ask, How much does he know? In New York, How much is he worth? In Philadelphia, Who were his parents? Sometimes they get answers.
Neal Boenzi, *The New York Times* (1965)

Philadelphia

"The orchestra," as they say here when they are not talking about "the university" or "the railroad," played a concert for the 108th anniversary of the Academy of Music Saturday night, and three thousand of the faithful were there. The festivities, including a champagne supper and ball for 1,600 as well as the concert by what is elsewhere known as the Philadelphia Orchestra, automatically emptied Rittenhouse Square, Society Hill, the Main Line and parts of Delaware. It also produced $130,000 for the enhancement of the academy.

The aristocratic invasion force was dominated by white-haired grandmothers who resolutely refuse to paint their eyebrows, eyelashes or lips. These stalwarts clomped in out of the sleet and snow wearing lace or brocade evening gowns, pearls and old-fashioned rose-cut diamonds, mink coats garnished with white orchids, and stadium boots.

In their wake were the regal-looking matrons with the short, simple hairdos, the classic evening gowns, the more elaborate jewel collections and the pre-Revolutionary ancestors. They were accompanied by their equally substantial and Ivy League husbands ("the university" is Pennsylvania, but Harvard is almost as acceptable) and their married or unmarried children.

"What gets us out," said the silver-haired Mrs. Alexander Biddle, "is

173

our sense of what is important. There's really nothing in the world like the academy."

Nor is there anyone quite like Mrs. Biddle. She is a descendant of Nicholas Scull, who mapped out Philadelphia and the State of Pennsylvania for William Penn only to have his daughter, Mary, marry a Biddle who named their son Nicholas.

"That was the end of the Nicholas Sculls," Mrs. Biddle said matter-of-factly. "All the Nicholases are Biddles now. We are related, my husband and I, once through our ancestors and once by marriage."

The Biddles, whose most illustrious forebear was the Nicholas Biddle who ran the United States Bank for President James Monroe, were among the more than one hundred guests who nibbled spinach and caviar canapés at Mr. and Mrs. Stuart F. Louchheim's preconcert reception and dinner in the academy's gold-and-white ballroom. Mr. Louchheim, president of the academy since 1957, circulated among his friends while his wife greeted them at the door.

"You honestly need two pairs of gloves to get through an evening like this," she said, tugging at the white kid glove on one arm. "I'm saving my longest ones for the ball."

Pearl Buck, winner of Pulitzer and Nobel prizes for Literature, was among the early arrivals. She swept in wearing a full-length white mink coat with a wide flounce of white fox.

Behind her were other academy admirers, such as Mrs. Francis Boyer, whose husband is chairman of the board of Smith, Kline and French; C. Wanton Balis, Jr., who heads Balis and Company, reinsurers, as well as the board of "the orchestra"; Mrs. Walter H. Annenberg, wife of the publisher of the *Philadelphia Inquirer, TV Guide* and the *Daily Racing Form,* and Mrs. John Wintersteen, president of the Philadelphia Museum of Art.

"I'm a music and art person," Mrs. Wintersteen said. "I'm sorry my brother had to miss tonight." Mrs. Wintersteen's brother is Henry P. McIlhenny, the art connoisseur and collector. He is in South America, gathering additional treasures. "I have works by Matisse and Degas, but I'm especially interested in Picasso," Mrs. Wintersteen said. "If I remember correctly, I have nine of his paintings and five of his drawings."

The dinner guests, who sat at long tables centered with gilded candelabra, white candles and fragrant fresh mimosa, were sipping coffee by the time the marbled corridors of the academy's downstairs lobby were beginning to brim over with concert-goers. And at 8:30 P.M., the two groups began to merge, spilling over the gold-and-white staircases and into the elaborate scarlet-and-gold auditorium that is Philadelphia's answer to Milan's La Scala.

Mrs. Thomas S. Gates, widow of the banker who was also president of "the university" through the 1930s, and stepmother of Thomas S. Gates, Jr., president of the Morgan Guaranty Trust Company, was in a curtained box, studying the program (Leontyne Price, Franco Corelli and Van Cliburn were soloists) long before the Pittsburgh Symphony's William Steinberg raised his baton. Two other determinedly cultural watchdogs, Mrs. T. Carrick Jordan and Mrs. Thomas D. Thacher, were not far away. Mrs. Jordan is the daughter of the late Mahlon H. Kline—the Kline of Smith, Kline and French—and the sister of C. Mahlon Kline, honorary chairman of the pharmaceutical company's board. She allows, she says, "everyone around here" to call her "Mommy J." Mrs. Thacher, whose good works range from committee responsibilities for the Devon Horse Show to sending food parcels to prisoners of war, is, as she puts it, "one of the Morrises."

"We are descended from Captain Samuel Morris," she said simply. "He was Washington's bodyguard troop captain during the Revolution. The Morrises have always lived in Philadelphia."

Eight generations of Morrises, including Mrs. Thacher, were born in the old Morris mansion, now a museum. And her father, the late Effingham Buckley Morris, was president of the Girard Trust Company and a trustee of "the university" as well as of "the railroad," which outsiders call the Pennsylvania Railroad. The late Mr. Thacher was President Herbert Hoover's Solicitor General.

The concert ended at 10:45 with a scramble at the check room, and before long the parade to the nearby Bellevue-Stratford Hotel had begun. Meyer Davis, who is almost as essential to Philadelphia as he is to New York, and his orchestra were stationed in the ballroom behind a hedge of fresh pink-and-red carnations. Every now and then, he would lean down to chat with such friends as Miss Enid Curtis Bok, daughter of Mrs. Curtis Bok of the publishing family.

"I'm like the father of the bride," Robert Montgomery Scott said as he shook hands at the ballroom doorway. "Mrs. George Cheston and I are co-chairmen of the anniversary committee, but I feel as if I hadn't done a thing."

The party was so large that it spread not only to the ballroom balcony but to six additional rooms as well—all within sound of the foxtrot and waltzes. And as the dancers swept around the floor, they were reflected in mirrors and in the tin foil that had been wrapped around the ballroom pillars.

The hotel had a staff of 170—110 waiters and sixty kitchen helpers—to serve the party, and there were twenty bartenders to pull the corks of a thousand bottles of 1961 Bollinger very dry champagne—and lots of bright young things to consume it. The proceedings did not end until 3 A.M. and at noon there were dowagers out on the Main Line who had still not had their breakfasts.

175

The rugged grandeur of the Big Sur is a lure to San Franciscans who love
the natural world. Mrs. Nathaniel A. Owings, the architect's wife, worked
her collages at their mountain-hugging retreat overlooking the Pacific, and
fought to save the sea otters.
Carl T. Gossett, Jr., *The New York Times* (1963)

San Francisco

The great tycoons are dead, and socialites do not shoot at one another anymore, but life in American society's Western outpost has lost little of its glamour.

San Francisco blue bloods, whose *Mayflower* may have been a covered wagon that stumbled into town in 1849, are as authentic as the gold their forebears sought, and almost as glittering. They are vigorous, acquisitive, outspoken, educated, well traveled, fashionably dressed and extravagantly housed. Although their money is relatively new, there's plenty of it. It is a small, opulent world with a Gay Nineties flavor, but good taste usually prevails, and nobody has more fun than its leaders, several of whom are only one generation removed from the gaudy, hell-raising pioneers.

At the top are such thoroughly different people as Mrs. George T. Cameron, Mrs. Adolph B. Spreckels, Miss Louise A. Boyd and William W. Crocker. They are sometimes out of touch with life as it is led by the easygoing younger generations, but it is these one-of-a-kinds who gave and continue to give this city its elegance, cosmopolitan feeling and many of its cultural institutions.

Mrs. Cameron, a petite dynamo who played the saxophone until her husband got rid of it, is in her seventies. She is the oldest of the three de

177

Young sisters, daughters of the late Michael Henry de Young, the fire-eating publisher of the *San Francisco Chronicle*. (The late Mr. Cameron also was publisher of the *Chronicle*). Being a de Young can be a problem.

"I go to an awful lot of board meetings," she said recently. "I don't want to be a member of anything unless I can be active. But there are lots of de Youngs. I suppose we should keep quiet now and then. Sometimes I try to."

Mrs. Cameron is concerned with everything from foundlings to the San Francisco Opera, which has its gala opening Friday night.

"Music is my first love," she said. "I used to have musicales here at the house, but I had to give them up. The guests kept retiring to play poker."

As she talked, Mrs. Cameron moved about the grounds of Rose Court, the pink stucco chateau she and her husband built in suburban Hillsborough in 1913. Whole rooms were bought in France, dismantled, shipped and re-assembled here. "At first, it was too small—all very *Ladies' Home Journal*," she said, grandly flicking an ash from the cigarette in her ebony-and-gold holder. "Then we added the music room."

Mrs. Cameron, whose constant companion is a black poodle named Piccolo, wears Balenciaga clothes and visits and is visited by the Duke and Duchess of Windsor. She adores the Ritz Hotel in Paris, and like virtually everyone in society's upper echelons, she's plagued by the servant shortage.

"I haven't had a footman in years," she said. "I had a Chinese cook for thirty-seven years. After that, I had seventeen cooks in three months. I think New York or Hollywood is getting all the good people."

Mrs. Spreckels, who can remember when there was no such thing as an Elsa Maxwell, is the widow of the sugar king. She lives in town in an ornate white-stone house. She is renowned for her gold plumbing, French commodes, a custom-built Rolls-Royce with a mink lap robe, and a deeply ingrained sense of community responsibility.

According to Miss Boyd, the mining heiress, polar explorer and first woman to be made a fellow of the American Geographical Society, a lot that's said and written about the Old Guard is not true.

"People are always exaggerating," she said. "They get carried away. For instance, it's not true I shot nineteen polar bears in one day. That's a crazy story. I think it was only five or six, and that was for food." For years, Miss Boyd lived at Maple Lawn, a vast, wooded estate in suburban San Rafael. The house with its fifty-seven-foot library had been in the family since 1872. Last year she sold it to the Elks and moved into town. "Big estates have outlived their usefulness," she said. "I'm having a hard time adjusting to the city—the fog and the fire sirens. But the house was too big."

Her new home, on the top floor of a luxurious apartment building, is crammed with treasures, including Coromandel screens, Irish chandeliers and a priceless collection of Queen Anne chairs. She no longer has room to entertain forty at a formal dinner. "All I have is a personal maid, a cook, a butler, and a cleaning woman," she said. "Well, no. That's not right either. There's the chauffeur."

Miss Boyd, whose debut took place a year after the 1906 earthquake and fire, has been presented at the British court, and she's exceedingly feminine despite her rugged adventures at the North Pole. She loves Mainbocher clothes, hats ("I've never thought of going without one unless it was to the dentist's") and flowers. "I don't feel dressed unless I'm wearing flowers," she said. "Even in Greenland, I'd find something and wear it with a safety pin."

Mr. Crocker, retired board chairman of what is now the Crocker-Anglo Bank, is the Groton, Yale and Harvard Law School-educated grandson of Charles Crocker, one of San Francisco's fabled Big Four. Shortly after the Civil War, when Eastern millionaires were acquiring their chateaus, racing stables, tennis courts and yachts, Mr. Crocker, Leland Stanford, Mark Hopkins and Collis P. Huntington were helping to build the Western railroads. By the time William was a young man, the Crocker millions were secure.

"I started at the bank as vice-president," he said. "I must say I was astonished. I hadn't expected it at all." Mr. Crocker is a founder of the San Francisco Museum of Art, which will be the scene of the Tiffany Ball, a museum benefit to be held after opening night at the opera. He also was the museum's first president.

The Crockers live atop a mountain in Hillsborough, in a house that's nearly as grand as William Randolph Hearst's San Simeon. Its kitchens alone are as large as a downtown hotel's, and its driveway is a two-and-a-half-mile curlicue. The family's first home is now the exclusive Burlingame Country Club.

To the Old Guard, there is no such place as Hillsborough, although it has had a post office for several years. When their families settled down in the early 1900s, the wooded hills down the peninsula were Burlingame, and Burlingame they remain. Only the new people call the area Hillsborough.

Whether it's Burlingame or Hillsborough, the suburb is one of San Francisco's most elegant. Its great estates are palatial, old and formal. All have extensive gardens and swimming pools. The elderly residents play endless rounds of bridge, and the very young ask to be excused so they can go to Candlestick Park and watch the San Francisco Giants. Woodside, a rustic area that goes in for horses, dogs and the outdoor life, is another recherché peninsula suburb. Its contemporary homes have understated furnishings and extensive landscaping.

William Wallace Mein, Jr., president of Calaveras, a division of the Flintkote Company, and master of the Los Altos Hunt, lives here with his wife. She is a popular, dark-haired beauty who is active in dozens of community endeavors. "We can't have foxes for our hunt," Mr. Mein said humorously. "They'd lead us all into a swimming pool." But the hunt goes

179

on. Coyote scent is dragged over the terrain. Then along come the hounds to lead horses and riders over the course. Mr. Mein, son of an international mining engineer, is a fourth-generation Californian. His conservative blue business suit, button-down shirt and silk tie are as Eastern as Harvard, his alma mater. But his belt may be strangely Western. He has a tooled calf belt with an outsize silver buckle commemorating a horse race he won.

On the eastern shore of the Bay are the suburbs of Berkeley, essentially a University of California town, and the social enclave of Piedmont. In Marin County, across the Golden Gate Bridge, fragments of society share Ross, Kentfield, Tiburon and Belvedere with artists, writers and executives on the way up. According to Reese Wolfe, Marin County author, there may be bright young members of the Junior League who've never heard of Mrs. Spreckels or Mrs. Cameron. Mrs. William J. Ferguson, Jr., wife of a physician and member of Belvedere's chic sailing set, is not so sure.

"We know about these people, and they are unbelievably glamorous," she said. "They help make San Francisco what it is. But if we had their money, we wouldn't buy full-length chinchilla coats. We'd buy another boat."

The Fergusons, who have nine boats and four children, live on a private lagoon. It is not unusual for a supper party guest to remove her high heels, step onto one of the sailboats tied to the dock that serves as an outdoor living room, and go sailing during the party.

The family goes to concerts in San Francisco, skis at Squaw Valley and in Switzerland and sightsees in the remote corners of Europe and Asia. It also reads books.

"We find our friends on an interest level rather than a geographical or social level," Mrs. Ferguson said. It is a philosophy shared by Mrs. Paige Monteagle, whose husband belongs to a prominent financial family.

"Sailing people get together," Mrs. Monteagle said, "and so do swimming people or tennis people. It really doesn't matter who you are but what you're interested in."

Aspiring socialites can learn a lot from Mrs. Monteagle. Almost everything she says and does is fashionable, whether it's lunching in the Captain's Room at Trader Vic's ("No one sits anywhere else"), bemoaning the loss of the St. Francis Hotel's Mural Room ("It was a tragedy when they closed it for lunch"), commenting on Oakland ("It's not San Francisco"), paying $40 a ticket for a ball ("In New York it's much higher"), selling her town house ("It became the British Consulate") or describing her taste in drinks ("I'll have a Suffering Bastard. It's a very dry rum drink with a cucumber in it").

Among other things that are "in" in San Francisco society today are living rooms full of potted orchids, skirts long enough to cover the knees, any kind of royalty, the twist, elephant jokes, Oriental servants, the Villa Taverna—a restaurant with members—Lake Tahoe and the St. Francis Yacht Club. Only "out" people complain about the fog.

There's something irresistible about a costume ball, and virtually no city is
without them. In Miami, Dr. and Mrs. George C. Menninger (left) and
Mr. and Mrs. Lloyd L. Dilworth celebrated "The Ziegfeld Era" with Dr.
Benjamin Fine dressed as an Arab sheik. Such events always require lots of
feathers, rhinestones as big as tennis balls and a straight face.
Carl T. Gossett, Jr., *The New York Times* (1965)

Miami

When Henry M. Flagler was developing Palm Beach in 1893, he said it was for his elegant friends, and that West Palm Beach across Lake Worth was for their servants. Two years later, he ran his railroad south, and Miami was incorporated without either his blessing or his curse. And thus it has remained—a youthful city of indeterminate social standing.

The adventurers who spent the first half of this century making fortunes in real estate, construction and mortgage banking are still going to the office, not yet having run out of ways of making money. And their wives, whose tastes do not include papering the walls with hot-pink silks, stalking about in feathered chaps or calling everyone "darling," find pleasure either in working for the community's budding cultural institutions or in going to luncheons where they play bridge for money and the privilege of taking home the floral centerpieces.

But despite Miami's reticence, recognition is on the way. Waves of newcomers have invaded this exotic, poinsettia-dotted oasis, bringing their big names, their corporate images and their status with them. And instead of organizing a posse to cut these invaders off at the pass, Miamians, being either polite Middle Westerners or even politer Southerners, welcomed them, offered them seats on their golf carts and let them buy real estate at only slightly inflated prices.

Hialeah Race Course, racing's Sparkle Plenty, has had a lot to do with the fashionable migrations. By running a socially acceptable track, Hialeah has attracted socially acceptable people, some of whom have bought houses so they can be near their socially acceptable horses. This contingent has taken to two of Miami's exclusive, man-made islands—La Gorce and Indian Creek. Each is a highly restricted commune surmounted by willful arrangements of greenery and mansions. And each has a police force not just to patrol the streets but to make sure that no one ventures across the bridges without an invitation or a summons from an inhabitant.

Fred W. Hooper, whose Hoop Jr. won the 1945 Kentucky Derby, has a new, faintly Mediterranean estate in Indian Creek Village. He is a Georgian who settled here after having contracted in 1943 to build the runways for Miami's International Airport.

On La Gorce, the list of stable owners is so long that the main road has been nicknamed The Winner's Circle. Included are William L. McKnight, board chairman of St. Paul's Minnesota Mining & Manufacturing Company (Scotch tape was followed by Tartan Farms and boats named *Scotchie*); John W. Galbreath, a Columbus, Ohio, realtor whose Chateaugay won the 1963 Derby, and Mrs. Gene Markey, the former Lucille Parker Wright—head of the Calumet Farm in Lexington.

"This is our fourth year in this house," Mrs. Markey said recently. "My husband and I have a dock, but no yacht. If our pool weren't heated it would be too cold to swim."

The Markeys, who consider New York a stop-off on the way to Europe, share their house with Timmy Tammy, an eleven-year-old Yorkshire terrier who has crossed the Atlantic Ocean eighteen times. The three are rarely separated. "My husband writes his books at home," Mrs. Markey said. "I'm at home, too. I talk with my trainers on the telephone."

Rear Admiral Markey, U.S.N., retired, writes in longhand. His latest work is *Women, Women Everywhere* (he had previously married Joan Bennett, Hedy Lamarr and Myrna Loy), and he is working on what may be called "The Girl at Maxim's." Neither he nor Mrs. Markey cares much for the mad, club-centered social life. But others do.

Typical of these is Mrs. William H. Stubblefield, a St. Louis woman who has lived in her La Gorce Island house for twenty-two of her thirty Florida years. She is the widow of a real-estate and mortgage banker who retired when he was thirty-eight years old. Besides being petite and red-haired, Mrs. Stubblefield is the kind of person Alfred I. Barton, a founder of the Surf Club, was thinking about when he said, "People past middle age want to have fun in a big way. They're out dancing every night." Mrs. Stubblefield's house contains the white wrought-iron furniture, the chande-

184

liers and the arrangements of plastic flowers that Miamians hold dear. She also is a member of Miami's not-yet-old guard.

"There is an old clique," she said. "We've been here. We've known each other for years. Miami is a new place. If you've been here twenty-five or thirty years, you're an old-timer."

Mr. Barton, a transplanted Philadelphian who is Miami's unofficial social arbiter, is another old-timer. He came here in 1902, when his aunt had a house on Biscayne Bay. Then in 1924, after helping Cecil B. De Mille produce the first film version of *The Ten Commandments,* he and his mother built their own house.

"I'll always be a Philadelphian at heart," he said as he sipped a Bloody Mary. "It took me years to sign Miami Beach on a hotel register."

The Surf Club, which is slightly younger and a lot snappier than the Bath Club founded by Harvey Firestone and his friends, has a thousand feet of beach on the Atlantic Ocean, a wilderness of full-grown trees in its hallways and carpeting ornamented with enormous red poinsettias—the club's trademark. During the Depression, the management hired boxers to fight in the dining room while members were having dinner. Not one of the club's six hundred families is Jewish.

Miami is a club-dominated city with more than a million residents in its metropolitan area. It has the third largest Jewish population in the world. However, there are no Jewish members in the Surf Club, the Bath Club or the Indian Creek and La Gorce Clubs.

When Miamians are asked what induced them to leave their home towns, most admit that the lure was money rather than the sunshine. Mr. and Mrs. Charles M. Moon, formerly of Atlanta, invested about $200,000 in real estate, survived the land boom that failed in 1926 and then settled down. Mr. Moon is a successful lawyer, and his wife is the only woman trustee of the University of Miami.

"Everybody down here does things in spells," Mrs. Moon said. "One week it's flower arrangements and the next it's orchids or roses. We used to have boats, and now we don't."

Mrs. Moon and Mrs. Stubblefield gave Miami its first charity ball in 1951 ("It was for the opera and we charged just $7.50—enough to cover expenses—and now they cost $50"). The city's newest gala, a follies in which social leaders are expected to take part, was the idea of Mrs. Elliott Roosevelt.

"We have the cutest theme," Mrs. Roosevelt said after announcing that the evening will be called Gold Coast Capers of 1965. "The musical part will be called The Great Society. Don't you love it? I just know we're going to make tons of money." The Roosevelts' gala, with Perle Mesta as an honorary chairman, will benefit the National Foundation, and it already has the blessing of Mrs. Joseph P. Kennedy.

Mrs. Kennedy, the only United States President's mother to appear on the best-dressed list, flung herself into a little white wool dress garnished with pearls, and a private plane, and came down from Palm Beach to help the Roosevelts recruit volunteer workers.

"I go where I'm needed," Mrs. Kennedy said.

REPUBLICANS DISCOVER "IT'S ALL SUCH FUN"

August 1972

The Republicans, whose national convention promises galas and social one-upmanship rather than political floor fights, are beginning to assemble. Private jets litter the airports. Yachts are moving into the marinas. Elegant clubs and villas are jammed with the rich and famous. A four-day party is about to begin.

"It's all such fun now," said Curtis de Witz, manager of the exclusive Palm Bay Club, the jet set's Miami outpost. "It's nothing like the Democrats."

When the Democrats met here six weeks ago to select their presidential candidate, they spent their time in caucus meetings, floor fights and blue jeans. They didn't play tennis or go yachting, and although Mrs. George McGovern did go to a fashion show, the scene was hardly up to Miami Beach's mink-over-bathing-suit standards.

From a social point of view, and that seems to be the prevailing view, the advent of the Republicans is better. They've made it safe to wear dinner jackets and diamonds, rent limousines and throw a little money around. Elizabeth Arden's beauty salon reports that bookings are up from the Democrats. Already some taxi drivers have replaced the Bermuda shorts and work shirts they wore for the Democrats with black trousers and white shirts.

The social prospects were so good that Cornelius Vanderbilt Whitney, the sportsman-industrialist, and Mrs. Whitney decided to abandon Deerlands, their vast cool upper New York State hunting enclave and brave the 99-degree heat and humidity after all. "I'm sure the convention will be fascinating," said Mrs. Whitney, who always knows about such things. "Everybody's going."

Mrs. Carling Dinkler, the real-estate heiress, obviously agreed. She had been skiing in Chile, and when it looked as if her luggage couldn't be moved fast enough she abandoned it on a mountaintop rather than have it delay the plane that would get her back in time to supervise the decoration of her yacht. Actually, Mrs. Dinkler has three boats, all committed to what is known here as "the Nixon navy." On Wednesday night, when the President accepts his party's renomination, the Indian River waterway leading to

Convention Hall will be filled with yachts proclaiming their support of the President and hauling the rich and elegant to the evening session. Mrs. Dinkler's boats are scheduled to participate.

Near the front of the flotilla, its tuna tower aquiver, will be *Play Bay B,* Mrs. Dinkler's diesel-powered fishing craft. Next comes her thirty-five-foot *Play Baby,* a $40,000 boat with an air-conditioned bathroom and an ice machine on the teak deck. Finally, if it's needed, there's the *Little Queen Bee,* the tugboat that Mrs. Dinkler ordinarily uses for running errands around Biscayne Bay.

Mrs. Dinkler is very particular about her boat's banner. She wants it to say HURRAY FOR NOW, which somebody mistook for a feminist declaration on behalf of the National Organization for Women. "Heavens, no," Mrs. Dinkler said. "Now is for the good job the President is doing now."

When they are not sailing, the yachts are being used for parties ranging from chic little sit-down dinners to massive cocktail receptions. W. Clement Stone, chairman of the Combined Insurance Company of America and, at $1-million plus, one of President Nixon's favorite 1968 contributors, borrowed the *Black Hawk* as a personal headquarters and setting for a buffet. Ronald Reagan, Governor of California, plans to have his party on a yacht, too.

The Reagans, along with such other California pacesetters as Alfred Bloomingdale, the Diners Club executive, and Walter Annenberg, Mr. Nixon's Ambassador to Britain, are houseguests of Leonard Firestone of the tire empire. They are counting on Frank Sinatra to join them.

The talk in such circles, besides whether to add more Tabasco sauce to the Bloody Marys or put up with the long drive to Raimondo's Italian restaurant, centers on such matters as whether Vice President Agnew will have his own helicopter, what Mrs. Tobin (Anne) Armstrong, co-chairman of the Republican National Committee, will wear for the evening sessions, and why Zsa Zsa Gabor canceled her convention reservations.

At this stage the best rumor is that Mr. Firestone will replace Mr. Annenberg in Britain if the President is reelected. The second best is that Mr. Stone has already been selected for the post.

There's even a rumor that Jane Fonda may turn up at a sangría party being staged, at $5 a head, to raise money for the Women's National Political Caucus, and that Henry A. Kissinger might appear at the convention after all.

Socially, the facts are equally consequential. James Stewart, Charlton Heston, Art Linkletter and Sammy Davis, Jr., all part of the entertainment, are available for parties. Only the select have been invited to a Miami physician's tea for Senator Robert Taft, Jr., of Ohio. The color scheme of Sunday's $500-a-plate gala is red, white and blue. And the convention's Monday evening session will definitely begin with the singing of "The Star-Spangled Banner."

187

The Villerés accompanied le Moyne, who founded New Orleans in 1718, and they are still going strong. Mrs. Russell Clark, the former Alma Villeré, is so Creole she thinks of her husband as an "American." "Americans" didn't arrive until *after* the Louisiana Purchase.
Allyn Baum, *The New York Times* (1964)

New Orleans

The Villerés have had better luck than the Mohicans. There are thirty-four of them listed in the New Orleans telephone book and all but one are believed to have sprung from the same historically significant and socially impeccable family tree. The exception is a Negro.

"His people probably were Villeré slaves," said Mrs. Alfred Grima, a sprightly widow whose mother was a Villeré. "After the Civil War, slaves often took the surnames of the families for whom they worked."

Mrs. Grima, an engaging, gracious and community-minded amateur historian, is the daughter of the late Fernand Claiborne and Marie Louis Villeré. This, she says, makes her part "American" and part Creole. And like all New Orleans aristocrats, she is quick to define her terms.

"Creoles are descended from children born here in colony days," she said, adjusting a pair of black-rimmed spectacles. "They are of French and Spanish ancestry. Americans are people who came here very much later."

Americans, according to present Creole usage, are "new people," although Mrs. Grima's own American ancestor, William Charles Cole Claiborne, was a native-born Virginian whose family actually arrived in this country before her French ancestors did.

But time of arrival in the country is not the point. What counts to a

Creole is the arrival date in New Orleans. And the Americans, including such outsiders as Claiborne, the first American governor of the state, did not begin to settle here until after 1803, the date of the Louisiana Purchase. The Villerés were here eighty-five years earlier.

As a Villeré, Mrs. Grima is related to such distinguished New Orleanians as Ernest C. Villeré, who is in the investment business, and Mrs. Russell Clark, the former Alma Villeré. Mrs. Clark, who is pure Creole, refers to her husband as an "American." He is associated with Fenner and Beane, the brokerage firm. All are descended from the de Villeré who accompanied Jean Baptiste le Moyne, Sieur de Bienville, when he landed here in 1718 to establish New Orleans, and from Jacques Philippe Villeré, the first Creole governor of Louisiana.

"A lot of us seem to have stayed put," Mrs. Grima said. "We have been a part of things for so long."

Joseph Villeré was killed in 1769 for his part in the Louisiana Revolution, an unsuccessful Creole uprising against the Spanish, to whom France had ceded the territory. And in 1815, Gabriel Villeré played a remembered role in the Battle of New Orleans. "He was at his plantation on the Mississippi River, shaving," Mrs. Grima said as if it had all happened quite recently. "In the mirror, he saw a Red Coat through the pecan trees. He knew it was the British. He rode to the city to warn them the British were coming."

It is a story the Villerés have told and retold. Mr. Villeré believes the British captured Gabriel, and that he escaped. And Mrs. Clark is not sure the Red Coat was in the pecan trees.

"People really don't care about old families anymore," Mrs. Clark said. "The world keeps moving and changing, and so it should. We Creoles have married and intermarried. We're really very American."

In their day, the high point of which was before the Civil War, when they lost land and slaves, the Villerés were plantation owners, patriots and statesmen whose money came from sugar. Like other Creole leaders, they played a prominent role in the business, civic, cultural and social life of New Orleans.

"My father was a gentleman," Mrs. Grima said when she was asked what he did for a living. "He was just a gentleman and a poet."

The Creoles, Louisiana's Knickerbockers, were a gay, sophisticated people who have been neglected by the history books. They imported opera from Europe long before New York got around to it. The fashionable women wore French clothes, gave gala parties and touched their cheeks with rouge— a practice that shocked some Puritan visitors from the North. They also surrounded themselves with French and English furniture, and never had much use for anything now called "Early American" or "Modern."

The Villerés still live in spacious, old, high-ceilinged houses, surrounded by antique furniture, crystal wall sconces, English silver, imported china and giant portraits of their colorful ancestors. There are fires at this time of year and, despite a recent freeze, there are camellias blooming in the gardens. "When I work in the garden, I wear blue jeans or slacks, and I'm mud from head to toe," Mrs. Clark said. "I'd hate to have someone come by and catch me that way."

Mrs. Clark, who is often dressed in an expensive, understated tweed suit with gold, diamond and sapphire jewelry and black alligator shoes, has thirteen grandchildren and a string of community responsibilities, including membership on two hospital boards. It is her interest in gardening, however, that prompted her to give a mild cheer for the gradual disappearance of the once necessary calling card.

"It's a nuisance," she confided, noting that debutantes still leave cards as part of the coming-out ritual. "Everybody calls up now instead of just dropping in. Tea is practically a lost art."

At Mrs. Grima's house, however, afternoon tea is still something of a ceremony, albeit an informal and irregular one.

"I serve iced tea in the summer in the garden and hot tea indoors in the winter," she said. "I think it's terrible to ask people in and then offer them nothing but drinks. Not that I don't like a cocktail now and then."

The Villerés are related by blood or marriage to dozens of New Orleanians, whose company they seem to enjoy. This tends to make parties accidentally familial. "I remember a big dinner at Antoine's, when the hostess said, 'Let's not put any of the relatives together,'" Mrs. Villeré said. "We all looked around and then we laughed. We were all related."

"Mrs. Villeré is a Delarond," her husband said. "She's not related to me, but then again, she is. But it's complicated."

It is not unusual at aristocratic gatherings to discover that the names of the guests coincide with the names that have appeared and reappeared in New Orleans history. But this, too, seems to make everyone feel at home.

"The same old names with different faces," Mrs. Villeré said. "That's the charm of it."

REX AND COMUS PROVIDE SPLENDOR FOR
NEW ORLEANS MARDI GRAS

February 1964

There's nothing chic about a Mardi Gras street mob, what with people fighting over souvenir trinkets thrown from passing floats, but the splendor of the ceremonial, invitation-only Rex and Comus balls is something else again. They're enough to make one believe that some New Orleans people really do have royal blood in their veins.

The private galas, the finale of the New Orleans pre-Lenten carnival, which started on January 6, were held in separate sections of the Municipal Auditorium. Each group had an elegantly costumed king and queen who presided over the festivities, and although Comus, the older and smaller of the two secret societies, traditionally draws the *crème de la crème* of old New Orleans society, Rex had its share of aristocrats.

Ernest C. Villeré and Mrs. Russell Clark were there.

"Everything's so busy we always say we're going to leave town at Mardi Gras time," Mrs. Clark said, "but we never do. It's been part of our lives since the beginning. We're Creoles."

Mrs. Clark had a special reason for attending this year's Rex Ball. It was the fiftieth anniversary of her presentation as a maid in Rex's court. Crawford H. Ellis, the 1914 Rex King of Carnival, was on hand, too. So was Mrs. Louis Sussdorff, the 1914 Queen of Carnival. Mrs. Sussdorff, the widow of a Foreign Service officer, is the former Flores Howard. Her father and grandfather were carnival kings. Mr. Ellis, whose lapel is ornamented with a small commemorative gold crown, is chairman of the board of the Pan-American Life Insurance Company. He is ninety-one years old.

"Of course I go to work every day," he assured a young upstart who asked the question. "I was president of the company for fifty years, and then they insisted I take the chairmanship."

Darwin S. Fenner, whose father was the cotton broker who founded the brokerage firm of Fenner and Beane, now Merrill Lynch, Pierce, Fenner and Smith, was another of the distinguished guests at the Rex Ball.

"Some Rexes belong to Comus and vice versa," Mr. Fenner said. "But only a Comus knows another Comus. Members are always masked at their ball. No one's supposed to be able to recognize them."

It is considered rude to ask a man if he's a Comus member, however, and if the matter ever comes up, he changes the subject. Theoretically, only the captain, a sort of permanent general manager of the organization, knows the identity of all the members. Keeping the names secret apparently is half the fun. It also contributes an aura of exclusivity.

The Rex and Comus also, like other postparade dances given during carnival, officially began with pageants comparable to those held at the French court when Versailles was still a palace. Trumpets sounded while the kings and queens were escorted to their satin and brocade thrones. Courtiers wearing gilded tennis shoes bowed as if their monarchs' titles and jewels were real. The orchestras played and replayed majestic-sounding music. It was a great night for the "Aïda" march.

Clayton L. Nairne, president of New Orleans Public Service, Inc., the gas and electric concern, was Rex King of Carnival. Miss Claudia Tucker FitzHugh was the Queen. John R. FitzHugh, her father, is in the oil business, and her mother is a member of an old New Orleans family. The Comus king's expression was one of permanent surprise. His identity was concealed by a mask.

Each ball had two kinds of guests, both formally clad. One group was invited to watch the proceedings from balcony seats. The other, including members of the host organization, their wives and daughters, sat in rows of chairs around the dance floor. When the pageants ended, persons in the latter group were permitted to dance if they felt like it, and most of them did.

The dancing in both ballrooms came to a halt with the midnight meeting of the Rex and Comus courts. This ceremony was held in Comus territory because that society has seniority. It came into being in 1857. Rex, organized to provide extra-special entertainment for Grand Duke Aleksei Romanov of Imperial Russia, was not founded until 1872. About nine thousand members and guests attended the two gatherings.

The sun shines bright on nearly everybody's old Kentucky home, not the least of which is Mr. and Mrs. George Headley's La Belle Farm, which has been in the Headley family for four generations. Besides horses, swans, orchids and Norwich terriers, they are famous for their hospitality. William Strode, *The New York Times* (1970)

Lexington, Kentucky

The grass is blue. Make no mistake about that. That it looks emerald green is beside the point. Let the native aristocrats have what they all call "that tinge of blue this time of year." Maybe it actually *was* blue once. What matters after nearly two hundred years is that the bluegrass is still around Lexington in abundance, covering miles and miles of rolling pastures and providing a properly Jeffersonian setting for stately mansions, gracious living and some of the world's finest race horses.

"Everybody thinks we just sit on the back porch and drink mint juleps," Leslie Combs 2nd drawled. "We don't at all."

The fact, of course, is that despite its nineteenth-century beauty, its traditions and its patrician ways, there isn't much time in the Bluegrass country for porch sitting. Horse farms are big business, whether or not they make a profit. And although nobody who's anybody has to repair his own barns or curry the horses, stables have to be inspected, payrolls met and thoroughbreds studied as continuously and closely as other men watch the stockmarket.

For Mr. Combs, whose ancestors fought the French and the Indians before the American Revolution, this is a full-time and exceedingly lucrative job. He breeds and sells horses at Spendthrift Farm, a 6,100-acre establishment involving 550 thoroughbreds.

Mr. Combs covers his vast demesne on the back of a Tennessee walking horse or behind the wheel of a silver Cadillac with red leather seats, a short-wave telephone and a small silver jockey affixed to the hood. At 5:30 P.M., he returns to his white-columned house for tea in a room overlooking his property.

"Mint juleps are a special thing," he said, "but they're mostly for visitors. We've got a lot of Scotch and martini drinkers now."

Mint juleps and the Kentucky Derby are synonymous, and with that racing classic bringing the American racing establishment to nearby Louisville, the time to baby the mint has arrived. It is a game Mr. Combs would rather not play.

"Ever' single mint julep has to be made separately," he said with some reverence. "Now what're you going to do when you have a house full of people?"

His answer is to serve other drinks to the crowds that come in for Derby Day feasts. But his secret recipe (all good julep recipes are handed down from father to son) includes at least two shots of bourbon to a drink, bruised mint ("For God's sake, don't crush it"), simple syrup and crushed ice.

"No water," he said, aghast at the idea. "'Course, one trouble with juleps is the glass. A glass will never bring out the flavor the way a silver cup will."

The really prestigious (and presumably tasty) silver julep cups were awarded to their owners as Keeneland Track racing trophies. A set of eight means eight successful races and eight are just what Mr. and Mrs. George Headley, Jr., have in their house behind the white plank fences at La Belle Farm.

Mrs. Headley is Cornelius Vanderbilt Whitney's sister. She has her stable. Mr. Whitney has his stable. And Mr. Headley has quarter horses and an Arabian horse. Together, the Headleys raise white swans for their lake.

"My great-grandparents lived on this farm," Mr. Headley said. "You say 'Headley' around here and a lot of people answer."

Mr. Headley also designs jewels and *objets de vertu* for which he and his wife built their own museum. Before he goes there each day, he stops by his greenhouse in his bathrobe to examine his orchids and geraniums.

"People who don't know about orchids think they're hard to raise," he said. "They're not nearly as hard as geraniums. Orchids like neglect. Geraniums like to be attended."

The attention and lack of attention have paid off. Huge orchid plants with twenty and thirty blossoms fill their house, and it won't be long before the potted geraniums are set out around the front door. In the meantime, the Headleys have to content themselves these balmy spring days with green lawns bright with dogwood, crab apple and viburnum blossoms, bluebells, tulips and masses of violets.

196

"It's still country here," Mr. Headley said, gazing across his sun-drenched fields. "We like the casual life."

Life may be casual during the day, but formal clothes are expected at dinner parties this time of year. Afternoon tea is a ritual right down to the homemade cookies and little cakes.

And there isn't an important drawing room that doesn't have crystal chandeliers, crystal wall sconces or both, at least some historic English furniture and an array of freshly polished antique silver. Until recently, such rooms were maintained by elderly black retainers who had worked in the same big households for forty and fifty years. But these Negroes, perhaps the last to call their employers "Mr. Sam" or "Miss Mary Jane" and be considered part of the family, are gradually disappearing.

No house is better kept than Westover, Mrs. James H. Alexander's home, and she speaks of her faded red damask curtains with great pride.

"They are 250 years old," she said. "Sir William Alexander had them in his house in Scotland."

The Alexanders are one of Kentucky's old families and Mrs. Alexander, a widow and the custodian of the family treasures, lives amid Jouett portraits of her husband's ancestors, crested silver, leather-bound books and horse memorabilia.

"We just talk party talk," she said. "No politics. No big controversial issues. One tries not to talk tobacco because it upsets the men. Oh, horse talk's all right. But I'm not very good at bloodlines. That's what horse talk is about."

Mrs. Alexander gardens, plays bridge for something like a tenth of a cent a point, writes her daughter (Lucy Alexander Winchester, Mrs. Richard M. Nixon's social secretary) and runs the family farms.

Mr. and Mrs. John A. Bell's Jonabell Farms is equally historic. Riley, the 1890 Derby winner, came off the farm, and the house with its great curving staircase dates from about 1820. Today, Jonabell's fields are filled with mares and foals, their manes flying in the breezes.

"This is our livelihood," Mr. Bell said. "Not a hobby. We expect to make money."

In good years, the Bells do make money not just from the thoroughbreds but from the cattle and tobacco behind their black fences. Black fences? Yes, black fences.

"There are two schools of fences in Kentucky," Mrs. Bell explained. "Black or white. We're of the black-fence school. We think they look better."

Essentially, the fence debate is a matter of aesthetics. Black paint lasts no longer than white paint and the costs aren't that different. Yet the debate rages on.

"I always believed in black fences," Mr. Combs said. "But my wife believed in white fences. I learned very early never to argue with her."

197

Charleston has long since become a lot more than white-pillared houses,
Southern smilax and exquisite manners. But in times past, it was a
community where ladies like Mrs. Benjamin R. Kittredge (right) could go
for leisurely picnics at Cypress Gardens.
Slim Aarons (1955)

Charleston, South Carolina

The women did not wear hoop skirts, and there were new wooden folding chairs in the ballroom, but aside from that, the St. Cecilia Society's annual ball was like something out of *Gone With the Wind*. It was held in historic Hibernian Hall. The publicity-shy society, whose dues are about $25 a year, is an aristocratic organization whose sole purpose is the giving of the ball. Its members are men, most of whose ancestors settled here nearly a hundred years before the American Revolution. The ball, an exclusive assembly ruled by revered but antiquated regulations, is a nostalgic remnant of things past but not forgotten.

The high-ceilinged ballroom looked as it might have looked in the 1840s, when it was new. Electricity has come to Charleston, of course, so there were small lights where candles used to be. But the fires in the fireplaces were ignited because the building has no central heating. The windows were screened, as is the society's custom, with long lace curtains, and there were miles of leafy green, Southern smilax. The vine, almost as ubiquitous here as Spanish moss, fried chicken and camellias, was festooned around the chandeliers, pillars, stairways and tall Georgian columns. It was the only decoration.

It was no accident that the ball was more like a simple English country dance than a New York gala, or that some guests were wearing ball gowns

199

that had been to St. Cecilia before. The aristocracy rarely worries about what's happening to its status. The ball began with a bit of a traffic jam on Meeting Street. In the old days, slaves drove their masters, but aristocrats drive themselves these days. Men wearing white ties, tails and the immaculate white gloves they weren't allowed to remove in the ballroom drove their equally formally clad wives and daughters to the ball, then went in search of parking places.

By ball time, all of the little white dance programs were filled out. The women, who had to keep their white gloves on, too, slipped their hands through the string loops and wore their programs like bracelets.

"Men are always supposed to be gentlemen, and women are supposed to be ladies," the scion of a distinguished Huguenot family said confidentially. "At this affair, you are a gentleman or a lady. We don't go getting up and walk out of the room when St. Cecilia's mentioned. We just don't like to talk about it. It's a tradition."

A former president of the society, writing to a member during the 1930s, explained the group's reticence this way: "As a member of the society I believe you understand many of its peculiarities. Chief among these is the objective of preserving the social distinctions, customs and traditions of bygone times. In a city as small as Charleston such an organization is truly an anomaly which a little emphasis would convert into an aggravation, and experience has proved that publicity concerning the society is injurious to the community as a whole because it tends to stir up jealousies and animosities which seriously impair the goodwill normally existing between members and nonmembers."

Despite this philosophy, there is nothing very secret or mysterious about this hereditary society or its ultraexclusive ball. Virtually anyone who is anyone in the South knows a lot about it. St. Cecilia, named for the patron saint of music, was formally organized in 1762. But its members, wealthy rice and cotton plantation owners and good friends, had been giving amateur musicales off and on since 1737. For years its meetings were held at 9 P.M. on Thursdays.

Detroit may have been founded by a Frenchman named Cadillac but it's
the Fords whom everyone wants to entertain at dinner. Henry Ford 2nd is
the tough, respected chairman of the empire who has also been known to
have fun. Anne Ford Uzielli doesn't miss much either.
Joyce Dopkeen, *The New York Times* (1973)

Grosse Pointe, Michigan

Anyone who thinks the natives get a little restless around here in the summer doesn't understand Grosse Pointe. It was a summer resort long before it became one of the nation's richest suburbs. And, as any affluent inhabitant is quick to volunteer, in many ways it still is a resort. The country clubs, instead of being at the end of a long drive out of town, are only minutes away from the behemoth houses. The houses themselves are air-conditioned, at least in part, and a lot have swimming pools. Private tennis courts are not unheard of, although club courts are a popular gathering place. And there are sailing, boating and water skiing on Lake St. Clair, which, to all intents and purposes, is in everybody's front yard.

"We don't have to go away," said Mrs. Allan Shelden, a native-born dowager who does. "Why should we? We're already here."

Gray-haired Mrs. Shelden, who pops in and out of such places as the Soviet Union and the Orient, is no longer an athlete. But she takes more than a passing interest in a granddaughter's horsemanship ("I don't like it when she falls off"). And in the autumn, she climbs into a leather pants suit to join the parties that go hunting for pheasant, duck and partridge in northern Michigan.

Mrs. Shelden, one of a handful of grande dames who give Grosse Pointe its glamour, is a senior member of a Middle Western sodality that

203

believes in hats, gloves and work. She says she doesn't care what people do "as long as they do things." And besides being a devoted patron of the Detroit Institute of Arts and the Detroit Symphony, she is what she calls "a violent gardener."

She negotiates the thirty-minute drive between her house on the lake and her downtown office in a Lincoln Continental ("We're friends of the Fords. I wouldn't dare not have one of their cars") and then walks the three blocks from the parking lot to her office and back again "because it's good exercise." The office, which she keeps because her civic and charity work is complicated ("and I wanted a place to run my own affairs"), is in the Buhl Building. It was named for her mother's family. Buhl ancestors were granted their land by King George III. In 1855, the family founded Buhl Sons Company, a major wholesale hardware business.

When she was a girl, a time Mrs. Shelden distinctly remembers as being before the advent of the automobile, Detroit's upper echelons lived in town and summered in Grosse Pointe. Since then, the automobile tycoons, manufacturers and corporate executives have joined the older lumber, shipping and banking families in taking over Grosse Pointe. Together, they have spent their old and new money making it into a deluxe bedroom community, run the population up to 55,000, and given over less important seasons to the business of travel.

They turn up in the capitals of the world, but Chicago, never Detroit's idea of the nation's second most important city, is rarely on their travel agenda. And except for such affable people as Mrs. Shelden, Grosse Pointers have little enthusiasm for either Detroit itself or the suburbs of Bloomfield Hills and Birmingham. "Everybody lives in Grosse Pointe," Mrs. Shelden said, then changed her mind. "Well, not everybody. There's a perfectly marvelous group in Birmingham and Bloomfield Hills—automotive people who do things in the companies."

Frederick M. Alger, Jr., President Eisenhower's Ambassador to Belgium, seemed to agree. His grandfather, Russell A. Alger, was first an Ohio and then a Michigan lumber king ("What's left of our so-called fortune derived from lumber") and President William McKinley's Secretary of War. His father, Frederick M. Alger, was a member of the group that bought the Packard company. "Detroit feels it's unique," Mr. Alger said in the comfortably furnished library of his big, ivy-covered red brick house. "If it doesn't operate, the whole economy folds up. We're the leading manufacturing town in the country—the backbone of the U.S. economy."

But this doesn't mean that he or his friends have to go into downtown Detroit.

"I don't much anymore," said Mr. Alger. "Except on Wednesday when I go to my club."

Neither he nor his son David Dewey Alger, a Harvard graduate who is going to the University of Michigan's School of Business Administration this fall to specialize in finance, can think of any good reason for visiting any other suburb.

"In my day, there wasn't much traffic between Grosse Pointe and Bloomfield Hills," Mr. Alger said, speaking of his youth. "It's an incredibly terrible drive—an hour and fifteen minutes."

"In my group of friends nobody ever goes to Bloomfield Hills," said David. "I don't even know anybody there."

Grosse Pointe, which is to Detroit what Bronxville is to New York, Lake Forest is to Chicago and Shaker Heights is to Cleveland, is not as insular as it sometimes seems. It's just that the ultimate goal is life as it is led in one of the five adjoining Grosse Pointes—preferably Grosse Pointe Farms.

The children go east to preparatory school and college when they can meet the academic standards, and a lot of them can. Then they come home and, in David's words, "marry each other, so there's an awful lot of in-breeding."

Most families belong to either the Country Club of Detroit, which has a golf course, or the Grosse Pointe Club, more familiarly known as "the Little Club." It has a marina for power and sailboats. By Palm Beach or Newport standards, no boat qualifies as a yacht.

"There used to be yachts," said the Countess Cyril Tolstoi. "It was much more glamorous in the past."

The countess, an elegant native who met her late husband in Paris, lives on property first owned by Alexander Lewis, her grandfather. At one time, it was a family farm. When the banks closed during the Depression, she and Count Tolstoi, Leo Tolstoi's cousin, came back to Detroit. "We thought it would be temporarily," the countess said, "but then there was the Spanish Civil War and World War II so we stayed. We always intended to go back to Paris." The countess, whose house is furnished with French, Italian and Belgian antiques, is a lot less gung-ho about Grosse Pointe than most of her friends. "Where there was one house there are fifty today," she said as she sipped iced tea. "Nothing interests me here."

This is not quite accurate. The countess, and such equally old-family women as Mrs. Phelps Newberry, whose husband's forebears made their money in drygoods, shipping, real estate and the law, are ardent fans of the Detroit Tigers. They go to the home games periodically, or watch them on television. And if a dinner invitation conflicts with a particularly important game, the countess is likely to refuse. The Frederick Sloane Fords, Jr., are far more interested in sailing.

"One of the nice things about Grosse Pointe is that we have so many different kinds of things to be interested in," said Mrs. Ford. "There are our churches and all our community work. We all do a lot of volunteer work." Mrs. Ford, wife of a naval architect and yacht designer whose family has long been involved in the manufacture of chemicals and glass (Libby-

Owens Ford Company), has the scrubbed good looks of a typical Grosse Pointe matron. She is lean and blond, blue-eyed and tan. She plays tennis ("three times a week before the children got out of school") and paddle tennis, and she skis, shoots and sails. Fifteen years ago, she resigned from the Detroit Junior League.

"It seemed so silly to pay a babysitter so I could do volunteer work," she said. "What I really wanted to do was work directly with the agencies the Junior League served."

Mrs. Ford, who is known as a "salt Ford" (salt was important in the development of both the chemical and the glass industries) to distinguish her from the "automotive Fords" (Mrs. Edsel Ford) and the "banking Fords" (the Frederick C. Fords), belongs to one of the two Grosse Pointe sororities, Sigma Gamma and Tau Beta. "We take in young girls when they've finished the ninth grade," she said. "We try to teach them to be good volunteers." Mrs. Ford is another advocate of the "everyone must do some kind of work" school. But she believes that unless it is constructive, work has no point.

"I want my son to travel this summer," she said, speaking of eighteen-year-old Frederick B. Ford, "and he's going to Europe. That's more valuable than working in a supermarket."

Her daughter, Susan, a student at Connecticut College for Women, is "working" too. She is enrolled in a creative writing course this summer at Harvard. For Mrs. John Lord, the former Rhoda Newberry, work consists of painting lessons ("Just one abstract. The rest are a lot like Grandma Moses") and tending her spacious backyard.

"We never hire people to make party decorations," said Mrs. Lord, who gets down on her knees to weed her garden. "We do them ourselves. We prefer it that way."

Mrs. Lord's house, which is the equal of villas along the Atlantic Ocean in Palm Beach, has the white walls and cream-colored carpets of a resort mansion. A crystal chandelier hangs over the French living room. The entrance hall is white marble. The bouquets are made of plastic flowers.

In contrast with this and other Grosse Pointe houses is the place W. Hawkins Ferry helped design and build for himself farther out on the lake. It's thoroughly contemporary, a blending of Le Corbusier and Yamasaki, and the glassed-in conversation area is dominated by a nine-foot Brancusi sculpture. Other contemporary artworks, including wall-size paintings, a Picasso and a de Kooning, are counterbalanced by such family heirlooms as a Victorian mahogany table, a pewter and gilded bronze chandelier and an imposing white marble bust of Mr. Ferry's grandfather, Dexter M. Ferry.

The senior Mr. Ferry, who came to Detroit in 1852, was first an errand boy and then a clerk at a book and stationery store. Later, he was a founder of the D. M. Ferry Company, a seed business. All of Mr. Ferry's flowers are real.

Edsel Bryant Ford 2nd's sister Anne Ford Uzielli was graduated from Briar-cliff, and he has *female* cousins who received degrees from "Radcliffe or some place like that" and Yale. But no matter.

After five and a half years of trying, twenty-four-year-old Edsel, as charming a young man as he is well mannered, finally completed the required courses at Boston's easygoing Babson College. Even though he doesn't get his diploma until next month, he is, as he is quick to point out, "the first male Ford to graduate from college," occasion enough for his friends and the Fords of the Ford Motor Company to celebrate.

Which explains the drink-and-dance moonlight cruise around Boston Harbor. That gathering, complete with rock bands, bars, confetti, crepe-paper streamers, big pictures of Edsel, and two hundred exuberant guests, was the long-awaited "graduation party of the century."

Actually, it was Douglas Leeds's idea. Mr. Leeds, a fellow Babsonian (Babsonite?) who made it in the usual four years, is Edsel's roommate. Together they own a house in suburban Dover. Together they drew up a guest list, which included Mrs. Lyndon B. Johnson, Princess Grace of Monaco and the Aristotle Onassises.

Mr. Leeds sent out 237 little newspapers extoling Edsel's accomplishments ("The Board of Trustees of the college voted unanimously to confer on Ford a newly created degree—Bachelor of Cars") and detailed the particulars ("black tie and sneakers"). And at 9:30 P.M., the guests, mostly young college friends from the Boston area, were boarding the excursion boat *New Boston*.

Edsel's father, Henry Ford 2nd, in black tie and navy blue sneakers, and carrying a properly chilled magnum of champagne, arrived with Mrs. Ford and Mrs. Uzielli. Giancarlo Uzielli brought his own white wine. William R. ("Billy") Chapin, son of Roy D. Chapin, chairman of rival American Motors, brought his rubber-soled black evening slippers. The host remembered the Edsel buttons.

"We had them made up special," Mr. Leeds said, passing them around. "This is a real celebration."

Mrs. Ford's button showed Edsel kissing her in living color. Mr. Ford's was a solemn black-and-white snapshot of his long-haired son. Other party-goers were awarded "The Edsel Is a College Graduate," "Edsel Has a Better Idea" or "Meet the 1973 Edsel" buttons.

Either Dr. Henry A. Kriebel, Babson's president, didn't get a button or he took his off. Somehow, he seemed just a touch above button-wearing.

"Edsel has proved that if he puts his mind to something he can do it, which he did," Dr. Kriebel said as the boat was about to push off.

A uniformed security man, hired to protect the party from crashers, challenged Edsel when he arrived. "But I'm the guest of honor," Edsel said jovially. "No, he isn't," shouted some of his best friends. Edsel did get through, bringing Cynthia Neskow, his date, with him. "She works for an ad agency in Boston which just happens to handle some of our advertising," he said.

The guests cheered Edsel's appearance on the gangplank, showered him with confetti and entangled him in paper streamers. "Dynamite," he cried, obviously pleased. "This is super."

By this time, the blast of the rock band deleted conversation. Young people writhed around the upper-deck dance floor, some with drinks sloshing out of plastic cups. The bars were jammed. Boston's skyscrapers disappeared in the distance. Guests who didn't dance sipped or just plain drank. And so it went for nearly three hours.

"Two of my most important professors are here," Edsel said. "One teaches the financial management course. It's the toughest—the one course I might have failed. The other was the first to give me an A. I got it in advertising management or introduction to advertising."

Arthur L. Godfrey, a Secret Service agent whom Edsel met through his interest in automobile racing, was there, too, and so was Herbert Bryant, assistant chief of Interpol, the International Criminal Police Organization.

"I have a sort of connection with Ford," the man from Interpol confided. "My grandfather, James Couzens, was a co-founder of the company."

Mr. Leeds stopped the music long enough for what Dr. Kriebel called "the first presentation I ever made on shipboard." It was a plaque commemorating Edsel's work on three Babson seminars.

Edsel thanked Dr. Kriebel, the professors who had worked with him on the seminars, and Mr. Leeds for having the party.

"And I want to thank my father for having me," he said. "I wouldn't have been here without him. And my mother. And I want to thank my stepmother."

Mrs. Ford beamed. Then it was Mr. Uzielli's turn. He said that under such circumstances, some colleges might expect "a library or a dormitory" but that Edsel had gone to "forty-seven schools, which comes to six dormitories, five football fields and a library."

"We don't need a football field," Dr. Kriebel said later. "But we do need a library."

Presumably, that matter will be settled if and when it's settled. In the meantime, Jim Croce took over. The rock star sang such favorites of Edsel's as "Rapid Roy the Stock Car Boy" and "Working at the Car Wash Blues."

At 1:30 A.M., the *New Boston* docked to release those huddled masses who were yearning to breathe free. True stalwarts, led by Edsel and his host, sailed off again for another cruise. They were surely home by Saturday.

And what did the chairman of the Ford Motor Company think of his son's graduation? "I am very pleased," he said quietly. "Very, very pleased."

In January, Edsel will follow his great-grandfather, Henry Ford, his grandfather and namesake, and his father into the company. He'll start in the product-planning area.

"I'm not really very mechanically minded," he said. "I could change the spark plugs or the oil, but I'm not much of an engineer."

Eventually, he hopes to work his way into the marketing and advertising side of the business. "Unfortunately, it isn't like it was in the days when a Ford just walked into the company," Edsel said. "I'll have to go out and prove myself, which I really want to do. I hope someday to run the company, but if I can't, I can't."

Texas near Dallas is flat and grassy, and covered with bluebonnets in the spring. Beyond Mr. and Mrs. Edward S. Marcus are fields and more fields. They raise Black Angus cattle on their ranch and serve French food in their art-filled house in town.
Jack Manning, *The New York Times* (1968)

Dallas

For a while there around World War II there were those who thought Dallas might become the money capital of the universe. But, as is so often the case with impossible dreams, it didn't work out.

And now, nearly forty years after the beginning of the great Texas oil boom, Dallas has pretty much given up its flamboyant ways and settled down to being just one of several affluent American cities with a social establishment to match.

What is special about Dallas, however, is the number and variety of its multimillionaires. Besides the solidly entrenched old cotton, cattle and retail families, there are the first- and second-generation oil operators and the new electronics and aerospace moguls. These men dominate Dallas politically as well as socially, culturally and economically. Not one of them is sufficiently immobile to fill the popular conception of an aristocrat. And they are known, depending upon the size of their fortunes, as "the little rich," "the big rich," or H. L. Hunt.

"A man who made $100-million, now he'd be fairly big money," explained Mrs. Everett Lee DeGolyer, widow of one of the greatest of the oil geologists. "Five million, well, that's small time." Even for a white-haired lady who is decidedly not small time, Mrs. DeGolyer was being a bit

211

severe. It takes $1-billion in assets (and an affection for carrying lunch in a brown paper bag) to be Mr. Hunt.

But one doesn't have to have $100-million to be "big rich"; $20- or $30-million will do. Yet $5-million fortunes are more nearly what Dallas is about.

Such fortunes are plentiful, however, and as the impeccable Stanley Marcus, president of the Neiman-Marcus Company and arbiter of all that is tasteful about Dallas, has pointed out, "You sell a $200,000 necklace today and there's no big story. It's not unusual."

Neither are the rows of suburban mansions, the fleets of Cadillacs, the rustic hideaways at Koon Kreek Klub nor the closets devoted to nothing but different kinds of fur coats. Dallas takes these, its private planes, its $1-million philanthropies, its family foundations and its ranches for granted.

The ranch, nearly the only real extravagance native to the Southwest, may or may not support the cattle for which it was intended. It doesn't matter. But most Texans would rather have a couple of thousand Black Angus, Santa Gertrudis or Herefords than a thoroughbred racing stable, a collection of artworks or an ocean-going yacht.

Mr. Marcus, who once said that the only kind of music he liked at dinner was the sound of the lute, is no such Texan. He has a Rolls-Royce instead of a Cadillac, and masses of paintings and sculpture. But even he can't get very excited about yachts and horse racing. "If I were staying at the Pierre," he said, "and if they were running the Kentucky Derby in Central Park and paying people $50 to go, I wouldn't."

The trouble with Mr. Marcus—and his brother, Edward S. Marcus, for that matter—is that they persist in going their own supercivilized way. Dallas is the home of Southern Methodist University and a hotbed of loyal University of Texas alumni. And yet the Texas-born Marcuses (known locally as the Marci) went to Harvard, which in Dallas has always been considered just this side of downright subversive. The Marcuses also are Jewish among fundamentalist Protestants, liberal among conservatives and cultivated in a culturally unfulfilled community. Edward Marcus, however, did have the good grace to leave Harvard in time to get his degree from the University of Texas. And he does have a ranch.

That 1,275-acre spread, no behemoth by Texas standards, is populated with Black Angus cattle, quarterhorses and a flock of peacocks. It has its own landing strip. And when foreign dignitaries appear, as they always seem to in Dallas, they are sometimes invited to get out and rope and tie the steers.

"It's the closest thing to a rodeo," said Mrs. Marcus, the former Betty Lee Blum. "We give everybody cotton gloves and nylon ropes."

Mr. and Mrs. Ethan B. Stroud, Jr., have their own way of going, too. He is a successful tax lawyer whose ancestors were Indian fighters when Texas was still a republic (1836–45). And she is the daughter of the late

John W. Herbert 3rd, a rich New Yorker who became even richer in the oil fields.

"We never wear boots and we never wear Stetsons," Mr. Stroud said emphatically. "We don't have a ranch and we don't go hunting."

What the Strouds do do, aside from ornamenting the walls of their contemporary house with the works of Rouault, Dufy, Vlaminck and Utrillo and summering at Southampton, is to immerse themselves in the cause of such institutions as the Museum of Fine Arts, the Dallas Council on World Affairs and the Dallas Symphony Orchestra. They also play chess with early eighteenth-century ivory figures carved to resemble Orientals on one side and Caucasians on the other. They'd like to study Red China first hand. And they are not particularly enamored of football.

Colonel D. Harold Byrd, by contrast, arranges his fall Saturdays so nothing will interfere with his devotion not just to football as it is played by the University of Texas, his alma mater, but to the university's Long-horn Band.

"It is," he said simply, "the best band in the world."

Thanks to its remarkable benefactor, a gregarious oil tycoon whose first fifty-six wells were a total loss, the world's best band has what is thought to be "the World's Biggest Drum." Until recently, when a one-way street made the gesture too difficult, the band marched to Colonel Byrd's office on the day of the Texas-Oklahoma game, stopped and then serenaded him with a rousing rendition of "The Eyes of Texas."

Colonel Byrd, whose military title reflects his service with the Civil Air Patrol (which he helped to found), owned his first airplane in 1926. Since then, he thinks he may have owned fifty-seven more. He isn't sure. He also collects Santa Gertrudis cattle. "Mattie and me have cattle named for us," he said. "Mattie C. is a prize cow. Colonel is a bull."

Mattie is Mrs. Byrd, and she is not poor. Her grandfather, William Caruth, came to Texas in 1848 with $100, a gold watch and a pony. Before he died, he owned not downtown Dallas, which wasn't much, but North Dallas—thousands of acres of the black waxy soil suited for cotton. Mrs. Byrd still owns a lot of land.

"I think it was 6,600 acres in the Dallas city limits," she said not long ago. "I suppose it's maybe half that now."

While explaining her real estate, Mrs. Byrd and her husband, who was done up in a jaunty red-and-black-checked suit he had custom-made in San Antonio, were being driven around her properties in one of their white Cadillacs. The car passed residential areas, industrial plants, a shopping center and what she called "my cemetery."

"Yes," she said, waving a gloved hand, "this is my cemetery. There's my rose garden. It has three thousand bushes. Over here's the Caruth family monument. Down there's my 'Little Mermaid.' It's an inch larger than the one in Denmark."

Colonel Byrd, a descendant of the Virginia Byrds and a cousin of Admiral Richard E. Byrd of the polar explorations, is like a lot of oil multimillionaires. He is so diversified these days that oil has become merely one of scores of financial involvements.

He is in farming ("I've got four thousand or five thousand acres of spinach, kale and cabbage"), ranching ("Maybe three thousand head of cattle"), gas ("I supplied Salt Lake City"), electronics and aerospace. He is chairman of the Space Corporation, which specializes in propulsion and ground control equipment for jets and missiles.

The Byrds' house is a seemingly endless number of elaborately furnished rooms with power draperies. Cocktails are often served in the trophy room over the bomb shelter. And it is here, seated on an elephant's foot ottoman with an antelope's foot for an ashtray and Mrs. Byrd settled in her jeweled maharajah's chair, that a visitor comes face to face with two enormous polar bears, a grizzly and a lion.

"I had me a time with that lion," Mrs. Byrd said. "I called Stanley Marcus's secretary and said I had the most bald-headed lion and would she please get a wigmaker."

Texas being Texas, the secretary wanted to know whether the lion was alive. Mrs. Byrd assured her that it wasn't. Predictably, Neiman-Marcus came up with a suitable Dynel wig and mane.

J. Erik Jonsson is rich, too. But not so it's very noticeable. The electronics tycoon, who remembers when he had to support himself, his wife and three children on $150 a month, is worth more than $82-million these days, and yet the only outward signs of such affluence is the big money he regularly gives to education.

Mr. Jonsson and his wife, whom he inevitably refers to as "the boss" or "the little lady," gave Rensselaer Polytechnic Institute, his alma mater, $1-million for its science center.

Later, they gave Skidmore College (their daughter's alma mater) a one-thousand-acre tract in Saratoga Springs for a new campus and $1-million toward its development. They can't seem to put their money into diamonds or wall-to-wall chinchilla.

"We have simple tastes," Mr. Jonsson said. "The one thing that makes a man go is his family. You have to set a pattern for the younger generation. You have to think about the future. It isn't where we will be, but where we should be that concerns me."

Mr. Jonsson is chairman and the managerial genius of Texas Instruments, the electronics empire, and Mayor of Dallas. He is as concerned with the future of his adopted city (he left New Jersey during the Depression) as he is with his business.

His plan has been to rethink Dallas's problems—including its image—set new goals and work toward accomplishing them.

"It's very like running a business," he said.

The Jonssons live in a comfortable pink brick house with no-nonsense furnishings and an informal terrace. It is as typical of Dallas as the elegant French formality Mrs. Katharine Pitman and Mrs. John William Rogers admire.

Mrs. Pitman, who calls herself "one of the oldest living debutantes" was presented to Dallas society in 1911. Her father was with the Texas Pacific Railroad. Mrs. Rogers, widow of the Texas author, is a transplanted Chicagoan.

"If you have to live some place besides Chicago," she said, "this is as pleasant a place as any."

Dr. Denton Cooley, the heart surgeon, plays the bass in the Heart Beats, an all-physician musical group that performs for Houston charities. He also does transplants. But when the astronauts went to the moon, he said he'd have given almost anything to go along.
Associated Press Wirephoto

Houston

The International Heart Gala at the new Neiman-Marcus store was far more than an extravagant dinner dance for hundreds of rich and elegant Texans. It was a rare gathering of heart surgeons, and they were a charismatic group indeed. Dr. Denton A. Cooley, Houston's resident human heart transplant surgeon, was among the first to arrive. He came across town with his blond wife and his bass viol.

And while ordinary mortals were examining Neiman's furs or getting themselves drinks from bars in such places as the men's clothing department, Dr. Cooley and twenty-one of Houston's other leading physicians and surgeons were off between the store wine cellar and its stationery department setting up their music racks, tuning up their instruments and then blasting "The Tijuana Taxi" throughout the store.

"They're the Heart Beats," Mrs. James S. Abercrombie fairly shouted over the music. "Aren't they divine?"

Mrs. Abercrombie, who wore a platinum and diamond pin over the beading on her white crepe evening dress, is the red-haired wife of the oilman and philanthropist. She divides her time between canasta ("I belong to a little bunch called the Powder Puffs. We play a lot of canasta, but we don't drink") and working for the Episcopal Hospital.

217

"That's where they do the heart surgery," she explained before gliding off to watch the Heart Beats play.

By this time, the orchestra had moved on to "I Think I'm Going Out of My Head," a big crowd was gathering and Mrs. George Zeluff was pointing at one of the trombone players.

"That's my husband," the internist's wife said. "He's the handsomest."

Well, maybe. But Dr. Cooley is all right in a tall, blue-eyed blond sort of way. Scores of ladies went out of their way to meet Dr. John I. Ochsner, chief of surgery at the Ochsner Clinic in New Orleans, even though he can't play any musical instrument.

Mrs. Zeluff probably hadn't yet seen Dr. Christiaan Barnard, the South African surgeon who did the world's first human heart transplant. The music had him wriggling around inside his nubby raw silk dinner jacket and tapping his square-toed black patent leather shoes until two committee ladies—one for each arm—arrived to take him away.

"I came here specifically for the gala," Dr. Barnard said at an earlier brunch. "Dr. Cooley and I are good friends."

At the time, Dr. Barnard was wearing a hand-stitched checked beige suit with a nipped-in waistline and a long jacket. He insisted that he could play the piano.

For a supper dance that night, Dr. Barnard switched into a black-and-white-checked dinner jacket, danced nearly every frug with his blue eyes closed and sang all the words to "Sentimental Journey" into one partner's ears. He was far more subdued at the gala.

After cocktails, the formally clad guests moved out of the store and into a tent set up on the parking lot. To get there, they had to pass through an enclosed corridor hung with a jungle of delicate little green cellophane ferns, miniature chandeliers and hundreds of little Italian lights.

David Merrick, the Broadway producer, escorted Mrs. Kenneth Franzheim 2nd, wife of the building tycoon, and in their wake came the various aristocratic Marcuses of Neiman-Marcus, James Lovell and Alan Shepard, the astronauts, and the incredibly suave Marquis de Villaverde. Aside from being Generalissimo Francisco Franco's son-in-law, the marquis is Dr. Cristóbal Martínez Bordiu, who performed Spain's only heart transplant. When he wasn't doing anything else, he was kissing ladies' hands and dancing more than his share of foxtrots.

"We have nothing like this in Montreal," Dr. Pierre Grondin said, visibly impressed. "Nothing at all." Dr. Grondin, chief surgeon at the Montreal Heart Institute, was referring as much to the tent's cream-colored draperies, the festoons of pale green foliage, the Italian lights and the seventeen chandeliers as he was to the other guests.

He sat next to Mrs. Michael E. DeBakey. Her husband, the heart pump pioneer who repaired the Duke of Windsor's abdominal aneurysm, spent the evening in the operating room at Methodist Hospital.

"He's always there," Mrs. DeBakey said.

Mrs. Frank Chapman, the former Gladys Swarthout, was at another table. The soprano, one of the greatest Carmens of them all, is one of Dr. Cooley's patients.

"He gave me a plastic valve," she said.

"She has a good heart," Dr. Cooley later said of Mrs. Chapman. "I know. I've been in it."

Jack Valenti was master of ceremonies when he wasn't hugging his old friends. Sid Caesar entranced everyone with his pantomimes. And Robert Mosbacher, the oil man whose brother Emil (Bus) Mosbacher, Jr., is the America's Cup sailor and President Nixon's protocol chief, had his say about his friend Dr. Cooley.

"He may be perfect," Mr. Mosbacher said, "but I can beat him at Ping-Pong."

At the program's conclusion, Dr. Cooley announced that the gala tickets, which had sold for $150, $250 and $1,000 per couple, had produced $100,000 for the Texas Heart Institute. But he was no sooner in his chair than he was up again at the microphone.

"A friend, a patient, just whispered something to me," he said.

" 'How much did you make?' he asked. I said, '$100,000,' and he said, 'I'll match it.' "

George Strake, yet another of Houston's many successful oil men, did come up with another $100,000, too. Which is a perfectly natural way to end an evening in Texas.

"If you're born and raised here, you think Dubuque is the best," says Mrs. Delbert Hayford, the official "Little Old Lady" of that Iowa town. The Hayfords celebrated their fiftieth wedding anniversary amid a flurry of good wishes and initialed cocktail napkins.
The New York Times (1970)

Dubuque, Iowa

When the late Harold Ross rejected the little old lady in Dubuque as lacking the sophistication to read *The New Yorker,* he inadvertently made her into a lasting symbol of American provincialism. She and her friends fought back by subscribing to *The Reader's Digest.* Forty-five years have elapsed since that somewhat tentative feud began. Since then, Dubuque, a picturesque town with the best of the gabled frame houses on the bluff overlooking the Mississippi River, has nestled even further into its hills.

The population, nearly 80 percent Irish and German Catholic, has reached 63,000, including perhaps forty blacks. A new generation of little old ladies has cropped up. And although these women are still something less than intellectually, culturally and politically with it—or hep, as they say in Iowa—their fight for what they consider the good life continues.

In the fifties, they decided Titian nudes and John Steinbeck's *The Wayward Bus* were obscene. In the sixties, they were reasonably successful in getting Christ back into Christmas. And in the seventies, they are after the producers of what they call "sex-ridden" movies.

"Why, it's a disgrace what the movies are today," Mrs. Delbert Hayford said. "There's entirely too much nudity. The stories don't do anything for you. Does the movie of today encourage you to marriage and a family? No, it doesn't. I don't approve."

221

Mrs. Hayford and her husband, a retired postal clerk, heard about "the new movies" and decided to see one for themselves. They went to *John and Mary,* which concerns a young couple who meet in a bar and then go to bed without knowing each other's names. The Hayfords were shocked. "We didn't like it at all," the sixty-six-year-old grandmother said, shaking her head.

Miss Emma Trenk had a similar reaction to *Gaily, Gaily,* the story of a youth who goes to a big city to live in what sixty-eight-year-old Miss Trenk correctly identified as "a house of ill repute." And at seventy, Mrs. Anthony Eberhardt is so upset she's boycotting the movies altogether. "We're being deprived of one of the great arts," Mrs. Eberhardt moaned. "I think my individual rights are being trampled. I believe in family movies—things like *The Shoes of the Fisherman.*"

What Mrs. Hayford, Miss Trenk and Mrs. Eberhardt say may not coincide with *The New Yorker*'s movie reviews, but their opinions matter in this comfortably isolated Middle Western town. Dubuquers, or Dubuque-landers as some natives also call themselves, respect and admire these women not just because they are senior citizens but because they, and such others as Mrs. Louise H. Halliburton, are to Dubuque what the Astors and the Vanderbilts are to New York.

What Mrs. Hayford says is particularly significant, however, for she is something of a celebrity—the only official Little Old Lady of Dubuque.

The Chamber of Commerce selected her in a contest six years ago, sent her to New York (which she didn't much like although she did meet television's Ed McMahon), and boosted her as representative of what Dubuque likes to think is wholesome about its community. Mrs. Hayford believes she's fairly typical.

"I was born and raised in Dubuque, and I expect to die here," she said. "My ties are very strong. I like living where I know everybody and everybody knows me. I'd be nobody in a big city."

Mrs. Hayford was wearing a lime-green knitted dress and jacket with a pink-and-white crocheted collar and cuffs. Her long white hair was up in a bun at the back of her head. Her forehead was obscured by wavy bangs. She had little curls over her ears. With the ensemble, she wore thin-heeled lime suède pumps, glasses with the mother-of-pearl plastic frames edged with rhinestones, silver earrings set with aquamarines, pink lipstick and pearlized nail polish. She was as chic as anyone in Dubuque.

"I was a flapper when I was a girl," she said. "I shocked my mother when I had my hair shingled. I wore boots with the buckles open. They went flap, flap."

Mrs. Hayford went to a Catholic girls school and on to Clark College for two years.

"In my day, if you weren't married by the time you were twenty-one

222

or twenty-two, you were dead," she said. "I went back later to study interior design."

The Hayfords' living room is their special joy. Gold satin draperies are bunched down the sides of the windows. The ornate Victorian love seat is brocaded in scarlet. The grand piano has been antiqued or maybe modernized with cream paint. The chandelier is baroque. The candles are wood with flame-shaped electric lights. Mrs. Hayford decorated the room herself.

"We're the little Heidelberg of America," she explained. "We have art and symphonies. Everybody's very culture-minded."

Aside from a Salvador Dali print or two, religious paintings, including portraits of Jesus Christ, and family photographs, the art in homes is mostly native to Iowa. There is no art museum, although exhibitions of local works are held now and then. But Dubuque does have an orchestra, three colleges, three theological seminaries and a Young Women's Christian Association that gave a short course in Negro history.

"If we wanted to see a play, we'd go into Chicago," Mrs. Hayford said, adding that Clark College has a lively dramatics department. "We see lots of television."

The Hayfords' twenty-seven-inch color television is on regularly between 7 and 10 p.m. They rarely miss "Family Affair," about a rich bachelor, his butler and how they're raising three orphaned children, and "The Carol Burnett Show" because Mrs. Hayford met and liked Miss Burnett.

Miss Trenk has a TV set, too, but she rarely turns it on. Instead, she reads travel books, the Audubon Society's magazine, the *National Geographic, Life* and *The Reader's Digest.*

"The people in Dubuque are racist," the retired schoolteacher said flatly. "They don't want to know what a Negro is like. If one gets to the city, he has a hard time."

For forty years, Miss Trenk taught economics, American history and "a little bit of everything in social studies" at the senior high school. She figures she taught 10,000 children, only six or eight of whom were black. "The racial issue was always a hard one for me," she said. "So many parents were prejudiced." When she wanted to show what discrimination was about, she divided a class into two groups. One blackened their faces. The others didn't. They then played out the stereotype roles.

"I think I did a pretty good job," she said, adding that her students had joined Vista and the Peace Corps. "I can hear my mother saying, 'Self-praise stinks,' but I *did* do a good job."

Like the other women, none of whom have ever confronted a thoroughly alienated young radical, Miss Trenk sees no real generation gap. "About revolution," she said, "I always say if you want revolution, you'd better build something, produce something better—not just destroy. If laws are bad, you work to change them."

Miss Trenk doesn't like long hair on boys because "it's so effeminate," but concedes that "Thomas Jefferson had a long wig, so I suppose it's all right." Her definition of a hippie is a drug addict.

While an increasing number of local homemakers look to prepackaged convenience foods, Miss Trenk grows her own fruits and vegetables and makes everything from soups to grape juice. She is famous for her strawberry shortcake and for clothes she bought on a trip around the world.

On a typical day, she's likely to wear a brightly flowered silk from Hawaii ("I wasn't sure I dared in Dubuque"), pearl earrings from Japan and a carved ivory necklace from India.

"Mrs. Halliburton and I made the trip together," Miss Trenk said. "We loved everything. We cried when we saw the Taj Mahal."

Mrs. Halliburton is a widowed artist. At noon on Wednesdays during Lent, she and perhaps thirty other residents might be found in a solemn line on the Washington Park sidewalk facing the Federal Building. Each wore a sign reading "Silent Vigil for Peace."

"We've been coming here on Sunday mornings since 1966," she said. "One Sunday it was 14 below zero."

A pacifist since she saw the first draft numbers drawn out of a fishbowl in Washington before World War I, Mrs. Halliburton has fasted for peace, picketed for civil rights and against the Vietnam war, leafleted at the Pentagon and consistently befriended Iowa's conscientious objectors.

"I'm a native of Dubuque," she said proudly, "but I feel very privileged that I've had an opportunity to live in other communities."

She went to the Corcoran Art School in Washington, married a Quaker economics professor and lived in Indiana and New Jersey. In recent years, she has refused to pay the Federal telephone tax because it helps finance the Vietnam war and urged her friends to boycott grapes on behalf of the Mexican grape pickers in California.

"I don't get into arguments," she said. "Nobody talks about what I do. The conversations are usually very uninteresting. People avoid discussing the real issues."

Mrs. Halliburton doesn't own a television, will not be drawn into the movie fight, reads *The Progressive,* exhibits her sketches of nudes, entertains black friends and defends Dubuque.

"So many people have lacked exposure to other viewpoints," she said. "They're turned inward to their families. But they're changing a little. I think maybe we're moving into the twentieth century."

While Mrs. Halliburton speaks hopefully of the future, Mrs. Eberhardt, a grandmother who spearheaded Christ in Christmas and the obscenity raids, plays "Love Me Tender, Love Me True" on her guitar, reads detective stories and talks about her European trip. She and her husband, a retired post office supervisor, took pictures of castles along the Rhine, admired St. Peter's in Rome, toured the Alps and were photographed in Paris at the base of the Eiffel Tower. "After it was all over," she said, "it was wonderful to get back to the old world charm of Dubuque. You know the hills here are very reminiscent of Switzerland. And, oh, our river! Now I've never seen anything, neither the Danube nor the Seine, that's as beautiful as the Mississippi."

Mr. and Mrs. Robert A. Uihlein, Jr., live in a Tudor house that overlooks rolling lawns and gardens. Mr. Uihlein, chief of the Schlitz brewers, is one of the beer barons who made Milwaukee famous. Now what's this nonsense about Coors?
The New York Times

Milwaukee

MILWAUKEE, AND THE BEER BARONS
July 1966

Robert A. Uihlein, Jr., one of the beer barons who made Milwaukee famous, gave a Fourth of July party as part of a four-day, community-wide celebration that may well have been the most elaborate in the nation. He and Mrs. Uihlein (pronounced EE-line) were host to 450 industrialists, bankers and civic leaders at the Memorial Art Center, an Eero Saarinen building some residents liken to a giant air-conditioner stuck out over Lake Michigan.

By 7:30 P.M., such guests as Robert Greenebaum, president of Inland Steel Products Company, and Mrs. Greenebaum had examined the cowboy and Indian paintings in the gallery where cocktails were being served. And by eight, the Uihleins, freshly dressed after their regular Sunday afternoon polo game—he plays and she cheers—had arrived.

"The Duke was marvelous," Mrs. Uihlein said after she had greeted some friends and ordered a martini. "He sent Lenny roses."

Lenny was Leonard Bernstein who, with the New York Philharmonic, had been imported to play a free celebration concert Saturday, and the Duke was Duke Ellington. The two musicians met for the first time on the Uihleins' rolling lawns, and promptly hugged each other.

"It was beautiful," said Mrs. Uihlein, a statuesque brunette who likes to fish and hunt big game. "They had a lot to talk about."

So did Mrs. Uihlein.

227

She said that when Mr. Bernstein visited them in 1963, she thought the helicopter that brought him in from the airport was going to land in one of their elm trees, but that the landing had been much better this time—despite the heat.

"It's terrible," she said. "Not like Wisconsin at all. If it was 96 in the shade by our lake, it had to be much worse in town."

Almost everybody was talking about the weather and not doing anything about it when Governor Warren P. Knowles materialized at the entranceway, accompanied by Mrs. Knowles. He, too, said it was hot. But Mrs. Knowles, who's redecorating the governor's mansion, said she didn't mind. "You get used to it," she said cheerfully.

Mrs. Knowles wore a short tent dress, a pair of false eyelashes and a wig that extended straight to her shoulders. She was the only woman at the party who looked as if she had stepped out of the pages of a fashion magazine. Mrs. Uihlein was more classically dressed in blue silk with her initials hand-embroidered across the bodice.

"You mustn't tell anyone I said it, but I don't drink beer anymore," said a delicate blond lady, who turned out to be Mr. Uihlein's mother. "I just don't have the taste for it." The senior Mrs. Uihlein is an Ilsley, and the Marshall and Ilsley Bank was founded here in 1847—two years before Uihlein ancestors organized the 117-year-old family-owned Joseph Schlitz Brewing Company, of which her son, the dinner host, is president.

The overhead lights blinked in the galleries to signal the end of cocktails and beginning of the buffet dinner. It was held in a huge hall on the center's third floor. All the tables were covered with red cloth and decorated with red, white and blue flowers. And the food, which had been trucked in from Gimbels-Schuster department store, included sixteen ounces of sliced filet of beef for each guest.

"You don't get much call for potato salad," said Jack Norman, the store's catering manager. "I have a lot of holiday parties and not one of them wants potato salad, hamburgers or hot dogs."

The speeches came toward the end of the dinner. Mr. Uihlein, a shy Harvard man who succeeded his uncle, Erwin C. Uihlein, as president of the brewery, said he was delighted not just by the presence of his dinner guests but by "all these people" who were in some way involved in the celebration.

Nearly 80,000 attended his concerts in Washington Park. Four thousand were invited to a picnic at his brewery. Another 450,000 were expected to see his gigantic circus parade. And thousands jammed the lawns outside the art center or were on little boats in the lakefront marina as he talked, waiting for what is billed in Milwaukee as "the world's greatest fireworks display." Several party-goers, who saw the fireworks from the center's rooftop, compared the celebration to Macy's Thanksgiving Day Parade in New York and the

Tournament of Roses in Pasadena. But whatever it was, it cost the Uihleins between $300,000 and $500,000.

If there were Millers in on the festivities, they went undetected, and the Pabst family, which is related to the Uihleins, had fled to the cooler lake country out of town.

"We are competitive," explained August Uihlein Pabst, Jr., whose great-grandfather, Captain Fred Pabst, married the daughter of the brewer Phillip Best, and turned the Best brewery into Pabst. "But I think some members of the family do go to the parade." Mr. Pabst, whose family still has some stock in the Pabst Brewing Company, recently sold his foreign-car agency and went to work for the brewery. He is the grandson of Mrs. Fred Pabst, the former Ida Uihlein. She is Robert A. Uihlein, Jr.'s aunt.

Despite their celebrity, the brewery clans are not the only families that have been in Milwaukee since the 1850's. Besides the Ilsleys, there are the Vogels, who were tanners; the Allises, who founded Allis-Chalmers, manufacturers of machinery and equipment; the Brumders, who went from German-language newspapers to banking; the Blommers, who're in the chocolate business; and the Plankintons, who were meatpackers. A hotel, an office building, a downtown avenue and a town in South Dakota are named for the Plankintons, and William Woods Plankinton, a colonel in the Civilian Air Patrol, never misses a Fourth of July parade.

"Our building's on the parade route," said Mr. Plankinton. "We can watch without getting out in the sun."

Cattlemen from all over the West always attended the late Winthrop
Rockefeller's two-day sale and parties. Bidders from the left include Gus
Wortham, Sterling Evans, R. W. Briggs, John Lynch and L. A. Nordan.
Afterward came the barbecue for three thousand and dancing.
Allyn Baum, *The New York Times* (1967)

Morrilton, Arkansas

Governor and Mrs. Winthrop Rockefeller's Santa Gertrudis cattle sale is what matters here socially, and it was a success this year even though Elvis Presley's parents didn't attend.

Thousands of other cattle fanciers, including cotton and pecan planters, oil men, bankers, aristocratic ranchers, construction tycoons and the dean of architecture at the University of California at Los Angeles, did show up on a recent weekend for the two-day sale—some in their own airplanes and some in chauffeur-driven limousines.

"We'd have had fifty planes if it weren't for the fog," Mrs. Rockefeller said unhappily. "Why, there's nothing out there on the field at all."

Mrs. Rockefeller, a statuesque woman for whom "Jeepers" is an all-purpose exclamation, is the granddaughter of D. E. Skinner, the Seattle shipping magnate. She was unhappy, she said, not about the airplane shortage—the Rockefellers have four planes of their own—but because of what the heavy fog could mean to the sale. "They don't like to drive," she said of the cattlemen. "If they can't fly, they'll skip the sale. That would be awful."

Mrs. Rockefeller's prediction did not come true. Aside from the Vernon E. Presleys, who have a cattle ranch in Alabama, and Colonel D. H. Byrd, a Dallas oil man who once described himself as "just one of your little rich—I

---

only have five or ten million bucks," everyone who was supposed to be in on the festivities was.

John F. Lynch, the lanky president of La Gloria Oil and Gas Company in Houston, was there in his black alligator loafers. L. A. (Les) Nordan, a San Antonio oil man, wore his mustard-colored Western suit with his white ostrich-skin boots. And Mrs. Harry C. Weiss, a Humble Oil heiress, brought along her Balenciaga coats and dresses, and a lot of her diamonds. "I get most of my clothes in Paris," she explained. "Mainbocher is only my American designer."

Edward (Pete) Crook, whose family has owned Quatro Milpas ranch near Paris, Texas, since the late 1840s, said he was as interested in cotton ("I'm a cotton picker but a high-class one") as he was in cattle. And Sasha Brastoff, a Los Angeles artist, wanted everyone to look at the Rockefellers' china collection. "I designed a lot of it," he said.

Mrs. Rockefeller, who runs the main house and all six of the guest houses at Winrock Farms, was well prepared for her guests. Her chef had ordered enough beef, chicken, lamb, pecan pie, crabmeat salad and vegetables for an army. The bedroom closets were stocked with everything from new toothbrushes and six shades of nail polish to French perfumes and postage stamps ("I never know what our guests are going to forget or want"). There were huge bouquets of fresh flowers everywhere. And when the first guests arrived, the only job left was the hanging of two dozen paintings.

"I don't know what CeeZee Guest does with her friends," Mrs. Rockefeller said, referring to New York's Mrs. Winston F. C. Guest. "But I put mine to work."

The gathering, which revolved around the sprawling wood, glass and stone main house with its walk-in fireplace, indoor plantings of hydrangeas and artificial waterfall, started on a Thursday night with caviar wrapped in blinis at a formal dinner for perhaps twenty houseguests.

Friday morning Mrs. Rockefeller took time out long enough to become honorary member of the Angel Flight, a girls' auxiliary to the University of Arkansas's Reserve Officers Training Corps. Then she made one last inspection trip (in her air-conditioned maroon Lincoln Continental) to the guest houses.

"I'm not happy unless I know everything's right," she said as she arranged some ashtrays.

By Friday afternoon, the house guest list had grown to forty, the dinner list to two hundred, and there was an orchestra for dancing in a big frame building the Rockefellers call "our playhouse." (Guests who didn't want to dance could have gone to the recreation building, with its squash court, four bowling alleys and pinball machine, but nobody did.) By Saturday, the day of the sale, the barbecue, and another dinner and dance, Mrs. Rockefeller had stopped counting.

"We feed two or three thousand at the barbecue," she said. "It's like running a hotel."

The barbecue, like the sale, is a public event open to anyone in the countryside who cares to turn up. It was held stand-up style in a red, yellow and blue tent at tables designed for men whose shoulders are at least five feet from the ground. Men in broad-brimmed hats and boots lined up beside women in linen dresses and flat-heeled shoes. They filled their paper plates with beef that had been cooking all night, mounds of potato salad, pickled peaches and homemade rolls. While they ate, they talked—sometimes about the weather.

"The sun's always come out for our sale," Governor Rockefeller said. "It won't fail us."

The governor, second youngest of the incredible John D. Rockefeller's six grandchildren, is as rich (reportedly more than $200-million) and as patrician as a Rockefeller is supposed to be. But he rarely looks it. He abandoned ordinary shoes and such New York haunts as El Morocco when he settled in the rolling green country in this the most western of the Deep South states in 1953. And his usual daytime attire at the farm, a 7,500-acre spread atop Petit Jean Mountain, consists of a Western hat, an Eastern white shirt, pants, a zip-up rancher's jacket, elegant high-heeled boots and a gold wedding ring with his WR brand inscribed on it.

"I regard myself as much an Arkansan as anyone who was born here," he said last year after becoming the first Republican governor since Reconstruction days.

The governor's passion for peanut butter sandwiches is well known here (hot peanut butter on toast was as important an appetizer at one of the many sale parties as shrimp with Roquefort cheese). And he dotes on Coca-Cola, the Southern staff of life, although he apparently is incapable of pronouncing it the way the natives do. They call it Koh-Kolah.

"I get a kick out of these things," Governor Rockefeller said, as millionaires and farmers crowded into the sale tent. "It's a very serious business."

When the tent was full, the sun came out and the tenth annual sale began. A big (2,620 pounds) rust-colored Santa Gertrudis bull plunged into the ring, glared at the crowd, tossed its sleek head and sniffed at the wood shavings on the floor.

Mrs. Weiss, who in 1966 bought such a bull as a gift for Texas Agriculture and Mining University, thought he looked "wonderful." Gus S. Wortham, a Houston insurance tycoon and cattle baron, said he was "mighty fine." The bidding started at $1,000, and climbed steadily. At $8,000, the bid went once, then twice, then the auctioneer's gavel came down. It was the first of fifty head of cattle sold for a total of $140,050.

After the sale, guests regrouped in a green-and-white tent on the lawn outside the main house. They stood in little groups, discussing beef prices while the sun gradually disappeared over the junction of the Petit Jean and Arkansas rivers, 1,100 feet in the valley below them.

Winrock Farms had not yet shoved Palm Beach, Newport or San Francisco's better suburbs completely out of the American society picture. But its grass will always be a little greener. The Rockefellers spray it with vegetable dye.

Mrs. Albert Jones Coleman, a descendant of Wyoming's cattle barons, is a child psychologist, philanthropist and ecologist who plays tennis and knows her Colorado history. She lives in Denver.
Bruce McAllister, *The New York Times* (1967)

Denver

The Arapahoes who pitched their tepees in the cottonwood groves where Cherry Creek joins the Platte River are gone, and so are the gaudy gold and silver kings who hung their stately mansions with chandeliers of amber, amethysts and garnets. But Denver survives—an "Eastern" city at peace with itself. What the once raw Queen City of the Plains lacks in opulence and the frontier spirit it has replaced with a serenity virtually unknown to Western cities except San Francisco. It takes its evening and weekend hunting, fishing and skiing in the nearby Rocky Mountains as seriously as its art museum and its symphony. And its community leaders, many of whom are the hopelessly aristocratic custodians of inherited fortunes, like it that way. They are only a generation or two removed from the restless pioneers who crossed the treacherous prairies in covered wagons. Yet they run the city as economically and socially as if it were an old Eastern establishment.

One doesn't have to control a bank to be decidedly upper caste. But it helps. It's also all right to own the Gates Rubber Company, if for no other reason than it may be the largest private industry in town. And nobody looks down on anyone in real estate because nearly all the old wealth derived at least in part from what is called either the "development" or the "exploitation" of the land.

The old order does admit newcomers, however—particularly if they are

237

financially sound members of old Eastern or Middle Western families. But rich Texans are something else. They are sometimes restless, often vigorous, but they have to prove themselves despite what their successes in the oil fields could contribute to the local economy.

Starting at the turn of the century, Denver depended upon such Eastern colleges as Harvard, the Massachusetts Institute of Technology, Vassar and Bryn Mawr to educate its young. Good children were expected to return after they received their degrees. If they married Easterners, they brought them home to Denver. But mostly, they married each other. They still do.

"If not the first time, then the second or third time," according to Mrs. William Pryor, the former Diana Knowles. Mrs. Pryor, here from San Francisco for a brief visit, is the daughter of Thomas B. Knowles, president of Van Schaack and Company, and she knows what she's talking about. Her late mother, a Van Schaack of the real-estate family, was her father's second wife. He was previously married to a Kountze of the Colorado National Bank. Her maternal grandmother, a Mitchell of the Denver National Bank, widow of Charles C. Van Schaack and arbiter in the selection of local debutantes, recently married Albert E. Humphreys, who heads a mining business.

It is the Evanses, however, who are awesomely regarded as the city's first family. They are descendants of the Dr. John Evans whom President Abraham Lincoln sent here as the second territorial governor. Dr. Evans arrived in 1862 after helping to found Northwestern University at Evanston, Illinois, a community that was named for him. By 1863, he was organizing the University of Denver. The third and fourth generations are represented by an engaging father and son team, John Evans and John Evans, Jr., neither of whom would be caught dead in anything so "Western" as a Stetson hat or high-heeled cowboy boots. Besides the First National Bank, the Evanses dominate the Denver Tramway Company, a real-estate concern, a family investment business and something like three hundred head of cattle. John, Jr., also is president of the University of Denver's board of trustees.

"I'm the fourth member of the family at the job," he said. "I'm following my father, my grandfather and my great-grandfather. None of us got our degrees there. I went to Princeton. My father went to M.I.T."

The senior Mr. Evans was born in 1884, a year after President Grover Cleveland distressed Denver silver miners by putting the United States on the gold standard. He delights in etchings and maps of Colorado in its earlier days.

"When I was a boy, it was a real trip to get to the mountains," he said. "Now it's only an hour or so, and you're there."

The natives have an understandable affinity for the majestic Rockies. The mines were there. And when Europeans and Easterners introduced the West to skiing, the mountains again paid off handsomely, particularly at such resorts as Vail and Aspen. But it is not enough that the snow-capped peaks and crags are there. The denizens have to be out in them. And when they come back to the city they want to see the mountains from their picture windows. They build their houses accordingly.

Such houses rarely have butlers, and full-time cooks are for the lucky few. Neither Mrs. Temple Hoyne Buell nor Mrs. Charles C. Gates, both of whom have access to millions of dollars, have all the help they'd like. "We wind up with the caterer," said Mrs. Buell, the chatelaine of a vaguely Tudor house filled with French and Italian furniture. "Usually it's French cuisine with black ties and long gowns." Mrs. Buell's father bought Cripple Creek land for fishing only to discover that it was loaded with silver. As a consequence, she was raised at Wolhurst, a fifty-two-room mansion that had sixteen bathrooms.

Her husband is an architect and real-estate developer who made so many of his own millions that Colorado Woman's College recently decided to honor him by changing its name. "The president came to me and said, 'Sandy, we're looking for a new name for the college,' " Mr. Buell explained. "He said, 'Temple Buell sounds alliterative.' He asked me if I'd leave the college some money in my will. I said, 'Hell, why not give the money now?' and I did. It wasn't less than $25-million."

Mr. Buell, a Chicagoan, was gassed in World War I. He came here in 1921, hoping that the dry, mile-high climate would relieve his tuberculosis. It did. He went on to build the city its Cherry Creek Shopping Center and to have his suits (with waistcoats) made on Savile Row in London.

"Colorado today is what California used to be," Mr. Buell said between puffs on one of his long cigars. "There are opportunities here for people who want to find them."

Mrs. Gates agrees. Her late husband built his rubber empire on a job he saw advertised in a newspaper. She thinks such enterprises are still possible for "people who aren't afraid to work."

"They tell me I have millions," she said. "But money itself doesn't mean a thing. You can't eat it or sleep in it. For me, it means that I can give people things they need."

The Gates family long ago decided to cut out what Mrs. Gates called "those $50 and $100 contributions." Instead, it has given the community a school science building and a swimming pool.

Its current project, a dream of the grandmotherly matriarch who wears silk brocade gowns, gold shoes and plenty of diamonds in the afternoon, is a planetarium in the park with head rests on the chairs so that visitors won't be uncomfortable looking up at the stars.

Mrs. Gates—"Mommie G" around the rubber company employees—entertains 10,000 employee children every Christmas. If she has a hobby, it's houses. She has three. The Siamese town house is noted for its hand-carved teak skylight coated with gold leaf, its Mexican brass chandeliers, its Cambodian ornamental dogs and its benches with turquoise-inlaid legs. She also has a residence in Honolulu and a hideout in the foothills. Unless her family really wants the hideout, it's to be burned when she reaches what she calls "the deep end." The house, of native rock, was built around a tree. Its great hall is sixty feet long and there are ten bedrooms, "with a bath for each, of course."

"Sometimes I think Denver forgets it was a mining town and the only women were dance hall girls," Mrs. Gates said.

Denver was more than that. In the 1890s, according to Mrs. Albert Jones Coleman, an amateur historian, "it was a culture center between St. Louis and California." It had a natural history museum before Washington had its Smithsonian Institution, and opera singers came to perform. It also has a history of being a healthful, beautiful and economically exciting place to go to get away from somewhere else. Mrs. Coleman's great-grandfather Swan, one of Wyoming's greatest cattle kings, was followed in later years by Lawrence C. Phipps, Pittsburgh's Carnegie Steel multimillionaire who later represented Colorado in the United States Senate.

Edward B. Close, Jr., a ski-minded New Yorker whose socially impeccable father was once married to Mrs. Marjorie Merriweather Post, came here after World War II because he "got tired of Greenwich and the caverns of Wall Street."

"My wife is from Denver, but I'm probably happier to be living here than she is," Mr. Close said.

Three of the late Senator Phipps's sons—Lawrence C., Jr., Gerald H. and Allan R.—have stayed in Denver, where they have been vigorous community leaders.

But it is Mrs. Coleman, a gray-haired child psychologist who wears knee socks and turquoise and silver Indian jewelry with her skirts and sweaters, for whom the West still seems to be Western. "We have twenty-four generations of family sorted out," the Bryn Mawr graduate and member of the Colonial Dames said as the sun streamed into her living room over a series of green plants near a huge picture window.

Mrs. Coleman's family gave Scripps College its chapel and Colorado Medical College its memorial library and a science building. But she has other philanthropic ideas: she plans to give Denver "a primitive area."

At this stage, the "primitive area" is Mrs. Coleman's country home at Lookout Mountain, a seventy-five-acre sanctuary for animals, birds, trees and plants, only twenty-five miles from downtown Denver. Her goal is to preserve this ecology as it is now—still not seriously disturbed by man.

"We're going to fence the people out, not the animals in," she said. "It's expensive to feed the mountain lion, but I do it. I don't want him going after something else and being shot."

Mr. and Mrs. Joshua Green played a significant role in the Seattle social order all the way into their nineties. Their baronial mansion was filled with trophies from hunting expeditions to Africa and Alaska, and there was fur everywhere.
Carl T. Gossett, Jr., *The New York Times* (1963)

Seattle

People are on the make economically, culturally and socially in this watery world of fish, shipping, timber and airplanes, and although there is, by San Francisco and New York standards, a lot of catching up to do, Seattle is not the end of the world. There are a few established families of wealth and prominence here, but they consciously turn the adjective "social" away from themselves and apply it to their institutions. Nobody seems to want anyone to think he is glamorous, rich or at all different.

They are a conservative, practical, outgoing and sometimes imaginative people who believe in "social responsibility," a firmly entrenched concept that seems to have sprung both from the not-too-distant pioneers, who had to work together to bring civilization to the wilderness, and from their Eastern and sometimes Puritan ancestors. It is a philosophy that keeps society's nose to the civic grindstone.

Until recently, one could quote Sir Thomas Beecham, who called Seattle "a cultural dustbin," and get away with it.

Not so today. Seattle insists, perhaps accurately, it has as much "culture" for its size (1960 census, 557,087) as any comparable community, and in some instances more. It has the Seattle Symphony, its own opera, an art museum and a new repertory theater. Society, denizens are quick to contend, may not always have supported the arts as it should have. But it did not go in for

243

drinking champagne from dancing slippers, having its own elegantly furnished railroad cars or hanging crystal chandeliers in the lavatory either. The reason? There never was enough money.

"The wealth came too late," said Mrs. Thomas H. Meadowcroft, whose grandfather, J. H. Bloedell, was a lumber and timber magnate. "It took a while to earn the money, and then it was 1920 and there were income taxes."

Mrs. Meadowcroft is a finely featured young woman whose clothes, hairdo, jewels and way of speaking are decidedly Eastern. She was educated at Chatham Hall in Virginia, Vassar College and the University of British Columbia. If she lived in a city with a *Social Register,* she would probably be listed.

"I did things because I'm interested in them," she said. "I'm nonclubby, but I like to work for the Seattle Symphony because ours is a working board. We don't just sit there."

Mrs. Meadowcroft's husband is an arts-conscious real-estate developer. Her brother-in-law, Bagley Wright, is a displaced Easterner who organized the financing for the Seattle World's Fair Space Needle. He may also be responsible for the recent run on commissioned artworks. Mr. Wright ran a contest for a sculpture design for a downtown building and persuaded the building's owners to buy the finished selection. Since then, all kinds of sculpture and paintings have been commissioned and labeled with the donors' names.

"Everyone wants a monument," Mrs. Meadowcroft said.

The Meadowcrofts live in her grandfather's spacious old mansion, which she is restoring to its earlier grandeur. It is on Harvard East, next to one of the city's many contemporary homes.

"I'm no longer a member of the Junior League," she said. "I resigned. My field is money-raising—especially for the symphony and the opera. The Junior League does not count the time I put in as 'volunteer service.'" Resigning or being asked to resign from the Junior League in a city the size of Seattle could plunge a woman into social oblivion. Mrs. Meadowcroft's social standing has not been affected. Among aristocrats, the Junior League is nice but not necessary.

A similar move would not tarnish the escutcheon of the distinguished Baillargeon clan either. It's been here since 1867—long before "The Fire." Pioneer organizations restrict membership to those whose forebears arrived before 1870. The next best thing is to have had an ancestor around in 1889, when a glue pot was ignited and the city went up in flames.

Cebert Baillargeon is chairman of the board and chief executive officer of the Seattle Trust and Savings Bank. His son, J. C. Baillargeon, Jr., is executive vice-president. It is not a family bank. K. Winslow, Jr., is president. The Baillargeons, who are "related to almost everyone in town," live in The

Highlands, a prestigious residential area. Father and son wear suits with vests and drive themselves to and from work. Chauffeurs are for the elderly or the ailing. There are fewer than twenty of them in the Puget Bay region. The elder Mr. Baillargeon's office is furnished with a rolltop desk, chairs, an Oriental rug, a pair of small American flags, medals struck in honor of President Kennedy and former President Eisenhower and an artist's sketch of a new branch bank. It is a walled-in world in which the arts have been discussed. The chairman's father was president of the symphony and so was he. Eventually, the job may pass on to his Princeton-educated son. Neither cares for Vincent Price's suggestion to Seattle that "man cannot live by fish alone."

"Mr. Price," said the elder Mr. Baillargeon quietly, "may be a nice man, but what else is he? An actor who sells paintings for Sears, Roebuck."

Some years ago, Seattle had a *Blue Book*. It was a commercial venture with social connotations—a list of the supposed elite. One of the first women approached was Mrs. Joshua Green, whose husband was president, then chairman of the board of Peoples National Bank. Mrs. Green, a fluffy-haired Southerner who is in her nineties, would have nothing to do with it. "We've never believed in that sort of thing," she said vehemently. "It's nonsense."

The book was published. But, apparently because of her opposition, her name was not included. She did not care until she later tried to cash a check in New York.

"They looked me up in the Seattle book and I wasn't there," Mrs. Green said. "They wouldn't give me any money."

Mrs. Green is a founder of the Sunset Club, the city's most exclusive social enclave. She also helped to organize the Winter Ball, a predecessor of the Christmas Ball for debutantes. And in her day she was a glamorous hostess. She still wears bright pink nail polish, plenty of pearls and high-heeled shoes. Her ninety-three-year-old husband calls her Missy and occasionally allows her to smoke a cigarette. Mr. Green and Seattle have grown up together. He came here from the South in 1886. He has been a post office clerk, a railroad worker ("we wanted to build our own railroad to Chicago and New York"), a steamboat purser and a shipowner. In 1926, he changed jobs again. "There was a little bank for sale," he said. "It could be bought for only a couple of hundred thousand dollars. I sold some of my steamer stock and became a banker."

In 1901 the Greens bought their baronial house with its heavy carved-wood doorways, huge fireplace and basement billiard room. Among its trappings are souvenirs of Mr. Green's various hunting expeditions to Alaska and Africa. A bearskin rug spills over a stairway. A chair has lion legs and paws for arms. An elephant's foot serves as an umbrella stand.

The Greens' son, Joshua, Jr., runs the bank today. A daughter, Mrs. Charles Pye Burnett, Jr., has served on the Christmas Ball's debutante-

245

selection committee. The number of debutantes grows every year. "Thirty of them are presented these days," she said. "In Mother's day, it was two, maybe three. The committee nearly goes out of its mind. It's not like the old days."

Victor Denny, a tall, slim partner in Blyth and Company, Inc., has more reason to be interested in the old days than almost anyone in Seattle. In 1851 his grandfather Denny guided the first pioneers to Alki Point, a spit at the entrance to the city's harbor.

For two years, Mr. Denny, who was once described as being "as conservative as an E Bond," was president of the United States Lawn Tennis Association. Today, he is the United States representative to the International Lawn Tennis Federation. His "social responsibilities" include the Museum of History and Industry. He is its president.

"In a city like this," Mr. Denny said, "the more people we can get to think they are pioneers, the better. We don't have millionaires to compare with those in the East. We depend on a great many people for the support of our institutions."

The list of "active contributors" to the arts is long. It includes almost anyone with social stature, pretensions or aspirations. Among its numbers is a woman the Sunset Club turned down "because she's only a teacher," a woman who put her press clippings on a bulletin board, and such social figures as William M. Allen, president of the Boeing Company; Mark Tobey, the painter; Dr. Richard Fuller, and Mrs. David E. Skinner.

Dr. Fuller and his mother, the late Mrs. Eugene Fuller, gave the city its art museum. Mrs. Skinner's husband is president of the Skinner Corporation, a holding company, and its subsidiary, the Alaska Steamship Company. She knows almost as much about ships, their routes and the international laws governing them as her husband does.

The Skinners raise race horses and children in Bellevue. They play tennis on their own courts and sail a forty-six-foot auxiliary sloop, *Kate II.* Among others who sail regularly are Mr. and Mrs. Charles J. Frisbie. In 1958 Mr. Frisbie took temporary leave of his insurance business, met his wife at a marina, climbed aboard the couple's comfortably furnished *Alotola,* unfurled the sails and headed halfway around the world to the Greek islands. The voyage lasted two years.

Walter J. Hickel came to Alaska with 37 cents in his pocket and went on to become a millionaire, governor and then Secretary of the Interior in the Nixon administration. He and Mrs. Hickel have his-and-her kitchens, each with its own appliances.
Carl T. Gossett, Jr., *The New York Times* (1966)

Anchorage, Alaska

There's nothing very old or established about the affluent pioneer élite that dominates the icy wilderness in this, Alaska's biggest and most prosperous city. But money is money, and the first- and second-generation residents who have it never seem at a loss for ways of spending it interestingly. Virtually everyone of consequence has his own airplane, a second house (on a bush-country lake accessible only by air, or in some warm place in what Alaskans call "the outside" or "the lower 48"), and enough hunting trophies (you must have shot the bear, moose, caribou, Dall sheep or walrus yourself) to stock a medium-sized museum.

When the going gets rough, and by outside standards that roughness starts when the temperature is in the teens and low twenties, the frozen ground is covered with snow and the pale sun rises at 9:30 A.M. and sets at 3:30 P.M., Alaskans insist upon business and pleasure as usual. But every month or so through the long winter, the women abandon their spacious houses and fly down to Seattle or San Francisco for a little shopping and a taste of warmer air. And whenever a couple decides to zip off to Tokyo, Copenhagen, Paris or on a trip around the world, it is almost inevitably during the winter.

Nobody, Alaskans are quick to note, came here rich, and the men who are making the first-generation millions, whether high school dropouts or Ivy League graduates, are self-proclaimed runaways from the outside. They came here as much to get away from an urban or rural civilization they didn't like as they did with the desire to make money and live a rugged outdoor life. Members of the born-rich second generation, most of whom have a Puritan dedication to work—both for themselves and for the community—welcome those they sometimes disparagingly call "new people," particularly if they are successful. The cheers that went up when Anchorage's own Walter J. Hickel became Alaska's first elected Republican governor came as much from the second generation as from all the other Alaskans who voted the self-made construction executive into office.

Such Alaska-born stalwarts as Mrs. Robert B. Atwood and her brother, Elmer E. Rasmuson, the banker, were Hickel advocates, although Mrs. Atwood is not a Republican and Mr. Hickel definitely is "new people." But his kind of "newness" is what established Alaskans admire most. "Why, he came up here with 37 cents in his pocket and look what he's done," said Mrs. Atwood, wife of the editor and publisher of the *Anchorage Daily Times* and the acknowledged arbiter of Anchorage society. "He's got vitality. He's doing something."

It's true that Mr. Hickel, the eldest of ten children of Kansas tenant farmers, is doing something. He was sixteen years old when he quit school and twenty when he left home in 1940, bound on making his fortune in Australia. But when he got to Los Angeles, he discovered that anyone under twenty-one couldn't get a passport. So he came to Alaska. Anchorage was a lively, wooded community then, just as it is now. It sits like a crescent on an inlet named for Captain James Cook, the explorer. And on a clear day, its 120,000 citizens can see snow-capped mountains on three sides and water on the other.

"I thought it was a challenging, young, dynamic country," Mr. Hickel said simply. "I wanted a frontier. I knew I could be somebody. I like to work and I like to accomplish things."

Mr. Hickel's first job was washing dishes. (He and his wife now have large his-and-her kitchens, each with its own automatic dishwasher, as well as his-and-her drawing rooms, and steamrooms.) Since then, he has developed and built houses, apartments, shopping centers, hotels and Turn-again-by-the-Sea—the city's most elaborate residential area. He became a multi-millionaire in the process, and when he decided to run against Governor William A. Egan, there was joy in the power élite.

Besides trying for what amounted to an unpopular third term, Mr. Egan, it is said in Anchorage's better drawing rooms, had two things against him. He was neither "imaginative" nor "progressive," and although he helped draft the state's first constitution, the grocery business he had before becoming the state's first elected governor was not successful.

"It's what anyone does—what kind of contribution he makes—that counts up here," Mrs. Atwood said. "We don't have all the precedent and tradition they have back East. There are no sacred cows. It's wide open."

Mrs. Atwood, a sleek, auburn-haired lady who gave black-tie dinners beneath three French crystal chandeliers until the 1964 earthquake swallowed up her $100,000 log cabin, braves the snows in high-heeled black alligator shoes, black stockings and nothing more substantial than a long-sleeved wool dress, a short blue sheared beaver coat, turquoise eyeshadow and diamonds. She doesn't feel cold, she says, even when the thermometer registers zero. And the only reason she doesn't walk around the town instead of driving is that nobody walks.

"If you did," she said, "someone would think you had a flat tire or were out of gas."

She believes in beautiful clothes, French furnishings and French cuisine. But she won't buy French wines because she doesn't agree with Charles de Gaulle. She thinks nothing of spending two days shopping for a dinner party ("We can live as graciously here as they do in San Francisco, New Orleans and Boston"), demands and gets perfection ("Artichokes must have their own plates; crab legs must be fresh") and fights to keep Alaska economically, politically and socially in what she calls the mainstream.

"I don't believe in putting on airs," she said, "but I don't see any reason why we have to be uncouth."

Besides founding the local League of Women Voters and the World Affairs Council, Mrs. Atwood's contributions include three books on Alaskan history ("I was around and I don't want people to get the stories wrong") and conversation as after-dinner entertainment instead of bridge or poker. She was not born poor.

But she remembers her early life in Skagway as being lit by kerosene, heated by coal and full of mile-long walks to school in the snow. Her parents, missionary teachers representing the Swedish Evangelical Covenant, came to Alaska at the turn of the century. And it is because of them and her upbringing, she says, that she still saves string.

"My dad didn't want to be a poor immigrant," she said. "He studied law and saved enough money to go to Minneapolis to study. He passed the Minnesota state bar and then came back to Alaska."

Before long, Edward A. Rasmuson was legal counsel for the National Bank of Alaska, and then its president. And before he died he owned a Palm Springs hotel. He sent his son, Elmer Rasmuson, now chairman of the bank's board, to Harvard for his bachelor of science and master of arts degrees.

"You can write a few pages of history here instead of reading it," Mr. Rasmuson said from behind the cluttered desk in his cedar-paneled office. "It's an exciting place."

Mr. Rasmuson, a gentle, soft-spoken man who in no physical way resembles the popular image of a frontiersman, is Mayor of Anchorage and one of the city's celebrated hunters. He has shot the so-called grand slam of wild American sheep—Dall, Stone, Rocky Mountain Big Horn and Desert Big Horn.

The gun rack made of the feet of these sheep was lost during the earthquake. But he managed to save the jade tiles he had had around his fireplace. He also is interested in the arts ("Our symphony and theater groups are quite creditable"), has Chagall and Picasso lithographs on his office wall, and values his Sydney Laurence paintings of the Alaskan outdoors.

The senior Mr. Rasmuson would have sent Mrs. Atwood, the former Evangeline Rasmuson, to Vassar. But she didn't want to go. She went to the University of Washington instead and on to the University of Chicago for her master's degree. For several years she was a social worker. She is not much for the Ivy League or the Eastern women's colleges.

"They have mannerisms that seem strange to us," she said. "When they come up here, they have to live down an Eastern college. They aren't always adaptable."

Neither Lowell Thomas, Jr. (Dartmouth), nor Barrie M. White, Jr. (Harvard), seems to be any the worse for their Eastern college degrees. But, like Mr. Hickel, they are considered newcomers. Mr. Thomas, son of the radio commentator and explorer, and his wife, daughter of Samuel Pryor, a retired vice-president of Pan American Airways, moved here with their two children in 1960.

"It was either that or be another New York commuter," said Mr. Thomas, who likes to climb mountains. "We love the out of doors and the chance to contribute to the growth of the state. Frankly, there's the frontier spirit." The Thomases live in the hills outside town in a post-earthquake tented frame and brick house. It is reputed to have cost more than a quarter of a million dollars.

The house has an old ship's wheel as its kitchen chandelier. The front hall is a purposeful arrangement involving a Scandinavian brass and glass chandelier, an early American corner cupboard, antique Spanish benches, Oriental rugs and Chinese wooden boxes. And Mr. Thomas has covered the filing cabinets in his study with Polynesian tapa cloth. The only outside things the Thomases miss are lamb, corn-on-the-cob and watermelon.

"Avocados are three for 99 cents," Mrs. Thomas said.

When the Thomases moved here, Mrs. Pryor sent her daughter lots of long, wooly underwear and advice about keeping warm. But neither was necessary.

"We're not deprived and freezing," said Mrs. Thomas, a Smith graduate who is writing a history of Alaskan churches. "Nobody ever believes life here has the comforts of the outside."

Until November 8, Mr. Thomas's chief occupation was lecturing, writing books and making films. But after two defeats he was finally elected to the Alaska State Senate. This means he will have to commute to Juneau, the capital, a distance he intends to fly in his Cessna 180.

Mr. White, who uses his airplane as much for hunting and fishing as he does for business, is involved in a series of ventures not the least of which is a real-estate investing concern. He also developed the city's sports arena, which is iced over in the winter so people can skate indoors or play hockey, and a newspaper delivery service. Like Mr. Hickel, he has washed his share of dishes.

"When I got out of college, the idea of being a stockbroker on State Street [Boston] just didn't appeal to me," he said. "I came up here to see what was going on."

He washed dishes because "in New England we were taught to live within our incomes and I didn't have one." Today, he and Mrs. White, the former Judy Finn of Montclair, New Jersey, live in a thoroughly New England white frame house with scarlet wall-to-wall carpeting. Upstairs in his study, he keeps a rug he had made from a polar bear he shot.

"Anyone who says Anchorage has an establishment is kidding himself," Mr. White said philosophically, sipping a drink from a glass bearing the Harvard insignia. "It's coming, of course, but it's not here. New people will come, and more new people. The present group could be engulfed."

Mr. and Mrs. Benjamin F. Dillingham 2nd live in an Oriental house in a
Japanese garden with a waterfall and a mock orange hedge. The drawing
room is an eclectic collection of French, English and Oriental treasures.
They are among Honolulu's very *kamaaina haoles.*
Carl T. Gossett, Jr., *The New York Times* (1966)

Honolulu

American society has all kinds of aristocrats, but none live more exotic lives then the once oligarchic *kamaaina haoles* whose ancestors were the New England Congregational missionaries who began to arrive in the Hawaiian Islands in 1820. When these Hawaii-born Caucasians, some of whom have a little Hawaiian royal blood in their veins, are not roasting and consuming quantities of suckling pig or shooting doves they later barbecue in soy sauce, they are dancing gentle hulas or installing French, English, and Indian antiques in their Oriental houses.

They are also body surfing in the middle of the night, raising money to restore Iolani Palace—the only royal palace in the United States—or chartering planes that whisk them off to one of their houses on the other islands. When they are not running around in their bare feet, they may have sable jackets over their shoulders. And they have lots of diamonds, but they don't wear them often because it's too hot.

Their missionary ancestors brought Yankee inventiveness, drive and capitalism to the islands as well as Christianity, public education and loyalty to Yale University. Later generations developed the sugar and pineapple plantations and the Big Five companies—C. Brewer and Company, Ltd., Castle and Cooke, Ltd., American Factors, Ltd., Alexander and Baldwin, Ltd., and

255

Theo. H. Davies and Company, Ltd.—which were merchants and plantation agencies.

Until World War II, the sugar and pineapple plantations were the mainstay of the economy. They were staffed with imported Oriental labor. And the men who owned the land and ran the Big Five controlled the islands politically, socially and culturally as well as economically. The latest descendants, most of whom are fourth- or fifth-generation islanders, inherited vast tracts of land—they still own most of downtown Honolulu—and their interest in the Big Five. They tend to be up and going between 5:30 and 6:30 A.M., sit on each other's boards of directors, and make their important business decisions either at the ultraexclusive Pacific Club or in one of the Big Five offices.

They are Republicans who deplore the postwar drift toward the Democratic (and increasingly Oriental) party. They marry each other or import their spouses from the mainland. And although they denounce anyone who suggests that the missionaries or their children took advantage of the Polynesian Hawaiians, they aren't much for ancestor worship. "I think each of us must stand on his own," said Richard A. Cooke, Jr., who was defeated in his fall bid for a seat in the state legislature. "We've got to move with the times." Mr. Cooke, who ran as Likeke Cooke because everyone who's born here has and uses his Hawaiian name, is a great-grandson of the Reverend Amos Starr Cooke, who landed with his wife in 1831. By 1839, the Cookes had started a school for the royal children. Later, he and S. M. Castle, a financial agent for the Board of Missions, organized Castle and Cooke.

"Everything my great-grandfather touched turned to gold," Mr. Cooke said. "He helped to start C. Brewer."

Until November 1, Mr. Cooke was associated with C. Brewer, the oldest of the Big Five. He resigned, he said, because he wanted to build and develop apartments. If he had been elected, he intended to devote himself to politics.

"We are the place of the blending of the races," he said. "We should lead. We should sacrifice financial gain for having what we want as a place to live."

Mr. Cooke thinks the Pacific Club should be opened to Orientals, that the old agricultural economy is nearly passé, and that everyone's going to have to get used to even more tourists in paradise.

He and Mrs. Cooke, the former Loraine Day of Beverly Hills, and their six children live in the fashionable Makiki Heights section of Honolulu in a house high up in the emerald green hills. They have what amount to three large living rooms. The lanai terrace has a bamboo tree growing in a pot on the crushed coral floor and paintings on two walls. The family room, as formal as any East Coast living room, is scarlet and gold with bookcases full of treasures from the Cookes' tours. And at the far end of the house is

256

the even more formal cream and white open-air Chinese drawing room. One of its Japanese screens dates to the fourteenth century. Mr. and Mrs. Benjamin Franklin Dillingham 2nd have Japanese screens, too, and the one in their dining room is supposed to be a national treasure. "When we sent it back to Japan for repairs, they didn't want to return it to us," said Mrs. Dillingham, the former Frances Andrews of Dallas. "Our house used to be a beach cottage. It was so light it had to have chains on the corners to hold it down."

The Dillinghams live at the foot of Diamond Head, which dominates the harbor, with the Pacific Ocean in their front yard. Their Oriental house has sliding glass doors as exterior walls and lanterns hanging from the eaves. The interior is a mixture of Oriental, English, Early American and French furnishings. When Mr. Dillingham was a boy, the house was in the country.

"The city has come in around us," he said. "We have to go to our ranch to get away from things."

Mr. Dillingham, who was twice elected to the State Senate and then defeated in 1962 in his only try for the United States Senate ("That's the only political job worth bothering with"), is the great-grandson of the Reverend Lowell Smith. The Reverend Mr. Smith's daughter married his grandfather, the first B. F. Dillingham. "He was from West Brewster on Cape Cod," Mr. Dillingham said. "He was in the China trade with his uncle. They stopped in Honolulu for provisions. On his third trip out, he went horseback riding and broke his leg. My grandmother went to read to him. You might say she was one of the earliest Gray Ladies."

The Dillinghams parlayed railroads, dredging and construction into what is now the Dillingham Corporation—an international empire headed by Mr. Dillingham and his brother, Lowell Smith Dillingham. It was never part of the Big Five, but is sometimes called the Big Sixth. When Ben and Lowell Dillingham were boys, their father, the late Walter Francis Dillingham, and late mother, the former Louise Gaylord of Chicago, ran what amounted to an international celebrity center. Walter was one of the few men in the world who called General Douglas MacArthur "Mac." And he and Mrs. Dillingham had Will Rogers in to dinner, Noël Coward in to play songs, and the Duke of Windsor—then the Prince of Wales—over from Britain to play polo.

"My father sat me on the prince's knee and made me sing 'Three Blind Mice' in Hawaiian," Mr. Dillingham said. "We all knew the words."

The Dillinghams, the Cookes and virtually every other *kamaaina haole* of consequence attended Punahou School, Hawaii's equivalent of the New England preparatory schools, and they all belong to the Hawaiian Mission Children's Society, the D.A.R. of the islands.

"But it's not a D.A.R.," said Mrs. E. C. Cluff, Jr., who runs the group and its museum. "All you have to do is prove you are descended from one of the missionaries. We have members with Hawaiian and Oriental blood."

Every time the Cousins Society, the name islanders have bestowed on their organization, has a major gathering, there's a battle among the Judds, Cookes, Baldwins, Rices and Wilcoxes to see which has the most relatives.

"There are an awful lot of us," said Mrs. James M. Richmond, who didn't wear shoes until she was in the seventh grade. "We have a joke in the Judd family. We say we came around the Horn in 1828 and we've been tooting it ever since."

When the Judd family loses a Cousins Society population count, it's usually to the Cookes. And although neither bears the name, Alexander S. Atherton and Michael Guard Sheehan are Cookes. Mr. Atherton, president of the Honolulu *Star-Bulletin*, a director of Castle and Cooke, and a director of the Hawaiian Trust Company, is the grandson of Joseph Ballard Atherton.

"He married Amos Starr Cooke's daughter," Mr. Atherton said of his grandfather. "He was a merchant, a bookkeeper, office manager and then president of Castle and Cooke."

The Athertons have weekend and vacation houses on the islands of Maui and Hawaii, but their main residence is high in Honolulu's misty vales on land that used to be a cow pasture. It commands a spectacular view of the city, Waikiki Beach and the ocean.

"We have a Filipino who comes in four days a week to do the garden," said Mrs. Atherton, the former Le Burta Gates of the Denver rubber family. "If we didn't have help, we'd be overgrown in a week." The Athertons' gardens, like others here, are heavy with the scent of plumeria, and there are mango trees, bright blue and orange birds of paradise, and pots of orchids. And when Mr. Atherton is in New York, he misses the tropical greenery. "He goes out and buys lots of flowers for our hotel room," Mrs. Atherton said. "After you've lived here a while, you have to have flowers around you."

The Sheehans, a pair of newlyweds, go on flower-picking expeditions. For their wedding in the oldest church on the island of Kauai last August, they gathered blue hydrangeas, jasmine, plumeria and ginger blossoms. Fragrant maile leaves, to wrap around the ushers' and bridegroom's shoulders in the old royal manner, were flown in from Hawaii. Mrs. Sheehan, the former Patricia Kualhelani Wilcox, carried leis of white ginger blossoms and her bridesmaids carried maile leaves and pikake. The reception was a luau at Grove Farm Plantation, her Grandfather Wilcox's estate.

"She's part Hawaiian," Mr. Sheehan said proudly. "She may be the first Hawaiian blood we've had in the family. We're Cookes, Athertons, Dillinghams and Rices."

Mr. Sheehan's father is Wade E. Sheehan, an import from Seattle and an executive at the Big Five concern of Alexander and Baldwin. His wife's family, descended from Lucy and Abner Wilcox, is to Kauai what the Roosevelts are to New York, and Mrs. Sheehan's mother is related to the Campbells, among the largest property owners in the state. When she was a child on Kauai, Mrs. Sheehan was the only *haole* in her class. She thinks Hawaiian music is superior to rock 'n roll, plays the ukulele and loves to hear the Lord's Prayer in Hawaiian.

"It was in Hawaiian for our wedding," she said.

So were the opening and closing prayers.

IV
Their International Cases

*W*e cannot end a book on the rich without some mention of the globe-trotting all-stars who, for want of a better definition, are usually identified as American members of international society. In the spring, they may be found in New York, London and Paris. In the summer, it's off to the South of France until the fall, when it's on to Spain or to Scotland for the shooting. The advent of cold weather finally completes the cycle, bringing them back to the world's capitals for a while before they once again fan out to the beaches and ski resorts.

We end where we began, except that the whole world has become the ultimate playground. It is typical of the newest international order that the most extravagant party of them all should be in Persepolis at the foot of the ancient ruins of a 2,500-year-old civilization. And why Persepolis? Because the Shah of Iran, in his own bid for acceptance and recognition, tried (and to some extent succeeded) in transplanting the whole scene—complete with Joy perfume, Porthault sheets and plastic chandeliers—into the Iranian desert.

So call them what you will: the "smart set," the "jet set," the "international nomads," the "beautiful people" or just plain society. These are the people who help create public taste while simultaneously serving as role models in a world that has always admired the rich and tried to emulate them.

A raft of international celebrities and heads of state showed up in Persepolis for the Shah of Iran's celebration of Persia's 2,500th anniversary. The Shah addressed the crowd, which included (left to right) Queen Ingrid and King Frederik of Denmark; Emperor Haile Selassie of Ethiopia; the Empress of Iran and Soviet President Nikolai Podgorny. Afterward, they all sent thank-you notes.
United Press International (1971)

Persepolis, Iran

The Shah of Iran, who thinks of himself as politically big league, established himself tonight as one of the world's great party-givers. For sheer grandeur, his gala in a silk tent will be hard for any nation to surpass.

Despite the noticeable absence of such obviously significant international leaders as Queen Elizabeth II of Britain, the French and American presidents and whoever is in charge of China these days, the guest list was impressive. Kings and princes, who don't wear crowns to parties anymore, mingled democratically with commoner presidents and prime ministers, while queens and princesses, most of whom still believe in tiaras, tried not to stare at one another. The grand dukes, sheiks and sultans weren't slouchy-looking either. They wore uniforms loaded down with gold braid and medals, white tie and tails, flowing robes or pants with sashed jackets. In all, the five hundred guests represented seventy nations.

The four-and-a-half-hour gathering, a ceremonial and very formal dinner celebrating Persia's 2,500th anniversary, began with a reception in the vast reaches of the scarlet and gold velvet hall built especially for the occasion. The Shah and Empress Farah received their guests here beneath twenty crystal and plastic chandeliers. The Empress, who was also celebrating her thirty-second birthday, was regal in a stiff brocade dress of gold embroidered in blue, the imperial colors. On her head was a towering wreath of diamonds. She had more diamonds at her throat and ears and on her fingers.

But hers were by no means the only diamonds. At least twenty first-class crowns passed through the receiving line, plus another dozen tiaras. Fifteen-year-old Imelda Marcos, daughter of President Ferdinand E. Marcos of the Philippines, wore a diamond necklace across her forehead. The Eastern European-bloc representatives, men in black silk suits with white shirts and ties, were particularly fascinated by the jewels, while Marshal Tito merely glanced at them through half-closed eyes.

Monarchs, whose families have been royal for centuries, didn't bother to bow to the Shah, whose father was little more than a peasant, but commoners did. Prince Bernhard of the Netherlands, perhaps the most gregarious of the visitors, did his best to make everyone feel at home. He hugged old friends and introduced them around.

Prince Philip of Britain, Emperor Haile Selassie of Ethiopia and President Nikolai V. Podgorny of the Soviet Union were the guests everybody wanted to meet, and the prince was very obliging. Haile Selassie stood impassively, his hands behind his back, waiting for people to come to him.

Easterners were quick to spot King Mahendra of Nepal. Westerners did better with the kings of Denmark and Norway, Frederik IX and Olav V.

"I think I might know five faces," said Sheik Abdul Aziz el-Khasmi, the Ambassador to Teheran from the tiny Trucial State of Ras al Haima.

Following cocktails, the elegant guests moved into the huge blue-and-gold tented dining hall for dinner under more chandeliers. The most important guests sat at a two-hundred-foot table. Some men sat side by side.

The Shah had Queen Ingrid of Denmark on his right and Queen Fabiola of Belgium on his left. This was according to protocol. Haile Selassie sat to the Empress's right and the King of Denmark was on her left. For dinner partners, Mrs. Spiro T. Agnew got the President of Pakistan, Ayub Mohammed Yahya Khan, and Prince Jean, the Grand Duke of Luxembourg. Vice President Agnew sat next to Mieczyslaw Klimastky, Vice President of the State Council of the Polish People's Republic, and Prince Carl Gustav of Sweden. The dinner, flown in from Maxim's of Paris, included partridge with foie gras and truffle stuffing, eggs and caviar, chicken stuffed with gold leaves, and filet of sole stuffed with caviar. The wines ranged from a pink Dom Perignon to a Chateau Lafitte from the Rothschild vineyard.

Two of Maxim's chefs supervised the preparation and serving of the meal assisted by 120 imported French captains, 175 other Europeans and 150 newly trained Iranians. One result of the celebration is that rich Iranians will no longer have to send out of the country for their waiters.

In his welcoming speech, the Shah said that man's eternal and changeless mission is an effort toward perfection. "Each one of us must try as hard as possible, as much as circumstances allow," he said, "to turn the world into one of love, peace and cooperation for mankind, a world in which every person may enjoy the full amenities of science and civilization."

Haile Selassie, whose empire is older than Iran's, gave the answering toast. The Iranian National Symphony Orchestra, with three American Peace Corps workers among its ranks, played selections the Empress herself chose.

King Hussein of Jordan appeared content though he and Princess Mona had tent problems. They had brought his sister, Princess Basma, and her husband with them, only to find single beds in each of the two bedrooms. Princess Basma and her husband spent the night on cots in the maids' room.

"They don't mind," the Jordanian ambassador explained. "It was supposed to be a camping out anyway."

Maximilian Cardinal de Furstenberg and Kai-Uwe von Hassel had tent problems, too. When the cardinal, the personal representative of Pope Paul, arrived, he was told that he could not have a tent. The cardinal put up a fight and finally got one. Mr. von Hassel, who is the president of the West German Bundesrat, was not so lucky. He was put up at a hotel.

Despite such contretemps, which the Iranians did their best to hide, everybody seemed to be having a reasonably good time. The subjects of serious talks, if there were any, were put aside. Countries that aren't on the best of terms showed no visible hostility. The Indians did sit down with the Pakistanis, although not side by side. The African nations did not walk out when they learned that South Africa was present. And if Prince Philip was in any way annoyed by the Shah's recent threat to wrest Abu Masu and two islands from Britain, he didn't show it.

The evening ended, as usual, with a blaze of French fireworks against a clear, star-bright sky above the stately pillars and sculptures of ancient Persepolis.

Then everyone who had a tent returned to it. In the distance, spotlights still shone on the silent ruins where Haile Selassie and his chihuahua Chicheebee had walked earlier in the day. While the eighty-year-old Lion of Judah stood silhouetted against the blue sky, Chicheebee scampered over the stone platforms, her diamond collar glittering in the desert sun.

NEIGHBORS GO VISITING IN IRAN'S TENT CITY

October 1971

The Ancient Persian city of Persepolis had been deserted since 330 B.C., when the armies of Alexander the Great sacked the place and loaded its treasures on the backs of 20,000 mules and 5,000 camels. With the creation of the Shah's Tent City on its outskirts, it became for a brief moment what several journalists called "Disneyland-in-the-desert."

Located more than thirty miles from Shiraz, the nearest real city, Tent City was perhaps the least accessible location for a party in modern times. Only those with permits could leave Teheran for Shiraz. Only those with passes that would get them by guards armed with machine guns were permitted to approach the tents, and there was no way to get there except by buses and cars, all operated by the Iranian government. Tent City itself was plywood and plastic, an enclave surrounded by barbed wire and tales of interior grandeur that never materialized. The tents, decorated by prestigious Jansen of Paris, didn't have the marble bathtubs that had been rumored and reported during the weeks before the party, nor chandeliers, nor eighteenth-century French furnishings.

They did have twin bedrooms (each with a single bed), his and her bathrooms with bidets, kitchenettes and maids' rooms, adequate supplies of Fauchon snacks, Alka-Seltzer, blue matchbooks with "Persepolis" stamped in gold on the covers, candles in case the electricity failed and portable radiators against the cold desert nights. They also had exquisitely handsome Persian carpets, Porthault linen (for the maids' rooms as well), Guerlain shaving preparations for the men and Joy eau de cologne and soap for the women.

Besides the guest tents, a couple of hastily erected fountains and lavish gardens that had quite recently been planted somewhere else, Tent City included the Shah's extra large tent (which *did* have marble tubs and gilded fixtures, thereby speaking to the host nation's priorities), a scarlet reception hall hung with twenty plastic chandeliers and the adjacent dining hall with the two-hundred-foot table, a club tent and work areas for the French hairdressers, the Swiss maids and Maxim's chefs, all of whom had been flown in for the occasion.

The morning after the great banquet, the city's fountains bubbled and the streets bustled with high-level activity. While nobody in the encampment troubled a neighbor for a cup of sugar, there was a small-town atmosphere to the place, even though the residents were kings, grand dukes, princes, sultans, sheiks and heads of state. Communications between the city and the outside world, however, were something else. Vice President Agnew tried and tried to use his tent telephone to reach Victor Gold, his press secretary, back in Shiraz, but never got through. Neither did Mr. Gold, whom the Iranians exiled to the press section. Only the city's intercoms worked.

Haile Selassie, the most sought-after and celebrated of the illustrious guests, gave audiences in his tent, while the Iranians fumed. "His country is the most backward of all," Iranian press officers kept saying. "Why does anyone care?" The Ethiopian Emperor, making what turned out to be one of his last international appearances, took no notice. In the morning, he took Chicheebee out on the lawn in front of his tent while he, himself, knelt in prayer.

Up the street there were lines of people waiting to see Marshal Tito. The Soviet's Nikolai V. Podgorny ordered Scotch in preparation for the arrival of Egypt's vice president. Handsome Constantine II, the exiled King of Greece, walked hand-in-hand with his pretty young wife, Queen Anne-Marie. The politicking and socializing went on all morning as waiters rushed about delivering breakfast orders in little yellow-and-black trucks and maids prepared to change those Porthault sheets.

By noon, the luncheon orders were being phoned to no ordinary room service, but to the team from Maxim's, which boasted it could produce anything anybody wanted, and pretty much did. The Sultan Qabus bin-Said of Oman ordered and got caviar and kebab. The Poles wanted beef-steak. King Olav V of Norway settled for a cold salad.

Frederik IX of Denmark and Queen Ingrid, the most regal of the imperial guests, went out, as it were, for lunch. They walked from their tent to the curb, climbed into the Rolls-Royce assigned them and motored the five hundred feet to the club tent.

After lunch, the illustrious guests dressed for the Shah's parade and climbed into buses that took them to the ruins. They sat in a single line of imperial blue and gold chairs strung out along the wide road that runs parallel to the ruins.

The parade, the highpoint of the 2,500th anniversary celebration, was organized to show the history of the Persian Empire's rulers from 500 B.C. to the present. It started with men dressed as Archaemenians, who ruled from 500 to 300 B.C., and continued on through the Saffarians, the Sapavyyehs and the Zaniyyehs to the Ghajaryyehs and finally to what is now known in Iran as the Pahlevi era.

The setting was spectacular. Men in Archaemenian gold and scarlet uniforms stood high in the ruins behind the guests but well in view of Western television cameras. Trumpets sounded in the hills. A band struck up Persian marching music, and the first of perhaps two thousand costumed marchers started down the roadway. Cavalry troops on matching black horses were followed by foot soldiers in link armor.

Oxen pulled copies of mobile battlements. The men on twenty-six camels wore plumes. At least two early sailing vessels motored by. The kings and commoners, who faced directly into the sun, were very hot. They shaded their eyes. The parade went on and on. Beginning with the Pahlevi era, the soldiers goose-stepped and the music became increasingly militaristic. Besides a rather obvious play for world attention, the celebration was also something of the Shah's international debut party. On the first day of the week-long party, when a crowd of his guests had gathered in the club tent for afternoon snacks, he walked in, looked all around and didn't seem to know what to do with himself. Spotting Prince Bernhard of the Netherlands, he walked over and spoke to him.

"Who are all these people?" he asked.

"They are your guests," Prince Bernhard said. "Now that is the King of Norway and over there is Frederik IX, and . . ."

One by one, Prince Bernhard, the guest, introduced the Shah of Iran, the host, to the other guests.

The inimitable Fleur Cowles paints pictures, designs china, writes books and lives amid the splendor of a London apartment she herself created. In private life she is Mrs. Tom Montague Meyer, and they may be found anywhere in the world where there's excitement.
Carl T. Gossett, Jr., *The New York Times* (1964)

London

WHEN A CASTLE NO LONGER FEELS LIKE HOME

July 1964

England is not going to the dogs socially, but things in the mother country seem to be getting just a bit out of hand. Only a few noble households bother to iron his lordship's copy of *The Times* of London before delivering it to him. Dozens of aristocrats have taken to wearing ready-made shirts and suits. The peacock population has declined along with the size and opulence of a great many city houses and country estates. And there are days when a man's castle no longer feels like home.

After World War II, when the cost of running the ancestral castles outstripped their owners' ability to pay, the lords allowed the residences to be turned into museums for paying sightseers. It was either that or sell the furnishings or the house.

The Duke of Bedford, a genial philosopher, faced this invasion of privacy with the reticence of a used-car salesman. He shocked his fellow peers by selling ice cream bars, installing a Ferris wheel on his front lawn and sitting down to lunch with Americans willing to pay about $25 for the privilege.

Most owners were less enthusiastic. They erected signs—"Please Keep Off the Grass" and "This Door Is for Paying Visitors, Not for Staying Guests"—hid out while tourists giggled at suits of armor and gold-canopied beds, and gratefully but quietly banked the visitors' money. They were stiff-upper-lipped and invisibly distressed. "I try not to think about it," said the Duke of Marlborough, master of Blenheim Palace. "When I do, I'm realistic. I know the day of big houses has gone, but I'm holding on to my treasures as long as I can. If it weren't for the visitors, I don't know what I'd do." The duke, a benign-looking man wtih blue eyes, pink cheeks and gray hair, is as much a Vanderbilt as he is a Spencer-Churchill, and he is not starving. Between 100,000 and 155,000 visitors pass through Blenheim's eighteenth-century splendor every year, and some of them buy his flowers.

"I am something of a horticulturist," he said as he puffed away on a fat cigar. "I grow things that are easy to sell. There is a pelargonium (geranium) which the Queen Mother showed many years ago. It seems to have become a favorite. The tourists like it."

Blenheim, whose staff never refers to it except as "the palace"—which it is—is falling apart.

"Some of the stone work is perishing and I'm having to get new," the duke said. "It's like what's happening to Oxford."

David George Brownlow Cecil, the Marquess of Exeter, is another nobleman who has made what are considered to be dignified concessions to the twentieth-century situation. Visitors at Burghley House, a 27,000-acre estate in Lincolnshire, may have tea in the Orange Court with its hand-painted wallpaper, but their dogs must be kept on leashes lest they run around scaring the peacocks.

"My chief interest is in the Olympics," the marquess said. "My wife and I are helping to get the money to send a team to Tokyo." As Lord Burghley, the marquess was an Olympic gold medalist. His skill as a hurdler brought him three English and eight British championships and the Olympic championship in 1928 in the four-hundred-meter hurdles. He is descended from Edward VI's Secretary of State and Elizabeth I's Lord High Treasurer.

"I have a cousin, George Cecil, in the United States," he said. "His mother was Cornelia Vanderbilt. My wife and I shall be seeing him on our way to Tokyo."

Mr. Cecil, a grandson of George W. Vanderbilt, spent part of his boyhood at Biltmore, the Vanderbilts' vast estate near Asheville, North Carolina. Lord Exeter visited the 12,000-acre property in the late 1930s. Like the English stately homes, Biltmore has become a museum but no one lives there.

"It's a beautiful place," he said. "It's almost as big as mine."

All signs of change disturb the aristocratic denizens of the historic estates. They are just as critical of the men who have made millions despite high taxes as they are of the taxes themselves. Such men, according to the Duke of Marlborough, are "competitive." It was not a compliment. The word is almost synonymous with "American."

"The class system is evaporating here without any revolution," said Mrs.

Tom Montague Meyer, the former Fleur Fenton Cowles. "There are no sharp signals. Britain is just sliding into classlessness. At the same time, Britons know the United States is going in the other direction."

Mrs. Meyer, who created and produced *Flair* magazine while she was married to publisher Gardner Cowles, is a part of an international set that is at home anywhere in the world. She is an American, but she has forsaken the "infinite variety and frenzy of New York" for London, "the delicious and glorious world where there is no contest."

"There are six hundred important American businesses here," she said as she strolled about the former ballroom that is now one of her two large drawing rooms. "Americans tend to stay together unless it's important business-wise to associate with the English. When my English friends sneer at this, I have an answer. I say, 'Remember India.'"

Mrs. Meyer is a shadow of her more familiar globe-trotting self. She zips off to Paris or Brussels for lunch now and then. But she divides the bulk of her time between Great Surries, her informal country house, and the London apartment.

And it is in the latter that she is more likely to be surrounded by a group of guests who might include a Brazilian government official, an Indian maharani, a White Russian, a British peer or two, an American diplomat, an English newspaperman and an assortment of titled and untitled Europeans.

Mr. Meyer, a timber and lumber executive, is an amiable host. He sees to it that the guests' glasses are refilled while his wife reviews the intricacies of Latin American politics or the situation in Vietnam. Her salons are comparable in brilliance, if not in their effect upon the British power complex, to those of Lady Pamela Berry and Mrs. Ian Fleming.

Lady Pamela, whose dark good looks earned her the nickname of "the Black Bee," is the wife of Michael Berry. He runs the daily *Telegraph,* a London newspaper. Mrs. Fleming, whose husband created James Bond, is one of Britain's great conversationalists.

"I like mixed personalities," Mrs. Fleming said. "The dullest thing in the world is six respectable married couples. The husbands and wives are always interrupting each other." Mrs. Fleming is thoroughly English even though she is not interested in horses, racing, debutantes, charity balls, calling cards, hats or the queen.

"England is the best country for good conversation," she said as she flicked cigarette ashes into a little silver tray. "It's quicker than America—quick-witted. Americans often say we're superficial. I like that. I believe in conveying serious things in a lighthearted way."

Nothing annoys Mrs. Fleming more than being stranded at a party with a group of women. But she is resigned to being what she calls "a member of the downtrodden sex."

"Englishmen like men's things and men's clubs and their own company," she said. "They like to go to the club and play bridge for high stakes. On the average, women are not as able intellectually."

Britain has never been particularly interested in educating its women, but there is a new trend toward college for everyone—women as well as men. Lady Gaitskell, widow of Hugh Gaitskell, the Labor party leader, believes that additional facilities are needed and that present ones should be expanded. It is a concept endorsed by an increasingly vocal segment of British society.

"The highly intelligent are in a minority everywhere," said Mrs. Richard Hare, "but there is no reason why we should not strive for more education. We have to build buildings and train teachers. It won't be easy."

Mrs. Hare, whose husband is professor of Russian literature at London University, is Dora Gordine, the sculptor and painter. Three of her works are in the Tate Gallery and another belongs to Thomas J. Watson, Jr., chairman of the board of International Business Machines. The Hares have lived and worked in the United States.

"Good art does not get the support it got in England before the war," Mrs. Hare said. "In America, private people are interested and support the arts. There is great vitality.

"By opening their large country houses to the public, the dukes are contributing something," she continued. "But it is not enough. The queen has arranged for her gallery to be open, but she doesn't collect. We who are artists have not had the real support of a monarch since George IV. Charles I worked at it, too, but he had his head cut off."

Mrs. Hare has discussed the arts with the Duke of Edinburgh. She found him polite but lacking in enthusiasm for the arts. But both the duke and Queen Elizabeth II have unveiled her works and publicly praised them. While Mrs. Hare was talking, another arts-minded Briton was doing her best to convince the nationalized telephone company that there was something to be said for having a white cord to go with her white telephone.

"I've been trying for three weeks to make them understand," the Countess of Jellicoe said later. "They said Princess Margaret was happy with gray, so why should I not be?"

Where the Duke and Duchess of Windsor went, the world went, and now she is alone. For years the Windsors shared the opulent house in the Bois de Boulogne in Paris. To escape the fuss and formality, the Windsors often had their dinners on trays in front of the TV set. Or they talked about clothes.
Carl T. Gossett, Jr., *The New York Times* (1964)

Paris

After twenty-seven years' residence in France, the Duchess of Windsor admits to a loneliness that comes of being constantly surrounded by people who do not speak her native language. Yet she denies that she would prefer to live in Britain or the United States. "France is our home," she said on the shaded terrace of her Bois de Boulogne house. "My roots are here. I'm really too old to change."

The duchess was on the verge of saying something else, when she was interrupted. Mr. Chu, one of her five pug dogs, came bounding across the terrace.

"Watch out. Watch out," she said as the dog jumped about excitedly. "He'll get your stockings. He doesn't mean to, but he likes to climb all over people."

After a few minutes, the dog sat down at his mistress's feet, pretended to snooze and then got up, stretched and trotted off in the direction of the drawing room.

"England is where I do my Christmas shopping," she continued. "People always like to receive things from another country."

The duchess, an intelligent and knowing woman, seems to have come to terms with life as it is, has accepted it and, at sixty-eight, is in full control.

She is smaller than her pictures would lead one to believe, looks younger than most women her age and speaks with a suggestion of an English accent. She spends her time, she said as she twirled a band of sapphires on the third finger of her left hand, in a variety of ways. She raises orchids ("I love them in their own pots"), shops for clothes ("At Dior, they let me change things around"), goes to the hairdresser ("Alexandre understands my hair"), has her shoes made ("I have no idea what size shoe I wear") and imports her stockings ("They cost $1.95 a pair and I get them all from the United States").

She also consults with her chef over the menus ("You don't get any original food if you don't work with a cook"), writes dozens of letters ("If someone takes the trouble to write, he deserves an answer"), worries about her American toaster ("It won't pop French bread") and wishes the French would produce inexpensive frozen cakes like those she has seen in American supermarkets.

"I keep remembering the name Sara Lee," she said, her generous mouth widening into a smile. "They were such good cakes. I wish there was some way to get them to Paris."

At least some of the russet-haired duchess's activities are what she calls "playing house," except that she plays at an exquisite level. The house on the Bois is actually a castle in miniature, and although its interiors and furnishings are classically French, the atmosphere is not cold, fussy or overly formal. The drawing room is predominantly blue, the duchess's favorite color. The walls and brocades are pale blue-gray. The Aubusson rugs are touched with deeper blue.

Large, full-length portraits of the Duke of Windsor in the robes of the Order of the Garter and of his mother, the late Queen Mary, are merely there. They do not scream for attention.

"We have collected a few things," the duchess said, her eyes wandering over a studied wilderness of bibelots.

There is a photograph of Queen Victoria, the duke's great-grandmother; a collection of Flying Tiger Meissen porcelain, and a seemingly endless number of enamel, gold, silver, porcelain and vermeil objects—some of which belonged to George IV.

Giant arrangements of flowers, none of which were grown on the property, decorate one doorway, and the two large windows look out over the terrace to the lawn—a lush sweep of grass, clover and little daisies.

"I found the dining room in a chateau," the duchess said as she walked through the cool, incense-fragrant drawing room. "It was really something to install."

This room is darker blue. Its painted wood walls were pried away from their original base and reconstructed in the Windsors' house. In the process, the construction decreased the size of the room, but by only a few inches.

"I can never seat more than twenty-six at dinner," the duchess said, shaking her head. "It's really quite small. But the whole house is small—only three rooms downstairs, a sitting room and but two bedrooms upstairs, and two guest rooms with a bath between them."

The other downstairs room is a red-and-yellow combination den and library. The sofa is yellow, and it is decorated with red cushions covered with fabric that once belonged to a cardinal's cape.

The dominant feature, however, is a portrait of the duchess. She is wearing a blue dress that almost matches her eyes. Her eyebrows are the thin dark pencil lines popular in the 1930s. And her hair is black and parted in the middle. She looks as she did in 1937, when she was married to the former British king.

There is also a baronial front hallway. The chief furnishing is a substantial table that holds a single object, a scarlet leather dispatch box with a gold lock. Printed on the box in gold capital letters are but two words, THE KING.

"I swim, but my only real exercise is running up and down stairs," the duchess said, returning to the comfort of a cushioned porch chair. "I have never been one to take exercise."

The former Bessie Wallis Warfield Simpson has other interests besides her house. She is occasionally involved in community affairs ("I'm deeply concerned by conditions at the slaughter house") and is one of the world's best-known party-goers ("I always say 'yes'—especially in the United States. But we don't go to parties all the time and we don't entertain constantly"). She also finds time for the arts.

"I have my dinner on a tray in the evening in front of the television," she said. "I like quiz programs, but of course everything is in French—Westerns, Bob Hope, Frank Sinatra—everything. It's an absolute scream."

She frequents art exhibitions ("There's always something new at the Louvre") and keeps up on current events by watching television and reading.

"We take *Life, Time, Newsweek, Vogue* and *Harper's Bazaar*," she said, ticking the magazines off on her fingers. "And *Réalités, Connoisseur, L'Oeil*—it has wonderful art—*Paris Match, Elle*—it lists such good buys—and a few English things for the duke including *Country Life* and political reports."

The Windsors' schedule varies little from year to year. They spend weekdays here and Saturdays and Sundays in the country at their Moulin de Tuilerie.

In August, they plan to go to Biarritz, where the duke will rejoin golfing chums and the duchess will visit friends. And then later, they may go off to Spain. They have bought property on the Costa del Sol.

"In the autumn, we shoot," the duchess said. "I don't really. I go out and sit behind the duke and watch."

In the winter, the couple is in France, shuttling back and forth between Paris and the mill. Before Christmas, the duchess goes to Britain on a shopping spree. The Windsors celebrate the holiday in France, often with Americans.

"It's hard to get up a party for Christmas," the duchess said. "New Year's is when the French celebrate."

They do not travel again until April, when they make their annual pilgrimage to Palm Beach. Toward the end of May, they move north to New York for their sojourn at the Waldorf Towers.

"We like to travel out of season," the duchess said. "We go away to relax, and you can't relax in season."

She seemed unaware that when she and her husband appear anywhere, everyone else wants to be there too—which almost inevitably creates a season whether one existed or not.

"I go away to get rid of the cares of housekeeping," she said. "I don't want to be jostled about. I don't fly, which means the train, and things can get complicated."

The Windsors cross the Atlantic Ocean by ship, usually by the liner *United States*. They are often accompanied by one or more of the pug dogs. The duchess says they are always glad to get back to Paris. They arrive in time for the season—a madhouse of society doings, some of which they attend.

"I don't like the word 'society,'" the duchess said. "It gives one a feeling of people who want to go to parties and who think of nothing else. Frankly, I'm not sure what 'society' is. It means different things to different people."

She paused, thought for a minute or two and then went on.

"I don't think 'society' is dead, and I don't think you can say a certain group is 'society' and another group isn't," she said. "Whatever it is, it has nothing to do with wealth. It is very open."

THE WINDSORS: WHERE THEY WENT, THE WORLD WENT

May 1972

When *A King's Story*, the late Duke of Windsor's filmed biography, had its premiere in New York in 1967, Mrs. Edwin I. Hilson, the banker's widow who was in charge of the gala benefit performance, was in something of a dither.

Somehow, like many Americans who knew the Windsors, she wanted the duke and duchess singled out for special attention. She thought maybe she could do it by having their theater seats decorated.

"I thought maybe red velvet," she said. "Something that would indicate that they were *their* chairs. But they wouldn't want anything like that."

Actually, the duchess would have loved it. She liked being the center of attention. It was the quiet, sad-eyed duke who didn't care for fuss, and for him the evening, like many others in the days when he was a celebrated social pet, proved more than a little trying.

When the documentary ended and the lights went up, shortly after the emotional "the woman I love" speech, the expensively jeweled and perfumed audience rose to applaud his former majesty. They turned toward where the duke and duchess had been sitting. The duke had disappeared.

The woman next to him had dropped her evening bag, spilling lipstick, mirror, house keys and other gilded paraphernalia in all directions, and the duke was down on his hands and knees, crawling along the floor trying to retrieve them.

Later, at a cocktail party among the main-floor handbag, scarf and sunglasses counters at Bergdorf Goodman, the duke stood stoically in a receiving line as hundreds of the well-to-do elbowed each other into racks of new umbrellas in an effort to meet him. Nor did he protest when Mrs. Hilson helped the duchess climb up on a shaking red platform to draw names for donated gifts. If the duke disapproved of such spectacles, and there was never any indication that he did, he didn't show it. For in the end, it was his lot to stand by while the duchess gave the newspaper interviews, described her clothes and drew raffle numbers for men's shoes and sets of Wamsutta Supercale sheets.

For nearly thirty years, he was international society's darling by virtue of having once been King of England, yet everyone with even the slimmest hope of social recognition was as eager to meet the duchess as well as the duke, and the two were inseparable.

"Wherever the duke and duchess go the world goes," Elsa Maxwell once said, and she was right.

Starting in 1940 when the duke was appointed Governor General of the Bahamas, the islands suddenly became popular. After World War II, the aspiring rich followed them to summers in Biarritz and springs divided between New York and Palm Beach. When they bought property on Spain's Costa del Sol, others sought out neighboring estates.

In the 1950s the Windsors were on the "most wanted" list of those whose names as honorary chairmen (they didn't have to attend and sometimes didn't) could sell out a charity ball or whose very presence at a party conferred special status not just on the host and hostess but on all who attended.

The real social distinction, however, was to be invited either to the Moulin de Tuilerie, their country mill, or their town house in the Bois de Boulogne. Yet by the 1960s, the guests were no longer limited to Europeans and patrician Americans, but included dress designers, hairdressers, newly arrived American tycoons and Harry Reasoner, who took the world on a televised tour of the Moulin after they put it up for sale.

In those years, the duke and duchess regularly came from France to

New York aboard the liner *United States,* whose officers once estimated that they had made nearly thirty crossings, and held a shipboard press conference. Because they refused to discuss anything political or controversial, such interviews inevitably took up the latest fads and fashions.

"I always wear double-breasted suits—except for sports," the duke once explained.

He also had his say on miniskirts. When they were new, he thought they were "rather nice on girls with good underpinnings." The next year, when miniskirts were ubiquitous, he seemed bored. "Miniskirts are too mini," he said.

He went on from there to talk about women in pants ("I'm not very keen") and the long skirts of the seventies ("I think the maxi is just dreadful"). Asked to comment on the influence young people seemed to be having on world affairs everywhere, he dismissed the subject as "too political."

By 1970, when President Nixon invited them to the White House, the Windsors, who had spent their lives at parties, admitted that they were not so socially active as they once were.

"There are parties every night, and we just can't go out like we did ten years ago," he said.

"We're just too old," said the duchess. "We even spent Easter in bed."

"Now, the duchess and I are a little past the age of being what they call with it," the duke added. "But don't for one minute imagine that we weren't with it when we were younger. In fact, I was so much with it that this was one of the big criticisms that was leveled against me by the older generation."

When Miss Maxwell said that where they went the world went, she said it all. But even Miss Maxwell's name, once synonymous with international partygiving, means little in the contemporary world. She made her famous observation in the early 1950's, when her parties mattered. She has been dead since 1963. Since then, international society has turned to such newer darlings as Elizabeth Taylor, Richard Burton and Aristotle and Jacqueline Onassis, but by 1976 the Burtons were divorcing and Mrs. Onassis was widowed again. No couple dominated society.

BARON ROTHSCHILD AND OTHER NOTABLES

June 1964

It was the Baron Guy de Rothschild's day even if the ultraexclusive Paris Jockey Club has never made him a member. His White Label streaked past thirteen other horses to win the coveted Grand Prix de Paris at Longchamp.

Before the race, the somber, blue-eyed chieftain of the Rothschild banking empire made a leisurely trip to the tree-lined paddock. He led his slim wife down the great double stairways from their seats in the upper stands, walked across the courtyard and passed the white gate that separates mere people from horses and their owners. Two jockeys were waiting for him.

The baron, like a good Rothschild, had taken no chances. He had not one but two horses in the race—Free Ride, the favorite, and White Label, which was not expected to do anything sensational. Both carried the historic blue-and-yellow silks of the Rothschild family shield. These same colors, which fly over dozens of Rothschild residences, have been familiar at Longchamp for more than fifty years. When a warning bell announced the race, the baron and all the other horse owners left the paddock. He wore a top hat and had a bunch of blue carnations at the lapel of his gray morning coat. And he was as solemn as he had been at Epsom, before his Corah IV ran (and failed to place) in the English Derby.

He was only a slightly different man after the race. When White Label was led into the winner's ring, he called to the horse, reached for his bridle and gave the sweaty three-year-old several affectionate pats. And there are those who insisted that the baron's aristocratic mouth was extended into a smile. Others were not so sure.

Longchamp is a fitting place for a Rothschild to win. The great brownstone pavilions have presided over the Bois de Boulogne since 1857—a time when the Rothschilds were cronies of French rulers and financiers to the world. The three grandstands, artistically superior to any in England or the United States, are so carefully designed and preserved they resemble a series of French chateaux. Queen Elizabeth II's own Ascot pales by comparison.

There is nothing rustic or informal about the gardens, either. They look as if they had been created by a giant with a sharp-edged cookie cutter. Pink petunias have been carefully rectangled away from blue hydrangeas, and scarlet begonias never come in contact with floppy yellow dahlias. The topiary trees are equally aloof. And aside from five blooming dandelions, whose precocity is reminiscent of the ancient Chinese insistence upon at least one flaw, all is perfection.

Before her death, Elsa Maxwell said the Grand Prix had lost its fascination for the beautiful people. She was only partly right. There are men in T-shirts and women in loafers, and the Duke and Duchess of Windsor rarely bother. But a lot of the elegant types do persevere.

Between races, the youthful Aga Khan stood cross-legged, his elbows propped democratically against the paddock rail—the very picture of what the beautiful people are supposed to be. Like the baron, he was in dove gray morning clothes from head to toe. And although he is the spiritual ruler of the many million members of the Ismaili Moslem sect (who will give him his weight in precious metals and jewels one of these days), he is very Harvard and more than somewhat horsey. His father was Aly Khan, and the bright-eyed Karim inherited the stable.

Tout Paris sat in the uppermost seats, naturally enough, communing with the view over the grassy turf and with each other. The Princess Lubomirski, the French wife of a Polish prince who is in the real-estate business, found that there were two other flowered hats like hers but managed to survive. "They come from Gilbert Orcel," she said. "It is the big hat place."

Mrs. Arpad Plesch, whose Waldmeister was a favorite among the expensively dressed, paused beside a green grillwork stairway long enough to pass the time of day with the Vicomtesse Paul de Rosière. The vicomtesse is the former Harriette Moeller of Columbus, Ohio. Her husband is associated with Harry Winston, the jeweler. The de Rosières commute between the Chateau de Barberey in the country east of Paris and a city apartment.

Lady Sassoon, the irrepressible widow of Sir Victor Sassoon, managed to get to Longchamp before the first race, but she was not sure how she had done it.

"I came in from Ireland this morning," she said as one of her horses came trotting into the ring. "The Irish Derby was marvelous."

Among others in the crowd were Mrs. John F. C. Bryce and Mrs. Patrick Guinness, the former Princess Dolores von Furstenberg. Mrs. Guinness, a tall blonde who is widely known for her good looks, is the daughter of Mrs. Loel Guinness of New York, Palm Beach, London and Paris. The former Princess von Furstenberg is the wife of the stepson of her mother.

The Maharanee of Baroda, who selects from among twenty-five perfumes
for the evening and fifteen for daytime, shares a lazy Monte Carlo afternoon
with her only child, the Prince of Baroda. Liveried Indian menservants in
white gloves hold her ashtrays. She takes her own naps.
Sabine Weiss, *The New York Times* (1969)

The Riviera

The Côte d'Azur is regularly accused of being a cenotaph of departed glories, and perhaps it is. But in the summer, when an international galaxy of superstars inevitably returns, the coast is the setting for the giddiest social season of them all—the Monte Carlo number.

There is Cannes, of course, and Beaulieu, Villefranche-sur-mer, Juan les Pins, St. Jean-Cap-Ferrat, Antibes and all the other little French villages along the turquoise Mediterranean. They offer exquisite and even palatial refuge for those moments when, as Gregory Peck put it, "the social ramble reaches the combat stage."

Monte Carlo is no such hiding place. Besides being the impeccably grand capital of a midget principality that could easily pass for Oz, the arrogant old city draws everybody who is anybody anywhere in the world now and then, and at this time of year, it's mostly now. The marina is jammed with enormous white yachts. The aging Hôtel de Paris has more than its share of tanned blond women whose chic seems to consist mainly of minuscule bikinis, see-through shirts, clingy dresses that never had much in the way of skirts, divinely trashy crepe pajamas and lots of diamonds.

The casino is a pampered opulence of the right big spenders gambling

289

their money away. The rocky beach and tented cabanas are littered with an anthology of sleek victors in the battle of the bulge. And the streets, restaurants and expensive shops are a perfumed hubbub of the rich, the elegant and the powerful. Men and women of noble origins, aristocratic birth or celebrated accomplishment mingle freely with those of uncertain provenance or wavering gender. The *vieillesse dorée* stays up as late as the gilded nymphets. It's not smart to sleep away the morning and miss the sun. And last night's galas are this afternoon's cocktail party talk.

"You see the same people for lunch, for cocktails and for dinner," Margaret, Duchess of Argyll, said at one of the scores of gatherings held last week. "It's one little informal party for fifty guests after another."

The duchess, the peripatetic former wife of the chieftain of Scotland's celebrated Clan Campbell, may be the only woman in Monte Carlo who assiduously avoids the sun.

"It's good for French, American and Italian skins," she explained, "but not for the English."

So while other guests at Mrs. Ernest Kanzler's butter-yellow Chateau St. Jean toasted their already browned bodies in the sun, the milk-white Duchess sat under an umbrella and talked about Mrs. Kanzler's mynah bird.

"He speaks French and Italian," she said. "I'm trying to teach him English."

Mrs. Kanzler is no slouch either. She's the irrepressible widow of the Detroit industrialist who was Henry Ford 2nd's uncle, and her chateau is frequented by French countesses, Italian playboys and virtually anyone named Ford.

"I don't pretend that life is peaceful here," she admitted, "but it's not interesting to sit in the sun alone."

Mrs. Henry Ittleson, Jr., rarely suns alone either, although she has a perfectly good terrace overlooking most of Monte Carlo and the privacy of her own gigantic fresh-water swimming pool.

"I love the salt water," she said. "I have to go to the beach."

While Mrs. Ittleson makes the rounds (sometimes lunching at La Vignie, a beach-side restaurant where she and her investment banker husband are so well known that their names have been stamped into a plastic sign that guards their table from would-be marauders), Mr. Ittleson is off at what he calls "my office."

"He means the casino," his wife said, "I love my salt water, and he loves his baccarat."

The Ittlesons live in a house that's the talk of the coast. The Europeans don't understand it because it's modern right down to the smooth marble floors, the custom-built California furniture and the absence of anything even vaguely French.

"You're not allowed to cut down the trees in France, so we built the house around them," Mrs. Ittleson said, indicating the pine growing up through the roof. "Why, even our cactus is a hundred years old."

The house is in hot colors throughout with abstract expressionist paintings on the walls. It's centrally air-conditioned and heated—still something of a novelty in the South of France—and the sliding glass doors, electric fixtures and the ice machine had to be brought in from the United States.

"We're lucky," Mrs. Ittleson said. "It only took us a year to build."

Princess Giovanna Pignatelli, whose brother heads Gulf Oil in Italy, is here too. And so is Her Royal Highness the Maharanee Gaekwar of Baroda, Georgie Jessel, Lady Sassoon of Nassau, Rudolf Nureyev, Edward J. Hand (American trucking), John Schlesinger (South African diamonds), and the Marquis de Villaverde, Generalissimo Francisco Franco's son-in-law as well as Spain's leading heart surgeon. They're the regulars.

Mrs. Lyndon B. Johnson and her daughter Mrs. Charles Robb are among the season's newcomers, and although neither of them seemed very comfortable in the presence of the nude dancers at a recent gala, they've managed to enjoy themselves. "I love it," said the frankly dazzled Mrs. Robb, paying some francs for what may have been her first gambling chips. "Mother never let me do anything like this before."

Lady Deterding, the Russian-born widow of Sir Henry Deterding, founder of Royal Dutch Shell, has long since stopped being dazzled. But she wouldn't miss her Monte Carlo stay for anything in the world. "I love to wake up in beautiful surroundings," she said shortly after one of the routinely brilliant cocktail parties she gives in her eighteenth-century French penthouse. "I have this for six weeks and then Paris the rest of the time. What more could anyone want?"

WHOOPING IT UP ON THE RIVIERA

September 1969

The Pirate is an outdoor restaurant in Cap-Martin with a roaring fire, flamenco guitarists, bare-chested waiters and the ambience of a gypsy camp, and dinner there is inevitably less than sedate.

But when the Marquis de Villaverde, Henry Ford 2nd and a raft of titled Italians and rich Americans vacationing on the Riviera appeared there the other night, dinner was the least of the evening's activities. The scampi, fish, steak and baked potatoes stuffed with caviar were barely out of the way before the guests joined the guitarists in singing Spanish and Mexican songs and at least one rollicking lyric in faint praise of Il Duce, the late Benito

Mussolini. By the time the dessert and liqueurs arrived, the waiters had put brightly colored paper streamers on all the tables and the evening's more serious war games began.

It is unclear just who threw the first unshelled almond, although there were those who suspected the Marquis de Villaverde. But it doesn't matter. In a minute or two the restaurant was a tangled web of streamers. Before long, guests were lobbing champagne glasses into the fire, roses at the musicians and nuts at one another.

The height of the action came when Count Giovanni Volpi, apparently tiring of what was happening on the ground, had what some thought was an even better idea.

The handsome young Roman millionaire, known for his land, his oil and his fondness for helicopters, took his plate of vanilla ice cream and raspberries, climbed into the Pirate's net rigging in the trees high above the tables, and dropped blobs of dessert on his friends below. This immediately cleared the tables.

Anne Ford Uzielli ran for cover under the narrow awning over the bar. Her sister, the unflappable Charlotte Ford Niarchos, watched the battle from beside a huge olive tree. Mrs. Ford squealed and threw her arms up over her face. Mr. Ford roared with laughter.

"Come on down, Foxy," Mr. Ford yelled. "You're going to get hurt."

The only attention the count paid Mr. Ford was to aim some ice cream at him. He missed. Mr. Ford, who calls the count Foxy because *volpi* is the Italian word for foxes, counterattacked by picking up a bottle of Perrier water, shaking it vigorously and squirting it into the rigging.

"You got him," said Mrs. Uzielli.

By this time, a girl in frilly black-and-white evening pajamas with a bare midriff was riding a burro that had wandered in among the tables. A man in a Mexican wedding shirt had an empty bread basket on his head— the better to protect himself from the ice cream.

Just when it looked as if there might be a lull, the Spaniard who owns the restaurant fired a cap pistol or threw another chair onto the fire.

Between toasts to nearly every pretty girl in the house, the marquis pulled curly streamers off his arms. Count Vega del Ren, the Spaniard who is working for Harry Winston, the jeweler, this summer, danced among the tables, pausing now and then to kiss a cheek or a passing hand. Don Carlos de Bourbon, a member of the Spanish royal family, joined Count Volpi in the rigging.

"That's Jack Daniels up there," Mr. Ford explained. "He's a lot of fun."

Mr. Ford, who took his brandy to a demilitarized zone shortly after the Perrier incident, said he always called Don Carlos Jack Daniels. "They're both bourbons," he said.

As Mr. Ford talked, mostly about how he loathed it when his private life is reported in the world's newspapers and magazines, Mrs. Ford was off near the minuscule dance floor, warming up to what may have been a rock 'n' roll flamenco.

"I'll never get her home after this," Mr. Ford said.

Which didn't turn out to be the case at all. After writhing around for a few minutes like a sea anemone (or Ava Gardner in *The Barefoot Contessa*), the inimitable Mrs. Ford and her husband were off in a herd of guitarists and violinists—on their way back to Monte Carlo and yet another night aboard their chartered yacht.

LA LEOPOLDA: FIT FOR A KING

August 1969

The sedately elegant inevitably occupy the better chateaux on the higher of the remote hilltops, and on a clear day, when the haze lifts off the Mediterranean and the little towns along the shore thousands of feet below, the view does indeed seem to go on forever.

But at Villa La Leopolda, Colonel C. Michael Paul's summer residence, it isn't what's way off down there through the two-hundred-foot cypress trees that matters very much. It's the chateau itself and its acres of terraced flower gardens, ornate sculpture, swimming pools, secluded courtyards, spacious terraces and—when least expected—the fountains. Leopolda is all of this and more, so much more that in a serious moment not long ago Colonel Paul paused as he walked over the intricate mosaic of the marble floors and got just a little philosophical.

"I feel as if I have a partnership with the Almighty," he said simply. "Only He can make this possible."

Maybe so, but Colonel Paul's millions enhanced the estate considerably. His sure knowledge of what is exquisitely eighteenth-century French certainly wasn't a hindrance. And Leopolda, once the residence of Leopold III, King of the Belgians, is decidedly not a place for those addicted to English sitting rooms, Danish modern furniture or plastic sofas. The chateau is one vast Empire drawing room or hallway after another: a palatial museum with Regency touches, Savonerie rugs (but never over the most elaborate of the marble floors), hand-painted flowers brightening up the blond velvets on the gilded chairs, enormous mirrors, hand-carved moldings, vermeil statuary and bronze dorée chandeliers strung with ropes of big crystal beads. French silk sofas, mirrored bronze dorée tables, Fabergé bibelots and a piano share the most comfortable of the drawing rooms. Stradavarius and Guarnerius violins Colonel Paul plays now and then are stored where the humidity won't get at them. Marc Chagall's self-portrait isn't far from Benny Goodman's signature in the guest book, and there's an elevator Colonel Paul rarely uses.

"I like the staircase," he said.

And well he might. The stairs are gray-beige marble, and they curve upward to meet more marble, tapestries, guest rooms and more French paintings.

Colonel Paul, who ignores most of what he calls "the summer turmoil around me," is an oil man turned financier-philanthropist. He is one of the great independents with drilling operations in Spain and Libya as well as Texas.

When he isn't running what he calls "my little empire" (either on the telephone in his baby blue and white bedroom office suite at Leopolda or his equally formal library in Palm Beach), he is giving his treasures away.

He recently gave $1-million to Lincoln Center for a recital hall in memory of his late wife, the former Josephine Bay. And his latest gift was an exceptional collection of nineteenth-century French sculptures that went to the Metropolitan Museum. "I live quietly," he said and meant it.

But he shows up at the palace in Monaco now and then, and he has been known to fling a little dinner or two, particularly if such friends as Alfonso Landa, the Palm Beach financier, or Danny Kaye, the Hollywood comedian, are around. He also is on friendly terms with French cabinet ministers, artists and writers of virtually every nationality, such American industrialists as Elmer Bobst, honorary chairman of the Warner-Lambert Pharmaceutical Company, and President Nixon.

"I think the President would like it here," he said. "He would have time to do a lot of thinking."

Colonel Paul, who has pictures personally autographed to himself from every American President since Woodrow Wilson, works between 9 A.M. and 1 P.M. He stops in time for soup, little sandwiches and a salad at lunch in the smaller and sunnier of his two dining rooms, and then frankly enjoys the esthetics of his estate. He swims in one of two pools ("One is salt. One is fresh water. Obviously what I need is a pool without water for people who don't swim"), cruises aboard the *Seven Seas Jr.* ("My first yacht was the *Seven Seas* and I guess this one is his son"), and contemplates such natural wonders as his 750 ancient olive trees.

"I have only about twenty acres of land," he said, "and if I wanted to I could be in a different kind of oil business—the olive oil business."

Colonel Paul usually finds some time to pamper the hollyhocks he brought from his Palm Beach house. And at least once a day he pushes the fountain button, which sends three jets of water spraying two hundred feet above his reflecting pond.

"It's a wonderful little world here," he said. And, of course, he's right.

She calls him Princey and he calls her Mama, and there's nobody like them anywhere, for she is Her Highness the Maharanee Sita Devi Gaekwar of Baroda and he is her only child, His Highness the Prince.

And in the summer, they usually can be found in and around Monte Carlo—she in a penthouse atop the Hôtel de Paris and he in his little villa. But more often than not, they are together because, as she herself is quick to explain, "Princey works for me."

It's not clear what Princey does, yet he was useful the day the Maharanee ran out of Cherry Mousse nail polish. She telephoned the beauty shop, but it was he who saw to it that her polish was immediately delivered. They both got just a touch ecstatic about the color.

"Perfect," Princey cooed, holding the bottle up to the light.

"Exactly," said his mother.

That was also the day the maharanee decided to rearrange the furniture. She had moved from another suite, she said from the depths of a sofa beneath an engraving of Louis XVI getting out of bed, and although the silks, velvets and chandeliers in her new salon were satisfactory, she was not much for the way the chairs were bunched up against the wall.

"I want it conversational," she said, shoving a gray velvet footstool toward the middle of the room. "I like it when there are little groupings."

Princey and a uniformed Indian man servant pushed furniture too, until finally the room was the way the maharanee wanted it. Then Princey was off to get his mother another pair of sandals. She wore yellow ones with her yellow, pink, blue, orange and green Indian silk caftan with the gold braid. He thought green sandals looked a lot better.

"He's so good about color," his mother said. "I trust his taste implicitly."

At this point, the maharanee sent Princey for champagne, settled herself among the sofa cushions, pulled out an L & M cigarette (she used to smoke cigars in a ruby-studded holder) and talked about life as she and Princey have led it.

Even though her father was the rich Maharajah of Pithapuram and she was a beautiful girl ("with ten to twenty maids and people to tutor us at the palace"), life really did not begin until she met the Maharajah of Baroda.

He was married and she was married, but they worked it out anyway. She divorced her first husband by declaring herself no longer a Hindu but a Moslem. He broke the Indian princely state of Baroda's antipolygamy law. And they were married.

That was in 1943, when he was "the world's second richest man" and their neighbor was the late Nizam of Hyderbad, "the world's richest man." Princey was born two years later.

"I sat on the left at the table and his first wife sat on the right," the maharanee said.

Aside from some friction between the wives, days in the five-hundred-room red-and-white sandstone Baroda palace seem to have consisted of polo, tennis, sitting for a 101-gun salute ("It's the same for the Queen of England"), exercising absolute power over nearly three million subjects and keeping track of the herds of ceremonial elephants. When the maharajah and his second wife traveled, which was most of the time, they often whirled about in a private plane, followed their thoroughbred horses to the internationally celebrated tracks, settled for twenty-one-gun salutes (which was all they were entitled to abroad) and spent millions of dollars.

In those days, the maharanee crushed her aspirin with an emerald five inches in diameter. She said the pestle with the ruby knob was "too small." But the days of absolute power in Baroda as well as India were coming to an end. In 1951, Prime Minister Jawaharlal Nehru sacked the prodigal maharajah for "defying the central government."

The maharanee was in New York at the time. Frantically, she boarded a plane and flew to London because, as she announced as she stepped off the aircraft, "I can't phone India from America, so I have come over here."

The maharanee divorced the maharajah in 1956 and kept most of the Baroda jewels. When he died in 1968, Yuvaj Fateh Singh, his eldest son by his first marriage, succeeded him as maharajah. Since then the maharanee and Princey have been very much on their own. Which doesn't mean that they are poor.

"I'm used to a kind of living and if you're used to it, you need it," the maharanee said. "I would not know how else to live."

She still has her racing stables and apartment in Paris, masses of behemoth jewels, a staff that on a good day may include "three maids, a cook, my secretary, the butlers, the chauffeurs, and I'm sure I've forgotten somebody," and enough money to assure her of deluxe treatment in her London, St. Moritz, New York, Paris and Monte Carlo haunts. She also has a creamy white Rolls-Royce that goes nearly everywhere she and Princey go. The Baroda crest has been embroidered on the gold velvet pennon that flies over the hood, and it appears again on the doors—supported by painted elephants. And no matter where she is, she keeps pretty much to a schedule.

"I never go to bed before six or seven," she said. "I wake at two, sometimes three. First is my massage. Afterwards I answer my phone calls and see my bankers, racing managers and lawyers—the usual daily chores."

At 4 P.M., she has lunch alone or with Princey. She may go out later in the afternoon, but she's usually back by 7:30 for her daily appointment with the hairdresser. And in Monte Carlo, dinner is at 9:30 or later—either at the hotel, friends' villas or Harry's Bar, a small Italian restaurant. Princey often accompanies her. Besides carrying his mother's jewels when they're traveling and advising her about her clothes, Princey's job is to decide which of their thoroughbred yearlings they will sell and for how much.

"My son works eight hours for me and then stays up all night," the maharanee said proudly. "Of course he's a playboy. But he's up at three and working—working very hard."

At twenty-four, the prince, whose full name is Sayajirao Pratapsinha, is almost as exotic as his mother. In the evenings, when she wears richly embroidered saris, sapphire and diamond earrings and four strands of enormous pearls, he wears brocade Indian tunics with jeweled buttons. In less formal moments, his pants are brightly colored and tight. His shirts are striped and open several buttons down from the collar. The gold charms on the chain around his neck clank as he walks.

"Sometimes people stare at me," Princey said happily. "I horrify them by taking my shoes off."

WHO'S A "SOMEBODY" DEPENDS ON WHO'S
DOING THE CHOOSING
November 1970

People come and people go, but the institution of the socially celebrated goes on forever. At last glance, the 1976 parade included Diana von Furstenberg, Barbara Walters, Tom and Joan Braden, Carl Bernstein and Bob Woodward, Yasmin Khan, Margaux Hemingway, Doris Kearns, Lally Weymouth, Mick and Bianca Jagger and various Iranian diplomats not the least of which is Princess Ashraf, twin sister of the Shah. For a summing up, however, professional autograph collector David Lefkowitz's list is as good as any.

Ward McAllister certainly wasn't the first American to make a list of those he considered better than everybody else, but since his invention of "The Four Hundred," an awful lot of people have made an awful lot of lists.

Inevitably, such lists raise the momentous (in some circles) question of who's important and who isn't, and the old question came up again not long ago at the New York City Cultural Council's black-tie theater benefit.

Crowds of New Yorkers lined up behind wooden police barriers to watch the rich, the celebrated, the elegant and the powerful stream into the Imperial Theater. The sidewalk audience cheered for Gina Lollobrigida.

But when Mrs. John F. C. Bryce (the A&P), Mr. and Mrs. Robert Scull (pop art), Mrs. Oscar Hammerstein 2nd (widow of the lyricist), Mr. and Mrs. Joseph A. Meehan (stockbroker), Pierre Arpels (jewels), and Mrs. Charles Shipman Payson (horses and the Mets) arrived, the crowd merely stared or commented on the clothes and jewels.

It took Mayor Lindsay's appearance to get the crowd cheering again and clapping their hands. And as the last of perhaps 750 theater-goers moved across the sidewalk and into the lobby, a man who had been watching the proceedings delivered what to him was the final appraisal of the guests.

"Nobody's here," he bellowed from somewhere under the marquee. "Mayor Lindsay's the only big name."

The booming voice belonged to none other than David Lefkowitz. And although his ruddy face, brown corduroy jacket and baggy blue pants probably aren't familiar to Mrs. Bryce, Miss Lollobrigida, Mr. Arpels or Mrs. Payson, he has been looking at them for nearly twenty years. Mr. Lefkowitz is a professional autograph seeker. Between April and the first of October, he doubles as a Good Humor man. In the winters, he may be found at virtually every highly publicized movie and theater opening or benefit in the Broadway area.

He disdains the French restaurants ("Nobody ever goes there") and the United Nations ("You can never get close enough to get an autograph"). Yet he's often at Sardi's issuing a passing verbal commentary on the wide variety of persons who go into that theatrical district restaurant for dinner, supper and first-night parties.

He has been known to stand outside the New York Hilton, the Waldorf or the Plaza when what he calls "something big" is happening. And although his contact with what passes for society is somewhat peripheral, he did "attend" Truman Capote's famous masked ball—a gathering he remembers as "only so-so."

In Mr. Lefkowitz's view, some people are better than other people, but, like most social arbiters, he's at something of a loss to explain why.

"It's up to me who's more important than another," he said. "Certain people I like. Certain people I don't like. I can't tell you why. It's a good question. Could be that some are more glamorous than others."

He didn't define glamorous (though it may be synonymous with his use of the phrase "big star"). But he did try to indicate how he rates the three or four thousand people whose autographs he has collected either for himself or for sale—at prices ranging from $2 for Joseph E. Levine, the producer, to $15 for the President.

"I like big people," he said. "I like mayors, governors, presidents. Those are big people. Or famous stars. Or Secretary of States. I don't go for businessmen. I wouldn't bother with Henry Ford or the president of General Motors."

Alfred Gwynne Vanderbilt, the sportsman and newly elected chairman of the New York Racing Association, is among those at the top of Mr. Lefkowitz's list at the moment.

Why?

"Because he's a millionaire," Mr. Lefkowitz said. "And he's a gentleman. I mean he's loaded; I can tell you that."

Governor Rockefeller is up there, too, not just because he's the governor but because he, too, is a millionaire "and money counts." Yet Aristotle Onassis, who has as much or more money than either Mr. Vanderbilt or Governor Rockefeller, is considerably lower down on the list because, as Mr. Lefkowitz put it, "I don't care for him. Now, Mrs. Onassis, she's all right."

But Mrs. Onassis "isn't as good" as Ingrid Bergman ("a big star") or Mrs. Richard M. Nixon, "because the President's wife is always more important" if they're in office rather than out—"no matter what party."

And presidents, in a male chauvinist contention that won't sit well with women's liberation, are "always better than their wives."

"Wives don't matter unless they're famous," Mr. Lefkowitz said, speaking of wives in general. "Sometimes I have to take their autographs to get their husbands'. But I wouldn't otherwise."

Now about William S. Paley, president of the Columbia Broadcasting System: Mr. Lefkowitz says "that's a good name"—hardly the highest accolade but better than some. Robert W. Sarnoff, president of the RCA Corporation, is "a good name" too.

Yet John Hay Whitney, former Ambassador to the Court of St. James's, racing enthusiast, member of an old and distinguished family, and former owner of the New York *Herald Tribune,* doesn't even appear on the list.

"I don't know him," Mr. Lefkowitz explained.

Mr. Lefkowitz has never heard of Mr. Whitney's sister, Mrs. Payson, nor of Charles Revson, chairman of Revlon, Inc. And despite a recent Gallup poll showing that Martha Mitchell's name was familiar to 74 percent of the population, Mr. Lefkowitz hadn't heard of her either.

"Who's that?" he asked.

Yet Mrs. Cornelius Vanderbilt Whitney got what amounted to a rave notice ("She's important"). Richard Ottinger, the Democrats' unsuccessful candidate for the United States Senate, rated "a big man" label—only slightly lower on the list than the "very important" Duke and Duchess of Windsor.

Mr. Capote seems to be somewhere to the south of such lofties as Mr. Vanderbilt, Mayor Lindsay, Raquel Welch, President Nixon, Governor Rockefeller and Gregory Peck. But he's above Joe Namath (who has refused to give Mr. Lefkowitz an autograph on four successive occasions) and Mr. Namath is well above Mr. Onassis.

"Now Bennett Cerf, he's around all the time," Mr. Lefkowitz said. "All he does is write books. And Leonard Bernstein. He's *always* around. It's the ones you never see who you want."

One of the loftiest of the lofty whom Mr. Lefkowitz actually yearned to meet, observe and ask for autographs was the late Charles de Gaulle ("I don't think he ever came to New York"). Two others are "Queen what's her name—the one from England," and Lee Van Cleef.

Lee Van Cleef?

Good gracious, yes. Mr. Van Cleef has played the bad guy in dozens of Western movies.

Index

301

Crocker, William W., 177, 179
Cromwell, Elizabeth, 72
Cronin, Thomas, 6
Cronkite, Walter, 90, 97
Cronkite, Mrs. Walter, 90
Crook, Edward (Pete), 232
Croquet, 37–39
Crosby, Bing, 25, 26
Crosby, Bob, 138
Cröy, Prince Maxim, 33
Cuevas, Marquesa de, 80, 90
Curtis, Charlotte, 90
Curtiss, Thomas Quinn, 90
Cushing, Frederick, 90
Cushing, Mrs. Frederick, 90
Cushing, Minnie, 90

Dali, Salvador, 6
Dallas, Texas, 211–215
Daly, John, 88, 90
Daly, Mrs. John, 88, 90
Dance Theatre of Harlem, 113–115
Daniel, Clifton, 90
Daniel, Mrs. Clifton, 89, 90
Daugherty, Mrs. Joseph, 57
Davant, James, 85
Davie, T. Bedford, 6
Davie, Mrs. T. Bedford, 6
Davies, Elizabeth, 96
Davis, Meyer, 175
Davis, Sammy, Jr., 86, 90, 187
Davis, Mrs. Sammy, Jr., 90
Day, Edward, 136
Dean, John, 3rd, 144
Dean, Mrs. John, 3rd, 141
DeBakey, Michael E., ix, 218–219
DeBakey, Mrs. Michael E., 218–219
DeGolyer, Mrs. Everett Lee, 211
Delheim, Robert, 90
Delheim, Mrs. Robert, 90
Delynn, Alan, 90
Democratic National Convention
    (1968), 134–136
Denny, Victor, 246
Denver, Colorado, 237–240
Derby, Earl of, 65
Deterding, Lady, 291
Deutsch, Armand, 90
Deutsch, Mrs. Armand, 90
Devon Yacht Club, East Hampton,
    39, 40
Dewey, Mrs. Albert B., 53

Dewey, Alvin, 90
Dewey, Mrs. Alvin, 90
Diaz, Justino, 64
Dickerson, Wyatt, 121
Dietrich, Mrs. Kurt S., 102–103
Dietrich, Marlene, 90, 97
Dillingham, Benjamin Franklin, 2nd,
    254, 257
Dillingham, Mrs. Benjamin Franklin,
    2nd, 254, 257
Dillingham, Lowell Smith, 257
Dillingham, Walter Francis, 257
Dillingham, Mrs. Walter Francis, 257
Dillon, C. Douglas, 16, 90
Dillon, Mrs. C. Douglas, 90
Dilworth, Lloyd L., 182
Dilworth, Mrs. Lloyd L., 182
Dinkler, Mrs. Carling, 186, 187
Dinwiddie, Ainslie, 90
Dirksen, Everett McKinley, 138
Douglas, Kirk, 28
Douglas, Mrs. Kirk, 154
Douglas, Mrs. Lewis W., 76
Douglas, Sharman, 90
Douglass, Mrs. Kingman, 90
Doyle, M. Dorland, 38
Doyle, Mrs. M. Dorland, 38
Drexel, John R., 3rd, 14, 54
Drexel, Mrs. John R., 3rd, 54, 80, 105
Drinkwater, Arthur, 167, 168
du Pont, Mrs. Richard, 64
Dubuque, Iowa, 221–225
Duchin, Peter, 17
Duchin, Mrs. Peter, 17, 88, 90
Dudley, Drew, 90
Dudley, Guilford, 12, 82
Dudley, Mrs. Guilford, 82
Duff, Peggy Scott, 92
Dufferin, Marchioness of, 90
Dufferin, Marquis of, 90
Dumphy, Jack, 90
Dunnington, Walter G., 44
Dunnington, Mrs. Walter G., 44–45
Dunphy, Robert, 90
Dunphy, Mrs. Robert, 90
Dupee, F. W., 90
Dupee, Mrs. F. W., 90

Eberhardt, Anthony, 224
Eberhardt, Mrs. Anthony, 222,
    224–225
Eberstadt, Frederick, 90

Eberstadt, Mrs. Frederick, 90
Edelman, Peter, 43
Egan, William A., 250
Ehrlichman, John D., 144
Ehrlichman, Mrs. John D., 144
Eisenhower, Barbara Anne, 101
Eisenhower, David, 137, 139
Eisenhower, Mrs. David, 101, 137, 139
Eisenhower, Dwight D., 25, 27, 138, 139
Eisenhower, Mrs. Dwight D., 25
El Morocco, New York, ix, 79–80
Elle, 281
Ellington, Duke, 227
Elliott, Osborn, 90
Elliott, Mrs. Osborn, 90
Ellis, Crawford H., 192
Ellis, Mrs. James, 140
Ellison, Ralph, 90, 96
Ellison, Mrs. Ralph, 90, 94
Elwood, D. C., 10
Energy crisis, 128–131
Engelhard, Charles, 90
Engelhard, Mrs. Charles, 90
Ennis, Jean, 90
Epstein, Jason, 90, 96
Epstein, Mrs. Jason, 90
Erpf, Mrs. Armand G., 123
Erwitt, Elliott, 90
Etherington, Edwin D., 16
Eudeville, Comtesse d', 82
Evans, John, 238
Evans, John, Dr., 238
Evans, John, Jr., 238
Evans, Rowland, Jr., 90
Evans, Mrs. Rowland, Jr., 90
Evans, Sterling, 230
Exeter, David George Brownlow Cecil, Marquess of, 274

Fabiola, Queen of Belgium, 266
Fahlstrom, Oyvind, 123
Fairbanks, Douglas, Jr., 90
Fall, Albert, 143
Farenga, William, 90
Farrell, Charles, 25–27
Farrow, Mia, 88
Faye, Alice, 26
Feiffer, Jules, 135
Feigen, Richard, 113
Feigen, Mrs. Richard, 113
Fell, Mrs. John R., 90, 111, 112

Feminine Mystique, The (Friedan), 36, 46
Fenner, Darwin S., 192
Ferguson, Mrs. William J. Jr., 180
Ferrer, Mel, 90, 97
Ferrer, Mrs. Mel, 90
Ferry, Dexter M., 206
Ferry, W. Hawkins, 206
Feymu, Bekim, 99
Field, Mrs. Marshall, 90
Fields, Mrs. Joseph, 153
Finch, Elizabeth Lathrop, 101
Finch, Maureen, 101
Finch, Robert H., 101
Finch, Mrs. Robert H., 101
Findlay, Wally, 8
Fine, Benjamin, 182
Finkelstein, Jerry, 42
Finley, Harry, 34
Firestone, Harvey S., 54
Firestone, Mrs. Harvey S., 54
Firestone, Leonard, 187
Fishbein, Jason Biddle, 90
Fischer, Bobby, 120–122
Fitzgerald, Frances, 90
FitzHugh, Claudia Tucker, 192
FitzHugh, John R., 192
Flagler, Henry Morrison, 7, 183
Flanner, Janet, 90
Fleming, Mrs. Ian, 275–276
Fonda, Henry, 90
Fonda, Mrs. Henry, 90
Fontaine, Joan, 90
Forbes, Malcolm S., 85–87
Forbes magazine, 85, 87
Ford, Mrs. Anne McDonnell, 65, 88, 90
Ford, Edsel Bryant, 2nd, 207–209
Ford, Frederick B., 206
Ford, Mrs. Frederick Sloane, Jr., 205–206
Ford, Henry, 2nd, 90, 202, 207, 209, 292–293
Ford, Mrs. Henry, 2nd, 88, 90, 138, 207, 208, 291–293
Ford, John B., 16–17
Ford, Mrs. John B., 16–17
Ford, Susan, 206
Forrestal, Michael, 90
Forrester, John W., 101
Fors, Mrs. Emi, 19–20
Forstman, Charlotte Ford, 130

Holbrook, Gerald C., 16
Holden, Milton W. (Doc), 38, 91
Holzer, Mrs. Leonard (Baby Jane), 79
Homans, Abigail Adams, 169
Homans, George, 170
Homans, Robert, 169
Homans, Robert, Jr., 170
Honolulu, Hawaii, ix, 255–259
Hooper, Fred W., 184
Hooper, Lucien, 85
Hope, Bob, 26, 152, 155
Hopkins, Mark, 179
Hornblow, Arthur, 91
Hornblow, Mrs. Arthur, 91
Horst, Horsl P., 91
Houston, Texas, ix, 217–219
Hoving, Thomas P. F., 98
Howar, Barbara, 145–147
Howard, Jane, 91
Howard, Jean, 91
Hughes, Emmett John, 91
Hughes, Howard, 143
Hull, Mrs. Lytle, 99
Humphrey, Hubert H., 85–87
Humphreys, Albert E., 238
Huntington, Collis P., 179
Hussein, King of Jordan, 267

Ilsley family, 228, 229
Imutan, Andrew, 41, 43
Imutan, Mrs. Andrew, 42
Imutan, William, 42
In Cold Blood (Capote), 93
Indian Creek Island, 184, 185
Ingermann, Keith, 12
Ingrid, Queen of Denmark, 264, 266, 269
International Debutante Ball, 99–102
International Heart Gala, 217–219
Irvin, Mrs. Effingham Townsend, 7
Isherwood, Christopher, 91
Ittleson, Henry, Jr., 28, 290
Ittleson, Mrs. Henry, Jr., 290–291
Iran, Empress Farah of, 264–266
Iran, Shah of, ix, 263–270

Jaffe, Mrs. William B., 115
Jagger, Bianca, 297
Jagger, Mick, 297
Jaipur, Maharajah of, 91
Jaipur, Maharanee of, 88, 91
Javits, Jacob K., 91, 116, 118, 121

Javits, Mrs. Jacob K. (Marion), 91, 115–118, 121, 124
Jean, Grand Duke of Luxembourg, 266
Jellicoe, Countess of, 276
Jessel, Georgie, 291
Johnson, Ellen, 124
Johnson, Mrs. F. Raymond, 78, 79
Johnson, Luci Baines, 146, 291
Johnson, Lynda Bird, 88, 89, 91, 94, 146
Johnson, Lyndon B., 27, 136, 146, 291
Johnson, Mrs. Lyndon B., 75–77, 146, 207
Johnson, Philip C., 84, 91, 96, 112, 129
Johnson, Rafer, 42
Johnston, Jill, 48–49, 124
Jones, Frederick E., 16
Jonsson, J. Erik, 214–215
Jonsson, Mrs. J. Erik, 214–215
Jordan, Mrs. T. Carrick, 175
Joyce, Beatrice, 100
Judge, Arlene, 80
Jupiter Island, 14–17

Kahane, Melanie, 128, 129
Kahn, Otto, 77
Kammerer, Julie, 45
Kanin, Garson, 91
Kanin, Mrs. Garson, 91
Kanzler, Mrs. Ernest, 290
Kask, Warren, 91
Kask, Mrs. Warren, 91
Katzenbach, Nicholas deB., 91
Katzenbach, Mrs. Nicholas deB., 91
Kavanaugh, Mrs. George Washington, 74
Kaye, Danny, 294
Kaye, Sammy, 138–139
Kazin, Alfred, 91
Kazin, Mrs. Alfred, 91
Kean, Benjamin, 91
Kearns, Doris, 297
Keith, Mrs. Kenneth, 91
Kelland, Horace, 91
Kempner, Mrs. Thomas, 129–130
Kennedy, Edward M., 91
Kennedy, Mrs. Edward M., 91
Kennedy, John F., 25, 27
Kennedy, Mrs. John F. *See* Onassis, Jacqueline Kennedy

310

Meehan, Joseph A., 91, 298
Meehan, Mrs. Joseph A., 91, 110, 298
Meehan, Marcia, 91
Mehle, Aileen, 91
Mein, William Wallace, Jr., 179–180
Mein, Mrs. William Wallace, Jr., 179
Melhado, Frederick, 91
Mellon, Paul, 66, 83, 91, 97
Mellon, Mrs. Paul, 83, 84, 91
Menars, Marquis Bernard-Alexis
    Poisson de, 124
Menninger, George C., 182
Menninger, Mrs. George C., 182
Menotti, Gian-Carlo, 91, 97
Merrick, David, 91, 94, 134, 218
Merrill, Dina, 45
Merrill, Robert, 91
Messmore, Mrs. Carman, 38
Mesta, Perle, 136, 185
Metcalfe, David, 91
Metropolitan Museum of Art, 98
Metropolitan Opera, 73–78
Meyer, Agnes E., 91
Meyer, Tom Montague, 272, 275
Meyer, Mrs. Tom Montague, 272,
    274–275
Miami, Florida, 183–187
Michener, James, 91
Michener, Mrs. James, 91
Milinaire, Caterine, 91
Miller, Arthur, 91
Miller, Mrs. Arthur, 91
Millis, Mrs. Walter, 91
Mills, James Paul, 16
Milwaukee, Wisconsin, 227–229
Mink, Patsy, 46–48
Minnelli, Vincent, 91
Minnelli, Mrs. Vincent, 91
Mitchell, Arthur, 115
Mitchell, Craig, 153, 154
Mitchell, Henry, 109
Mitchell, James, 80
Mitchell, Martha, 299
Mona, Princess of Jordan, 267
Montalembert, Countess Hughes de, 34
Monte Carlo, 289–291
Monteagle, Mrs. Paige, 180
Montesquiou-Fezensac, Duc de, 82
Moon, Charles M., 185
Moon, Mrs. Charles M., 185
Moon, Mrs. Henry, 115
Moore, John, 91

Moore, Marianne, 88, 91
Moore, Thomas, 91
Moore, Mrs. Thomas, 91
Moorhead, William S., 91
Moorhead, Mrs. William S., 91
Moreira-Salles, Walthes, 91
Moreira-Salles, Mrs. Walthes, 91
Morgan, Edward P., 91
Morison, Samuel Eliot, 163, 165
Morison, Mrs. Samuel Eliot, 164, 165
Morning Telegraph, 62
Morrilton, Arkansas, 231–234
Morris, Effingham Buckley, 175
Morrow, Winston V., 86
Mortimer, Stanley, 91
Mosbacher, Emil (Bus), Jr., 219
Mosbacher, Robert, 219
Mudge, Ann, 91, 95
Mulligan, Richard, 127
Muñoz, Antonio, 42
Murray, Mrs. Natalia, 91

Nairne, Clayton L., 192
Namath, Joe, 299
National Geographic, 223
National Horse Show, 73, 82
National Organization for Women, 46
Nelson, Mrs. Donald, 45
Neskow, Cynthia, 208
New Orleans, Louisiana, ix, 189–193
New York, x, 71–131
New York Association for the Blind, 99
New Yorker, The, 221, 222
Newberry, Mrs. Phelps, 205
Newhouse, Samuel I. Sr., 91
Newhouse, Mrs. Samuel I. Sr., 91
Newman, Ruby, 166, 168
Newport, Rhode Island, 3, 51–58
Newport Casino, 52
Newsweek, 143, 182
Niarchos, Mrs. Stavros, 88, 91, 97–98,
    292
Nichols, Mike, 84, 91
Nidorf, Michael, 30
Nidorf, Mrs. Michael, 30
Nine O'Clock dance club, 104–106
Nixon, Julie. *See* Eisenhower, Mrs.
    David
Nixon, Richard M., 22, 27, 128, 130,
    136–144, 186–188, 294, 299
Nixon, Mrs. Richard M., 136–137,
    139, 299

313

Roosevelt, Mrs. Elliott, 185
Roosevelt, Franklin D., Jr., 84, 85
Rosenquist, James, 123
Rosenthal, Nancy Beth, 100, 101
Rosenthal, Stephen, 100
Rosenzweig, Richard, 136
Rosière, Vicomte Paul de, 286
Rosière, Vicomtesse Paul de, 286
Roth, Philip, 92, 95
Rothschild, Baroness Cecile de, 92
Rothschild, Baron Guy de, 92,
    284–285
Rothschild, Baroness Guy de, 92
Rough, Valerie, 167
Roundtree, Richard, 121
Rousseau, Theodore, 92
Rubinstein, Artur, 155
Russell, Mrs. Edwin F., 38
Russell, Rosalind. *See* Mrs. Frederick
    Brisson
Ryan, John Barry, 3rd, 92, 127
Ryan, Mrs. John Barry ("D.D."), 3rd,
    54, 77, 92, 125, 127
Ryan, Mrs. John Barry, Jr., 92
Rybar, Valerian Stux, 156

St. Cecilia Society Cotillion, ix,
    199–200
St. Jacques, Raymond, 113, 114
Saint-Subber, Arnold, 92
Salinger, Pierre, 83
San Francisco, California, 177–180
Sanford, Stephen, 7, 13, 63, 65
Sanford, Mrs. Stephen, 7, 13–14, 61,
    63, 65, 66–67, 81, 82
Santa Gertrudis cattle sale, 231–234
Sarotoga Performing Arts Center,
    64–65
Saratoga Springs, New York, 61–68
Sargent, Herbert, 92
Sargent, John, 92
Sarnoff, David, 86
Sarnoff, Robert, 92, 299
Sarnoff, Mrs. Robert, 87, 92
Sassoon, Lady, 286, 291
Sassoon, Vidal, 82
Savitt, Mrs. Liberman, 85
Scaasi, Arnold, 82
Schiaparelli, Elsa, 106
Schiff, Frank, 92
Schiff, Mrs. Frank, 92
Schippers, Thomas, 92

Schippers, Mrs. Thomas, 92
Schlee, Mrs. George, 92
Schlesinger, Arthur, Jr., 83, 88, 92, 95
Schlesinger, Mrs. Arthur, Jr., 92
Schlumberger, Jean, 92
Schorer, Mark, 92
Schorer, Mrs. Mark, 92
Schrader, Abe, 43
Scott, Robert Montgomery, 175
Scott, Mrs. Zachary, 92
Scranton, William, 16
Scranton, Mrs. William, 16
Scull, Ethel, 36
Scull, Nicholas, 174
Scull, Robert, 46, 48, 124, 298
Scull, Mrs. Robert, 46–48, 298
Seabra, Nelson, 92
Sears, David, 164
Sears, Eleonora R., 64
Sears, Richard, 164, 165
Sears, Mrs. Richard, 164–165
Seattle, Washington, 243–246
Selznick, Daniel, 92
Selznick, Mrs. David O., 92
Selznick, Irene, 92
Shah of Iran's gala, ix, 263–270
Shapiro, John, 154
Shapiro, Mrs. John, 154
Shaw, Artie, ix, 118–120
Shaw, Carolyn Hagner, 143
Shaw, Irwin, 92, 97
Shaw, Mrs. Irwin, 92
Sheehan, Michael Guard, 258
Sheehan, Mrs. Michael Guard,
    258–259
Sheehan, Wade E., 258
Shelden, Mrs. Allan, 203–204
Shepard, Alan, 218
Sherwood, Mrs. Robert E., 92
Shiva, Gil, 105
Shiva, Mrs. Gil, 92, 105, 153
Shore, Dinah, 26
Shultz, George, 141
Sidey, Hugh, 141
Siegel, "Bugsy," 128
Silvers, Robert, 92
Simbari, Nicola, 11
Simon, Neil, 127
Simons, Pollard, 28
Simons, Mrs. Pollard, 27–28
Sims, Agnes, 92
Sinatra, Frank, 26, 88, 92, 136, 187

315